AF624825

THE WORLD TRADE ORGANIZATION

The World Trade Organization

Changing Dynamics in the Global Political Economy

Anna Lanoszka

Viva Books

New Delhi | Mumbai | Chennai | Kolkata | Bangalore | Hyderabad | Kochi | Guwahati

Copyright © Lynne Rienner Publishers, Inc.

First Indian Edition 2010

VIVA BOOKS PRIVATE LIMITED

- 4737/23 Ansari Road, Daryaganj, New Delhi 110 002
  E-mail: vivadelhi@vivagroupindia.net, Tel. 42242200
- Plot No. 76, Service Industries, Shirvane, Sector 1, Nerul, Navi Mumbai 400 706
  E-mail: vivamumbai@vivagroupindia.net, Tel. 27721273, 27721274
- Jamals Fazal Chambers, 26 Greams Road, Chennai 600 006
  E-mail: vivachennai@vivagroupindia.net, Tel. 28290304, 28294241
- B-103, Jindal Towers, 21/1A/3 Darga Road, Kolkata 700 017
  E-mail: vivakolkata@vivagroupindia.net, Tel. 22836381, 22816713
- 7, Sovereign Park Apartments, 56-58, K. R. Road, Basavanagudi, Bangalore 560 004
  E-mail: vivabangalore@vivagroupindia.net, Tel. 26607409, 26607410
- 101-102 Mughal Marc Aptt., 3-4-637 to 641, Narayanguda, Hyderabad 500 029
  E-mail: vivahyderabad@vivagroupindia.net, Tel. 27564481, 27564482
- First Floor, Beevi Towers, SRM Road, Kaloor, Kochi 682 018, Kerala
  E-mail: vivakochi@vivagroupindia.net, Tel: 0484-2403055, 2403056
- 232, GNB Road, Beside UCO Bank, Silpukhuri, Guwahati 781 003
  E-mail: vivaguwahati@vivagroupindia.net, Tel: 0361-2666386

Published by arrangement with

Lynne Rienner Publishers Inc.
1800 30th Street, Boulder,
Colorado 80301
USA

All rights reserved. No part of this book may be reproduced or transmitted in any form or by any means now known or to be invented, electronic or mechanical, including photocopying, recording or by any information storage or retrieval system without written permission from the publisher.

This edition is licensed for sale in the Indian subcontinent only. Not for export elsewhere.

ISBN 978-81-309-1243-1

Published by Vinod Vasishtha for Viva Books Private Limited, 4737/23, Ansari Road, New Delhi - 110 002. Printed and bound by Anand Sons, Delhi - 110 092.

Contents

Acknowledgments

I am grateful to many people for their help and encouragement with this project. Very special thanks must be given to my colleagues and teachers who over the years stimulated my interest in international political economy: Theodore H. Cohn, William D. Coleman, Robert O'Brien, Louis W. Pauly, Timothy Shaw, Denis Stairs, and Gilbert R. Winham. My greatest debt is to Sylvia Ostry, however, who has forever inspired me to relentlessly examine new options and alternative points of view about the world's economy, its hazards, and its new emerging economic giants in the developing world.

I would like to acknowledge the support and help of my colleagues whom I met when working in the Accessions Division of the World Trade Organization: Arif Hussain, Cato Adrian, Renzo Franco, David C. Hartridge, Edwini Kessie, Patrick Low, Renée Mailloux-Huxtable, Peter Milthorp, Jean-Daniel Rey, and Jan Woznowski. Their knowledge about the finest technical details of the international trade system is astonishing. In my efforts I have also benefited from the thoughts and insights of many incredible people such as Florian Bail, Chi Carmody, Patricia M. Goff, Simon Kow, Donna Lee, Åke Lindén, Patrick Macrory, John S. Odell, Jasper A. Okelo, Ernst-Ulrich Petersmann, Jan Aart Scholte, Jeffrey J. Schott, J. P. Singh, Heidi Ullrich, Marc Williams, and Bob Wolfe. For constructive comments I would like to thank the two anonymous reviewers. I am also grateful to Lynne Rienner, who is truly a remarkable person, and to everybody at Lynne Rienner Publishers, with special thanks going to Lesli B. Athanasoulis. These individuals contributed to the strength of the book; all possible weaknesses are mine.

I must thank Nick Hopkinson for inviting me to a most intellectually stimulating conference at Wilton Park in May 2007. The conference was a rare gathering of top practitioners and scholars dealing with crucial issues related to international trade. These long, thought-provoking discussions that I feel privileged to have attended greatly motivated my work and further convinced me that we are indeed living through a transformative stage of global economic relations. Generous financial support came from the Social Sciences and Humanities Research Council of Canada. The Secretariat of the World Trade Organization was always ready with open doors and to help me find any necessary documentation.

Special thanks go to marvelous friends and brilliant scholars, Suzan Ilcan, Maureen Irish, and Myra Tawfik, who kept my enthusiasm up during this endeavor. My acknowledgments would not be complete without thanking my son, Alexander, who despite being very busy pursuing his degree in international relations still provided invaluable research assistance, and, most important, asked many insightful questions that helped shape this project. Finally, I would like to thank my wonderful husband, Mark, for helping me to sustain the momentum, for his patience, and for taking care of Chancellor (our Boxer) and our two needy cats, Truman and Abigail, when I was away on research.

—Anna Lanoszka

CHAPTER 1
Introduction

This is a book about the changes that have taken place in international trade over the past twenty years. The point of departure for this inquiry is the time when more than 100 countries sat together to negotiate a new multilateral trade pact that culminated with the creation of the World Trade Organization (WTO). The establishment of the WTO, however, was just the beginning of a long process that is still far from over. This process involves a multilateral attempt to respond to the transformations in the world economy. It also includes dynamics of adaptation and resistance that characterize the behavior of many WTO member states as they are trying to position themselves in the new trading environment. The changes introduced by the WTO reflect, on the one hand, the rearrangement of power relations in the global economy and, on the other hand, the intensification of the linkage between global economic integration and local socioeconomic development.

But why should we care about these changes? What is the importance of international trade in general and the WTO in particular?

Why Study Trade?

The capricious world economic trends ensure that trade remains one of the most fascinating aspects of international relations. Over the generations, trade never failed to demonstrate its importance and create new controversies. When Aristotle contemplated the essential elements of the ideal city-state, he listed five classes of professions. One of them was the class of traders. It is striking to realize that at the beginning of our civilization, over two thousand years ago, the philosopher's considerations about commerce were inevitably connected with his plan for a well-functioning and secure society.

> The same, then, is true of the forms of government which have been described; states, as I have repeatedly said, are composed, not of one, but of many elements. One element is the food-producing class, who are called husbandmen; a second, the class of mechanics who practice the arts without which a city cannot exist; of these arts some are absolutely necessary, others contribute to luxury or to the grace of life. The third class is that of traders, and by traders I mean those who are engaged in buying and selling, whether in commerce or in retail trade. A fourth class is that of the serfs or laborers. The warriors make up the fifth class, and they are as necessary as any of the others, if the country is not to be the slave of every invader.[1]

Since time immemorial, international trade epitomized the engagement with the world beyond the known borders. It represented both necessity and luxury and was pursued in the name of survival and progress. Trade also stimulated our human curiosity about foreign lands and customs. This worked best if countries respected each other as equal partners. Sometimes, however, the economic progress of one nation came at the expense of other nations, fueling conquests and wars. Faced with a multiplicity of challenges posed by the realignment of power relations in the global economy, we must strive to address inequality and exploitation in international trade. Economic progress will only make sense if it is supported by trade agreements that take into account the developmental needs of societies. One may argue that the WTO is only a technical agreement with no place for development concerns. This is a fallacy. From its beginning, trade always influenced the economic development of societies. Ultimately, the legitimacy of the WTO depends on the responsibility of its members to ensure that such progress is sustainable and that some nations are not advancing their economic development by taking advantage of others.

Nowhere is the intricacy of international trade better conveyed than in the story of the Silk Road. The Silk Road was a complex system of trade routes that served to exchange goods and technology between the people of ancient civilizations. Geographically, the Silk Road stretched over the vast territory between China and Western Europe. Contemporary traders still travel similar routes, although they no longer use camels as their means of transportation. On the occasion of opening the Silk Group Project at the Art Institute of Chicago, Karen Manchester, the Elizabeth McIlvaine Curator of Ancient Art, skillfully summarized the historical legacy of trade:

> Although it still evokes fantasies of lush desert oases and distant crossroad settlements teeming with multinational merchants and other travelers, the

> Silk Road has become, in our time, a metaphor for the harmonious exchange of culture among people from diverse societies, distant places, and different faiths.[2]

Indeed, despite the numerous controversies that continue to surround the world trade system, we can still celebrate its unintended positive consequences: the cross-cultural encounters that have taken place over two millennia of international trade.

The Birth of the WTO

The creation of the WTO marks a beginning of a long process of attempting to govern ever-increasing international trade flows in a concerted and multilateral way. The architects of the WTO wanted it to be open to all countries. The legal underpinnings of the WTO do indeed point to an inherently democratic character of the organization. The lingering question is whether the WTO lives up to its democratic promise, particularly with respect to equality among its members. The record speaks differently on quite a number of issues. I will demonstrate throughout the book the gaps that exist between the organization's lofty goals expressed in the preambles of WTO agreements and the harsh realities of implementing these agreements. Our evaluation of the WTO's internal conflicts, external criticism, and unexpected developments will also shed light on the growing complexity of the world economy.

The decision to create the WTO in 1995 at the conclusion of the Uruguay Round of negotiations under the General Agreement on Tariffs and Trade (GATT) reflected an uneasy consensus among the negotiating countries to enlarge and strengthen the multilateral trading system in order to address the new realities of the global political economy. The provisional 1947 GATT has been replaced by the WTO, which concerns itself with much more than GATT ever did. Areas such as intellectual property, services, investment, and even agriculture were seldom mentioned under the old agreement. In contrast, under the WTO, new separate agreements now deal with each of these issues. After all, GATT was exclusively about trade in goods. The WTO is about trade in goods, services, intellectual property, and other trade-related issues. Its agreements often penetrate inside the borders of WTO members and influence areas that used to be under the sole jurisdiction of individual governments. In a way then, the WTO is well positioned to play a significant role in managing the increasingly interconnected global economy.

The scope of the new organization and its strong legal features surprised many scholars and practitioners when it was first created. It would be difficult to find an expert in the early 1990s who would, with some certainty, predict the future trajectory of the world trading system under the WTO. The agreement was signed by a record number of nations to create the first formal global organization. It was a momentous event in the history of the world economy, although some diplomats, skeptical about its level of ambition, were quietly calling the WTO project "an escape into the future" because of the many issues that were left unresolved at the time the organization was born. Ironically then, the organization that was considered to be a long-awaited achievement on the path of global economic integration was, from its beginning, rushing toward an uncertain future. Only now, after more than a decade of its existence, can we evaluate the WTO and ponder whether it was an appropriate multilateral effort in the face of a global economic makeover.

As we approach the end of the first decade of the twenty-first century, the record of the globalizing economy is mixed at best. While some communities have been able to take advantage of global market integration, others blame globalization for lost jobs and widespread socioeconomic insecurity. It is difficult not to acknowledge the economic successes of China, India, and Brazil. However, the unprecedented increase in the price of oil and gas, growing food shortages, and an enduring instability of financial markets continue to shake economies worldwide. These problems affect local communities, but because of their global nature they require a coordinated international action. The question is whether the WTO lives up to its promise of addressing at least some of these predicaments.

Themes and Theories

There are three interrelated themes that I follow throughout this book. The first considers the WTO as a response to the geopolitical and socioeconomic transformations that began to manifest themselves toward the end of the 1980s. In an attempt to respond to these transformations, the WTO was given new untested responsibilities and agreements. Some of the new WTO agreements overburdened member states, thus causing tensions between their WTO obligations and their developmental priorities. The second theme considers the WTO to be an unfinished project, especially when it comes to its decisionmaking processes. As the WTO was rushed into existence at the end of 1993, insufficient attention was paid to its institutional structure. Despite its new legal status and its enlarged scope, the WTO still operates according to the procedures first established under GATT, when the membership was smaller and the agenda much less complex. Thus, the current institutional structure of the WTO is ill-equipped to deal with the multiple challenges posed by the changing world economy. The third theme focuses on shifting power relations in the international trade system. Previously marginalized under the GATT system, developing countries as a group have taken advantage of their equal legal status under the WTO to play an active role in setting the agenda within the WTO. The new global division of labor, together with innovative ways of organizing today's international trade and investment flows, resulted in reduced domination of historically powerful industrialized countries. As a multilateral forum for conducting global trade negotiations and a mechanism for managing trade among its 152 members,[3] the WTO has become an interesting battleground in this respect.

For much of the postwar period, the Western industrial nations had shaped the GATT system, and that arrangement did not always work for all the countries involved. Developing countries remained outside its decision-making practices. GATT was essentially a clublike contract that reflected the preferences of the dominant nations and was characterized by the inherent pro-Western and antidevelopment bias. The WTO, by contrast, has promised to be more inclusive and sensitive to the developmental needs of all its members.

A break in the historical continuum of postwar trade relations that came with the decision to create the WTO has to do with legal guarantees and obligations that are now embedded in the WTO framework. They place certain constraints on countries belonging to the WTO, but they also offer opportunities for equal participation in the system that previously openly favored the major developed countries. As a result, these new guarantees and obligations can significantly influence the way WTO members interact with each other and hence, by extension, they alter power relations in the world trading system. One is the principle of *single undertaking* that requires the acceptance of the whole package of WTO agreements by each WTO member, and the second is the principle of *judicial equality* of all WTO members that gives every member an equal voice in the decisionmaking processes of the WTO. These two principles came into existence as the result of the Uruguay Round and they changed how international trade is managed multilaterally by the WTO.

Because of these developments, the WTO has also become a test for economic multilateralism. This is why consequences of the WTO will be long lasting, no matter how effective or, alternatively, how unsuccessful the organization turns out to be. The effectiveness of the WTO would have to be measured by its ability to manage international trade to the advantage of all WTO members with no major conflicts. It would also have to be an effective forum for conducting new negotiations and for addressing the needs of all its members. The WTO agreements should facilitate international trade flows without discrimination and without causing economic hardship in WTO member countries. Furthermore, the WTO should be able to rely on rules and transparent procedures. Finally, it should be able to effectively discourage power games and intimidation by those members that are economically powerful. If the WTO passes the above test, it will be a great victory for the multilateral trade system. If it does not, the failure of the WTO should be confronted accordingly. We may be forced to reevaluate our multilateral approach to managing world trade relations.

Theoretically speaking, this book is grounded in the institutionalist interdependence approach to international relations. The idea of complex interdependence among nations goes back to the examination of interstate cooperation and institution building during the post–World War II era, and it speaks primarily in opposition to realist theories of international relations. Structural realism, one of the leading forms of realist theory, is based on the premise that the anarchical structure of the international system compels states to either maintain or enhance their power for the sake of self-preservation.[4] And yet despite the realist assumption that states are guided by their self-interested logic that questions the utility of any collaborative initiative, states have continued to cooperate internationally on a variety of issues.

The liberal institutionalist theory, which stresses interdependence among nations, was first formulated by Robert Keohane and Joseph Nye. It makes a claim that stability and order in the international arena emerge from cooperation among nations through the medium of international regimes.[5] This leads to a famous definition: "Regimes can be defined as sets of implicit and explicit norms, rules, and decision-making procedures around which actors' expectations converge in a given area of international relations."[6] Keohane later goes beyond this definition by urging us to pay attention to the nature of the regimes and the state actors that shape them according to their needs. States seek to create international regimes because the networks of international cooperation benefit them in return. In fact, international cooperation has persisted with, or without, the existence of a dominant hegemonic state capable of providing a strong leadership leading to the establishment of common norms and institutions. According to Keohane, the functional need for international regimes leads to deepening international integration and allows states to function without a hegemonic state. The existence of international regimes can be a powerful motivator of international cooperation in the absence of a single large state able and willing to enforce rules and regulations within the system (hence the title of Keohane's book *After Hegemony*).[7]

According to the above theory, international organizations, such as the WTO, are based on norms that become their standards of behavior as defined in terms of rights and obligations.[8] In turn, these general obligations and rights guide the behavior of states in the formulation and implementation of rules. Legal rules vest these rights and obligations in international law. This is why it is particularly important to study the WTO, because it is the first global economic organization that is fully legalized by its adherence to legal rules and its principle of judicial equality. The WTO is also theoretically significant because it illustrates the limitations of the regime theory in addressing the tension between states' need for international cooperation and their subsequent vulnerability to become dependent on other states. This dependency is often directly related to institutional and legal constraints imposed, as in the case of the WTO, on its member states. Such constraints can be in conflict with the preferences expressed by some domestic groups, but they do not mean that the state becomes completely powerless.

Still, some observers worry that economic interdependence and the concomitant globalization have at least reduced the autonomy of the state. The claim is made that economic globalization supported by the WTO forces the state to eliminate its protectionist policies, relax environmental regulations, and reduce social programs in order to be more globally competitive. The subsequent global "race to the bottom" would ensure that the state becomes less of a relevant actor domestically and perhaps even internationally because of a strong dependence on the performance of the global economy.[9]

Proponents of this view of international economic relations emphasize the shift in thinking about the state's role in the economy from an interventionist Keynesian perspective to a neoliberal free-market approach based on the work by Fredrich von Hayek. John Maynard Keynes developed a theory of macroeconomics that attached importance to the government as being a source of stability in the economic affairs of the country. After all, the hazards of unrestrained free-market, laissez-faire economic liberalism were demonstrated well after the Great Depression in the 1930s. State intervention and the establishment of social programs were thus deemed necessary to protect the economy and the society from the uncertainty of unregulated free markets.[10] However, years of deficit spending and high costs of state subsidies accumulated into burdensome debts, which led some economists to call into question the wisdom of Keynesian macroeconomic theory. Milton Friedman, and other academics whose names are associated with the Chicago School of economics, revived the ideas of Hayek when they contended that government intervention in the market not only stifled individual liberty, but was inefficient and hindered competition.[11] Neoliberalism, as this economic movement came to be known, became particularly salient during the late 1970s through the 1990s when governments annulled many barriers to trade and capital movement and reduced some spending. According to critics of the neoliberal trend in the global economy, governments are getting smaller and the state, by extension, is becoming a less meaningful actor on the international stage as a result—especially when it comes to economic affairs.[12]

Such arguments, which often predict the complete demise of the state, are problematic on two counts. First, they overemphasize the ideological strength of neoliberalism in international economic affairs and thereby fail to appreciate the adaptability of the state. Laissez-faire capitalism, after all, reached its apex not in the later part of the twentieth century but rather in its beginning. Studies have shown capital flows were far greater before World War I.[13] Moreover, the scope of the state back then was much narrower, as defense had accounted for the lion's share of government budgets. Related claims regarding the power of contemporary multinational corporations also appear somehow exaggerated when one reads of the liberties afforded to imperial charter companies in nineteenth-century Asia and Africa and the activities of the United Fruit Company in Central America during the 1950s.[14]

Second, and perhaps more crucially, empirical studies have revealed that there is a positive correlation between the openness of the economy and the size of government. The famous finding by economist Dani Rodrik shows that states whose gross domestic product contains a higher share of trade tend to have larger government expenditures.[15] It is a correlation that is counterintuitive to the expectations of both advocates of free markets and their critics. The warnings of critics that reduced barriers to trade would require states to disappear have proven to be unfounded, whereas the judgment of the neoliberals that government size can negatively affect trade is also groundless. At the same time, it should not be surprising, given the record of countries that experienced laissez-faire capitalism in the face of the turmoil of the international market, that states should seek to shield themselves from its potential risks. Indeed, political scientist John Gerald Ruggie has emphasized how, in the aftermath of World War II, government intervention was determined necessary to maintain domestic economic stability and the smooth operation of a multilateral global economy. He has called this phenomenon "embedded liberalism."[16] While one might expect that the argument behind embedded liberalism has been weakened by the collapse of the Bretton Woods monetary system in the 1970s, the subsequent challenge to US economic hegemony, and by the neoliberal shift, Robert Keohane has argued that it continued thereafter, and the empirical evidence provided by Rodrik's research shows that governments remain reluctant to loosen their support systems to shield their populations from adverse market conditions.[17]

I rest my argument upon the recognition that the state continues to be an important actor on the international scene. Although joining an international organization such as the WTO may somehow reduce its autonomy, this is done to advance international economic cooperation that is expected to benefit the state. In fact, given the transformations taking place in the global economy, the state has an important role to play. The state is expected to deal with many conflicting pressures that originate outside its borders

In his book about globalization, Jan Aart Scholte talks about global tensions characterized by the spread of transplanetary and supraterritorial connectivity. The state should not abdicate its responsibility. It should try to resolve growing tensions brought about by globalization, which after all "is about contests between interests and competing values."[18]

Craig N. Murphy observes that globalization offers a possibility for establishing a substantially more democratic global polity. However, to seriously contemplate its current prospects we must pay attention to the central feature of the global polity that "can be identified along three dimensions: the policy realms it affects, its institutions, and its social nature, that is the social forces that it privileges or curtails."[19] In that sense, the WTO is an interesting case study because it provides a forum where economically and socially diverse countries can compete over the shape of its policies, its institutional structure, and its social consequences. Furthermore, the WTO claims to be a global organization with universal membership, which as Peter D. Sutherland observes, "means that it is ideally placed to contribute to new cooperative arrangements at the international level aimed at promoting global coherence in economic policymaking, not only in trade relations, but also more generally in other aspects of economic policy."[20]

Consequently, the WTO's ambitions must be scrutinized not only from the institutionalist perspective as a functional outcome of interstate negotiations. The WTO must also be investigated from within, as a bureaucracy with its own internal dynamics. Here the recent work by Michael Barnett and Martha Finnemore presents us with great insights by recognizing that each international organization has its own internal autonomy. The authors note that most theories of international relations assume that an international organization being created by states would exist and act in the way states want them. In contrast, their premise is to treat international organizations as autonomous actors that "often produce inefficient, self-defeating outcomes and turn their back on those whom they are supposed to serve."[21] This approach can help us examine certain unexpected developments in the life of the WTO that appear to have a detrimental effect on the operation of the organization.

Organization of the Book

This book is organized in the following way. Chapter 2 provides important historical background to the current events in the international trade system. It would be very difficult to understand the magnitude of the changes that have occurred both on the institutional level (creation of the WTO) and on the substantial level (new industries, new trade issues, new actors) without going back to the origins of the multilateral trade system. The chapter consequently takes the reader throughout the decades when trade relations were managed by the provisional GATT agreement until the momentous Uruguay Round of multilateral negotiations, which after prolonged negotiations, gave birth to the WTO.

Chapter 3 examines principles, structures, and practices of the WTO with the focus on the main obligations and responsibilities given to its members. The chapter takes a close look at the decisionmaking bodies of the WTO and shows the extent of the transformation from the GATT system to the rules-based WTO. My investigation reveals an apparent paradox of the organization—that as it becomes more democratic internally, it also becomes less effective in terms of advancing its goals. The WTO has provided legal opportunities for developing countries to shape its agenda, but it did so at a price. Developing countries are no longer willing to accept the demands by the historically dominant economies, which, in turn, are not ready to relinquish their control over the trading system. The outcome is an ongoing struggle within the organization that asks for institutional reforms of the system.

Chapter 4 concentrates on the first pillar of the WTO: trade in goods. It specifically focuses on the most controversial agreements included in the first pillar, namely the agreements on agriculture, textiles and clothing, and antidumping. Agricultural trade was poorly dealt with under the old GATT, despite the fact that it constituted a vital part of the economy in many countries. Over the years a number of exemptions allowed under GATT distorted the way countries conducted trade in agricultural products by keeping this sector effectively outside the multilateral rules. In a similar way, international trade in textiles and clothing remained outside GATT despite being of vital importance to developing countries. The chapter provides a historical explanation as to why this was the case. It also explains and critically analyzes the mentioned agreements.

The second pillar of the WTO, trade in services, is the subject of Chapter 5. It centers on the General Agreement on Trade in Services (GATS). It is a very unique agreement that permits countries to design their own liberalization strategy when opening services sectors to foreign competition. The flexibility afforded to WTO members under the GATS, however, can become counterproductive since the agreement requires considerable technical knowledge to conduct liberalization within its framework. Furthermore, because barriers to trade in services are related to a range of domestic regulations, the opening of services sectors to foreign competition requires collaboration between different ministries and private business groups. Overall, this chapter tells the reader about the magnitude of problems associated with services liberalization and explains the limitations of the GATS in advancing a thoughtful plan for achieving this.

Chapter 6 is about the third pillar of the WTO, which is also the most controversial part of the organization: the Agreement on Trade-Related Aspects of Intellectual Property Rights (TRIPs). TRIPs is an attempt to set global standards for protection of intellectual property rights at a level that is comfortable with the demands expressed by a number of industries. Regrettably, by emphasizing the private monopolistic rights of titleholders, TRIPs represents an approach that is very narrow and industry driven. It does not take into consideration the impact of implementing TRIPs in poor developing countries. TRIPs is also insensitive to the different cultural and social attitudes expressed toward the concept of intellectual property, which in fact contradicts the idea of free and open trade. The chapter provides a brief negotiating history behind the agreement, explains its main provisions, and discusses the various controversies surrounding it.

Chapter 7 talks about the attempts to enlarge the scope of the WTO by negotiating agreements on new issues. As the WTO was established, many countries felt that the negotiations were unfinished because issues such as investment were not successfully dealt with. In addition, the idea of including provisions within the WTO concerning the environment and labor standards was at the time gaining widespread support among civil society groups in the major industrialized countries. Following the first WTO ministerial meeting in Singapore in 1996, several working groups were established to advance future multilateral negotiations on a set of new issues. So far, however, there has been little progress in this area. Developing countries reject the inclusion of new issues in the WTO. They fear that such standards would only be used for protectionist purposes, thus restricting access of many products and services from the developing world. In response, the developed countries are seeking to broaden the scope of the existing multilateral obligations by placing additional demands on the countries acceding to the WTO and by negotiating bilateral trade agreements outside the WTO.

Chapter 8 focuses on developing countries and on the linkages between trade and development in the WTO context. The transformation of the world trading system from GATT to the WTO started with the promise implicitly conveyed by the new organization to integrate all countries under its legal framework. The integration of developing countries, however, has encountered numerous challenges. In this context, a number of developing countries expressed their reservations over an unbalanced WTO implementation process and asked that more emphasis be placed on their developmental needs. This was recognized in the 2001 WTO Ministerial Declaration that launched the Doha Round of multilateral negotiations aimed at addressing the ongoing concerns of developing countries. Events that have been dominating the agenda of the WTO since its establishment point out how influential a number of developing countries have become. Throughout the pages of this book, it is often demonstrated how the positions taken by India and Brazil, in cooperation with other developing countries, have changed the priorities within the WTO. In this chapter, special attention is paid to China, or specifically to the consequences of the Chinese accession to the WTO. China spent over a decade negotiating its entry into the WTO. Even before it completed its accession in 2001, China became a powerful new global economic player. Its current position and its stance on many important issues influence the world community. The conclusion of the book speculates about the future prospects of the WTO, the world economy, and more generally about the options for multilateralism during the time of ongoing global transformations.

Notes

1. Aristotle, *Politics,* Book Four, Part IV, written in 350 BCE.
2. Karen Manchester, "Silk Road and Beyond: Travel, Trade, and Transformation," opening speech of the Silk Group Project, February 2, 2007.
3. As of May 2008.
4. John J. Mearsheimer, *The Tragedy of Great Power Politics* (New York: W. W. Norton, 2001), pp. 19–21.
5. Robert O. Keohane and Joseph Nye, *Power and Interdependence: World Politics in Transition* (Boston: Little Brown, 1977), p. 19.
6. Stephen Krasner (ed.), *International Regimes* (Ithaca, NY: Cornell University Press, 1983), p. 2.
7. Robert O. Keohane, *After Hegemony: Cooperation and Discord in the World Political Economy* (Princeton, NJ: Princeton University Press, 1984).
8. Krasner, *International Regimes,* p. 2.
9. Anita Chan and Robert J. S. Ross, "Racing to the Bottom: International Trade Without a Social Clause," *Third World Quarterly* 24, no. 6 (2003): 1011–1028.
10. Elaine Hartwick and Richard Peet, *Theories of Development* (New York: Guilford Press, 1999), pp. 37–40.
11. Milton Friedman, *Capitalism and Freedom* (Chicago: University of Chicago Press, 1982), p. 9.
12. Donald W. Bray and Marjorie Woodford Bray, "Beyond Neoliberal Globalization: Another World," *Latin American Perspectives* 29, no. 6 (2002): 117–126.
13. Paul Hirst and Grahame Thompson, "The Future of Globalization," *Cooperation and Conflict* 37, no. 3 (2002): 249.
14. Stephen D. Krasner, "Sovereignty," *Foreign Policy* 122 (1991): 26.
15. Dani Rodrik, "Why Do More Open Economies Have Bigger Governments?" *Journal of Political Economy* 16, no. 5 (1998): 998.
16. John Gerald Ruggie, "International Regimes, Transactions, and Change: Embedded Liberalism in the Postwar Economic Order," *International Organization* 36, no. 2 (1982): 399.
17. Keohane, *After Hegemony*, p. 187.
18. Jan Aart Scholte, *Globalization—A Critical Introduction,* 2nd ed. (Basingstoke, UK: Palgrave, 2005), p. 83.
19. Craig N. Murphy, "The Historical Process of Establishing Institutions of

Global Governance and the Nature of Global Polity," in Morten Ougaard and Richard Higgott (eds.), *Towards a Global Polity* (London and New York: Routledge, 2002), p. 169.

20. Peter D. Sutherland, "Globalisation and the Uruguay Round," in Jagdish Bhagwati and Mathias Hirsch (eds.), *The Uruguay Round and Beyond—Essays in Honour of Arthur Dunkel* (Berlin: Springer Publishing, 1998), p. 152.

21. Michael Barnett and Martha Finnemore *Rules for the World: International Organizations in Global Politics* (Ithaca, NY: Cornell University Press, 2004), p. 2.

PART 1

The Foundations of the World Trade Organization

CHAPTER 2

Postwar Multilateralism: The General Agreement on Tariffs and Trade and the Road to the Uruguay Round

Although traders have been creating and establishing trade routes since ancient times, it was only in the twentieth century that the formal coordination of international commerce was first sought. Throughout the Industrial Revolution, governments were quick to collect taxes generated by foreign trade, but they would not engage in any negotiations on forging multistate trade treaties. The era of formal multilateral trade agreements started only quite recently. This is not to say that international commerce was outside the long historical processes that underpinned the development of international law. On the contrary, as one scholar put it, "one of international law's most enduring instruments—the interstate treaty—arose from the desire of states to make agreements to foster friendship, commerce, and navigation."[1] Hugo Grotius's *Mare Liberum*, arguably the founding text of modern international law, advocated the freedom of the seas to open up trade amongst nations. Still, up to the latter part of the twentieth century, free-trade treaties were mainly signed to facilitate commercial relations between two countries. The unique exemption to this rule appears to be the Hanseatic League of merchant associations established in the fourteenth century within the cities of northern Germany and other nations located around the Baltic Sea. On a darker side, free-trade accords were also sought by various European imperial powers that used the threat of force to strengthen their requests.

The need for multilateral collaboration on trade matters gained a sense of urgency only after World War II. The interwar era saw the appearance of some multilateral talks among nascent central banks of Western great powers to facilitate and control capital flows. Nevertheless, their attention was mainly directed toward finance rather than the exchange of goods and services. After the carnage of World War II, countries were determined to create institutional linkages among them to coordinate international flows of trade and finance. But trade matters proved to be difficult to manage. It took an additional fifty years before a formal trade organization of global reach, the WTO, was born in 1995. No law of destiny guaranteed its arrival; rather, a combination of many factors eventually led to the establishment of the WTO.

First, the multilateral system over the years had outgrown its provisional GATT framework, which by the end of the 1980s appeared to be too limited to effectively accommodate the enlarged membership and resolve trade disputes among them. Second, the global spread of new telecommunication technologies has created modern knowledge-based and communication industries that pushed for the expansion of multilateral trade agreements into the territories like services and intellectual property. In addition, new technologies have allowed speedy cross-border transfer of payments and flow of capital that have significantly accelerated international exchanges of goods and services. Finally, the geopolitical changes that have occurred since the end of the Cold War have encouraged a turn away from the ideologically charged rivalry that once played out between the capitalist West and the communist East toward a unified rule-based system of international economic governance. As a result, the rule of law has begun to play an important new role in the organization of international economic relations.[2]

The evolution of the postwar world trading system in the direction of a substantial legal organization was a victory for legally oriented trade experts.[3] They favored a legal approach to trade matters because it was considered to be more predicable, transparent, and fair. A diplomatic approach, on the other hand, was burdened with a notion of power politics habitually characterized by unpredictable outcomes and deals done behind closed doors. GATT's mode of diplomacy also appeared to be ineffective in dealing with an unprecedented number of new developing countries interested in joining the system. Nonetheless, the legal victory was not quite definite and it came after many years of uncertainty. The WTO was established as a result of the Uruguay Round of multilateral trade negotiations, which took more than four years of preparations and seven more years of talks to complete.[4]

The main goal of this chapter is to provide a historical background to the world trade system from the beginning of GATT in 1947 to the Uruguay Round of multilateral trade negotiations (1986–1993) that resulted in the creation of the WTO. It relates to the main argument of the book that considers the events surrounding the Uruguay Round as a transformative stage in the history of international trade relations. This is why this chapter necessarily concentrates on trade issues, although there was so much more to the post–World War II multilateralism. The investigation on how the Uruguay Round resulted in the WTO is justified, in my view, because the WTO was such a unique multilateral effort to deal with geopolitical, technological, and economic challenges of the changing world. Still, despite its significance, the WTO remains an unfinished project. The first decade of the WTO existence revealed many cracks in the system and created uncertainties about the prospects for multilateralism, and the prospects for meaningful integration of small and weak economies into the global trade networks. Over the postwar era, international trade had evolved into a complex legal system fueled by international finance. The question for the future is whether the system is becoming truly global to serve the needs of all its member countries or whether international trade of the future will be subject to power politics and unilateral decisionmaking.

Postwar Negotiations and the Bretton Woods System

When the Uruguay Round of negotiations began in 1986 the world was still divided along ideological lines. The so-called communist camp led by the Soviet Union practiced the orthodoxy of a state-run planned economy; it was hostile to the concepts of private property and free market exchanges based on supply and demand, and it perceived trade liberalization with great apprehension.[5] The West was not quite unified in terms of ideology, but it was generally accepted that the United States often provided leadership as the most economically powerful state. The liberal democracies of this camp continued to function according to free market principles, although there were clear differences among them with respect to the degree of state involvement. For over forty years the world was characterized by the unpredictable rivalry of the Cold War.

The need to reconstruct the world economy after World War II and the experience of the interwar period put pressures on political leaders to coordinate their postwar economic policies. The interwar period saw a particularly devastating economic depression resulting in a number of states introducing ruinous unilateral economic initiatives that perversely deepened the crisis. The Great Depression of the 1930s and the hostilities that followed led many political leaders to believe that: "the absence of an institutional framework allowed countries to pursue opportunistic policies that compounded their neighbors' problems."[6]

Consequently, there were four main priorities that framed discussions about the postwar economic order. The first priority was to construct a stable institutional framework that would encourage cooperation among nations. The second concerned the reconstruction of Europe. The third was to achieve stable economic growth, financial security, and full employment. The fourth priority was to pursue a liberal economic order on the international stage while allowing the state to retain its autonomy in conducting domestic economic policies. This last principle was later termed "embedded liberalism" by John Ruggie in the context of the subsequent development of the welfare state.[7] Focusing on these priorities helped the pursuit of common international objectives and led to the series of meetings at Bretton Woods, New Hampshire.

In July 1944, representatives of the forty-four countries meeting in Bretton Woods drafted and signed the Articles of Agreement of the International Monetary Fund (IMF) and the International Bank for Reconstruction and Development (IBRD), better known today as the World Bank. Despite the focus on monetary issues, one of the important objectives of the Bretton Woods talks was to facilitate international trade flows in the postwar era. The negotiated articles of the IMF demonstrated the acknowledgement of clear linkages between financial and trade issues. Article I of the IMF lists six main purposes of the organization. The first one is to promote international monetary cooperation, but the second one is to facilitate the expansion and balanced growth of international trade. All six IMF goals are interrelated in a sense that without financial and exchange stability and without multilateral confidence building, international trade would never take off among countries devastated by the war and in desperate need of loans to pay for essential imported goods.[8]

Scholars frequently point out the decisive role played by certain officials during international negotiations, although they often disagree about the degree of their influence.[9] There were two such dominant personalities at the steering wheel of the Bretton Woods talks: John Maynard Keynes of Britain and Harry Dexter White of the US Treasury. Keynes was a famous British economist, who revolutionized the field of economics by demonstrating how a government can help to avoid economic recessions and stimulate growth with the use of fiscal and monetary policies. In his 1936 book *The General Theory of Employment, Interest and Money,* he outlined the fundamental principles behind what would become known as "macroeconomics." As the chief British negotiator at Bretton Woods, Keynes prepared a proposal that reflected, first of all, the need for restoring domestic growth. Keynes believed that the IMF should never be able to intervene into domestic policy making. White, who was the chief international economist at the US Treasury, was instrumental in preparing his country's position on the IMF, which favored a stronger organization with the power to interfere in the domestic policies of its members in order to promote greater openness of the world's markets.[10] The negotiations centered on these two positions.[11] The final Bretton Woods compromise came closer to White's proposal, which favored less-restrained economic liberalization. When the IMF was inaugurated in 1946, US president Harry S. Truman named Harry Dexter White the first executive director of the IMF.

The negotiating parties at Bretton Woods agreed to peg their currencies to the US dollar, which in turn was pegged to gold at US$35 per ounce. The pegging of a preeminent currency to gold was deemed necessary to maintain trust and confidence in financial transactions. A stable financial system was a prerequisite necessary to address the apparent challenges of the postwar reconstruction efforts. The negotiators at Bretton Woods who attempted to design a new peaceful world order were aware that without restoring trust in the international economic arrangements, domestic economic institutions, and policies aimed at reviving industrial production, they would not be able to rebuild infrastructure, reduce unemployment, and halt inflation. But to become trustworthy, the new, emerging postwar economic institutional order also needed a guarantor. It would have to be a country with a large working economy and stable currency.

The US economy was the only economy that not only remained largely unscathed as a result of the war, but in fact, inevitably benefited from it as orders, first for weapons and then for a variety of industrial and food products, multiplied from the economically exhausted Europe. As Europe slowly tried to rebuild itself, the United States emerged after the war as an unchallenged powerhouse whose share of global wealth and production was skewed by the sheer destruction brought upon the economies of Europe and Asia. The convertibility of the US dollar to gold constituted the fundamental mechanism of the system, further supported by the new leadership position of the United States in the world. This unique position of the US dollar made it into the postwar dominant currency and the backbone of the IMF.

Implicitly, the signatories of the Bretton Woods compromise hoped that the IMF would gradually revitalize international trade by allowing its members to borrow money to pay for their foreign purchases. Every member of the IMF had to contribute its assigned quota in gold and its own currency to the Fund. The quotas were calculated first for the original members and later for the new members upon their accession to the IMF. The calculations that established the quotas took into account the size and strength of the individual economies. These quotas were to be paid on an annual basis of 25 percent in gold or the US dollar and 75 percent in the member-state currency. A similar formula is still in place today. The size of the quota has historically determined the IMF member's voting power.[12] But due to the growing unpredictability of the US dollar to gold exchange (eventually abolished in 1973) caused by the huge expansion of international trade and disastrous balance-of-payments deficits in the United States,[13] the IMF members decided to create in 1969 special drawing rights (SDRs), a type of international monetary reserve currency. Presently, while the SDRs have very limited use as reserve assets, all IMF accounting is done in SDRs. Countries started to trade with each other as soon as the war was over. The demand was mainly fueled by the reconstruction needs and shortages of many essential commodities and food items. The quick rise in the volume of international trade flows was also attributed to IMF loans used by countries to pay for foreign purchases. With time the strengthening of the banking industry in Europe would see the growing influence of private loans. However, in the early postwar years, it was the IMF that made trade possible. The IBRD was designated as an institution for lending money to finance the development projects. However, under its charter, it was not allowed to lend to countries that were unable to pay their external debts. The bank was designed to help rebuild Europe. As the Bretton Woods talks commenced, a large part of Africa and Asia remained politically and economically under colonial control. This situation would have profound consequences on developing countries once they became independent. By the nature of its early years, the World Bank would remain institutionally ill prepared to deal with developmental problems in the third world, as it was never part of its initial mandate. With its focus on market economies, the Bretton Woods institutions were lacking any mechanisms for rescheduling debts or for managing international capital flows.[14] These organizations were also essentially silent about the issues related to economic development, especially in the poor regions of the world. These weaknesses would develop into serious problems for the IMF, the World Bank, and eventually for the world economy as a whole following the debt crisis in the 1970s.

The negotiators at Bretton Woods realized the importance of trade, but specific negotiations aimed at establishing a trade organization followed their own trajectory. While it was relatively straightforward to negotiate an agreement on monetary matters and postwar financial architecture, the trade talks were difficult. Facing vastly different socioeconomic realities, the US and British negotiators—the representatives of the two countries that shaped the postwar economic order—subscribed to somewhat different visions about the scope and purpose of the international trade regime. The British team was preoccupied with the reconstruction costs and its focus was on domestic economic development. This meant that the British plan regarding the postwar international trade regime was limited and secondary to the urgent need of rebuilding the destroyed economy.

Because of the devastating impact of the war, it was clear that it would take years before any of the European countries, including the UK, would be able to compete on the world markets. In contrast, the United States was emerging as an economically powerful country that was to benefit greatly from the prospects of free trade, especially given the growing prominence of the US dollar. Despite these divergent ideas on international trade, both sides initiated the talks as early as 1943, but the negotiations reached momentum only in 1945 when a document entitled "Proposals for Consideration by an Intergovernmental Conference on Trade and Employment" was released. This document contained a proposed charter for the International Trade Organization (ITO).[15] To facilitate the negotiation process, the ITO Preparatory Committee was created under the umbrella of the UN Economic and Social Council. As soon as the committee began to hold a series of meetings in 1946, the divisions among the negotiating parties resurfaced.

The ITO was a US initiative, first conceived as part of the Bretton Woods system. The ITO proposal rested on the following six principles: (1) Trade liberalization should be encouraged to increase the volume of international trade seen as a means for maintaining employment and benefiting economies of the countries around the world; (2) Private enterprise is rendered superior to potentially distortive government policies as far as private enterprise can ensure the competitiveness, progress, and efficiency of trade; (3) A multilateral trade system is considered superior to bilateral trade relations because, among other benefits, it "protects the weaker bargainer against the stronger one. It places emphasis on economic, not on politics"; (4) The principle of nondiscrimination should guide all trade relations in a way that "every nation should afford equal treatment to the commerce of all friendly states"; (5) Countries should be aware of a close connection between domestic economic policies (stabilization programs) and trade policy; (6) Countries must recognize the crucial importance of international consultation and cooperation.[16] These principles support a vision of an international organization that places emphasis on fairness and cooperation among nations. It also expresses the view that international trade is indeed important, but it should be seen primarily as a means for achieving economic progress to benefit people in all countries.

The nondiscrimination principle, otherwise known as the most-favored-nation (MFN) principle, has remained a cornerstone of the trading system until today. Also called the "favor one, favor all" principle, the MFN treatment simply means that once a particular state (a signatory to a treaty) grants a certain trade concession to another state (also a signatory to the same treaty), this concession is automatically given to every other signatory of the treaty. The postwar trade negotiations were launched with the hope that once the ITO was established it would help to build a system where a preferential treatment could only be given on rare occasions, allowing member countries fair market access to each other's markets on a nondiscriminatory basis. Other principles, like multilateralism, international cooperation, and importance of private business were implicitly adopted by GATT, but the principle that acknowledges the close relationship between the trade and developmental policies of individual states would become less prominent under GATT. And despite its adherence to the idea of nondiscriminatory trade, GATT would gradually allow the MFN principle to be distorted, especially in the context of agricultural trade.

The first round of negotiations on the ITO proposal took place in London in 1946. The talks concerned the freezing of the existing trade preferences so the principle of nondiscrimination could be maintained. Also, at the table the negotiators were discussing whether countries should make a commitment to continue with progressive reductions to tariffs and other existing barriers to trade in the future. Another set of talks concerned the virtual ban on the use of quantitative restrictions. At the second round in Geneva in 1947, trade practitioners and negotiators engaged in what turned out to be the major event on the path toward regulating the postwar trading system. In Geneva the trade negotiators conducted extensive technical negotiations resulting in significant tariff cuts.[17] The significance of this initiative would only become clear when talks concerning the institutional arrangements of the ITO started to lose support of the main trading partners. The final meeting took place in Havana. Its goal was to negotiate a charter that would establish a formal organization.

The trade negotiations were turning increasingly difficult, but they did nevertheless result in signing the Havana Charter in March 1948. The charter constituted the legal basis for the creation of the ITO. Regrettably, throughout 1947 the global political environment was changing and countries were shifting their economic priorities. The US Congress was becoming increasingly protectionist as the attention of the new US administration under President Truman was being diverted to dealing with the uncertainty of the policies of the Soviet Union. For example, the Soviet Union participated in the Bretton Woods talks and signed the IMF treaty in 1944, but it refused to take part in the ITO negotiations in 1946. Furthermore, the new US administration was faced with growing opposition from business groups. Some were unhappy about certain provisions of the Havana Charter, while others were contesting the idea of a formal institution governing international trade altogether. As a result, President Truman never even risked sending the ITO Charter to the US Congress for ratification. And since the rest of the countries waited for the US to ratify the Havana Charter, the ITO never materialized.[18]

The ITO was supposed to deal with trade issues in a comprehensive way. The organization was to be given a broad mandate to manage international trade including tariffs and preferences, quantitative restrictions to trade, development, employment, subsidies, competition policy, agriculture, restrictive private business practices, commodity agreements, and investment. The ITO was to go beyond simple commercial considerations in dealing with the plethora of trade-related matters. The ambitious goals of the ITO are perhaps best expressed by citing the words of its US negotiator, Clair Wilcox, and one of its most devoted supporters:

> It is the central purpose of the Havana Charter to contribute to the improvement of living standards all around the world by promoting the expansion of international trade on a basis of multilateralism and non-discrimination, by fostering stability in production and employment, and by

> encouraging the economic development of backward areas. It will be the purpose of the International Trade Organization, which is established by the Charter, to substitute cooperation for conflict, in international commerce, in industrial stabilization, and in economic development, by providing a medium through which nations may regularly consult with one another concerning the international consequences of national policies.[19]

The Havana Charter for the ITO was never ratified. It is possible that the charter fell victim to its elaborate scope. Since the trade talks had been difficult from the start and many conflicting demands were presented in Havana, the proposed charter represented a peculiar compromise. As Peter Kenen once wrote, "In drafting an agreement that was too ambiguous to offend anyone, the negotiators succeeded merely in alienating everyone."[20] Kenen believed that the United States did not approve of it because the charter allowed for too much government intervention. Other countries pointed out its excessive exemptions that in effect nullified the idea about having a fundamental set of rules.

The collapse of the ITO Charter could had been quite detrimental for the world trading system if it were not for GATT, which was already in place at the time of the Havana conference. GATT was made possible because after 1946 trade negotiations were conducted in two streams. In parallel to the institutional talks concerning the charter of the ITO, a set of technical meetings took place between January and February 1947 in Lake Success, New York. During these talks GATT as a legal agreement was concluded.[21] This turned out to be a momentous development that would ultimately rescue the postwar multilateral approach to international trade, despite the ITO fiasco. GATT listed the provisions aimed at liberalizing the trade relations among its contracting parties by reduction of tariffs. Later that year the talks moved to Geneva, where the representatives from twenty-three countries conducted 123 bilateral tariff-cutting negotiations resulting in about 50,000 tariff cuts, with the average tariff being cut by 35 percent.[22] Most important, however, the negotiators agreed to protect the value of the tariff concessions by early acceptance of GATT by means of adopting the Protocol of Provisional Application, which was completed on October 30, 1947, and came into force on January 1, 1948.

One thing is worth mentioning on the occasion of the final stage of the postwar multilateral trade negotiations. The North-South discord that emerged during that time would continue to trouble the world trading system. The first notable disagreements erupted over the desire for maintaining the system of imperial preferences by Britain, the establishment of new preferential systems, the use of agricultural quotas and agricultural subsidies, the employment of potentially trade-restricting development strategies (especially the use of quantitative restrictions with the aim of protecting domestic infant industries), and the use of other trade restrictions.[23] In particular, it was the group of what we may now call developing countries (India, China, Lebanon, Brazil, and Chile) that pressed hard for the clause that would allow countries to promote domestic industrialization by imposing quotas on imports. Therefore, it was at this early phase of the postwar multilateral trade system that the enduring North-South friction over the link between international trade and domestic development had first arisen.[24]

The World Trading System Under the Provisional GATT

In the absence of other formal institutional arrangements, the multilateral trading system since World War II has evolved under the provisional GATT. The collapse of the ITO, however, meant that many important standards and provisions of the proposed organization were never made operational. As a result, GATT had several weaknesses. The first major weakness stemmed from its provisional legal nature. GATT had no binding interpretative powers. This weakness influenced the way trade disputes would be settled. Without the power of making formal and legally binding interpretations, GATT's dispute settlement mechanism became voluntary. The Havana Charter contained specific provisions (Chapter VIII) that provided the ITO with a mechanism for ensuring that dispute settlement decisions and interpretations would be legally binding. Since the ITO failed, GATT had no such authority. Under its rules, a contracting party was not obliged to accept an outcome of the dispute panel that it found disagreeable and unsatisfactory. The provisional character of GATT also meant that new legal norms would be difficult to establish.[25]

The second major weakness of GATT resulted from its limited scope. After all, GATT was derived from and closely resembled only one (Chapter IV on Commercial Policy) out of the original nine chapters of the Havana Charter.[26] GATT represented the minimum acceptable set of provisions necessary to manage international trade multilaterally. In contrast to the Havana Charter, which contained 106 articles, the provisional GATT was left with 38 articles.

There was one important part of the original Chapter IV of the ITO that was removed when using it as a template to create GATT. It was Article 17, which among other things defined the principle of reciprocity.[27] Reciprocity meant that all the trading member countries were expected to extend similar trade concessions to each other to balance the system. In other words, no one country would be required to lower its trade tariffs on certain goods, unless other countries would lower their tariffs on some goods as well. Although Article 17 of the ITO was not part of GATT, the principle of reciprocity still guided the GATT negotiations on tariff reductions.[28] Nevertheless, the absence of a formal provision regarding reciprocity in

GATT created some difficulties for developing countries (which will be further discussed in Chapter 8) since a legal basis in support of a more balanced trade system was no longer there. Among the most important issues absent from GATT were the following: the maintenance of industrial stability and fair labor standards, development, international private investment, restrictive business practices, and intergovernmental commodity agreements.

One of the crucial achievements of the ITO was that the Havana Charter not only applied to governments but also to private businesses. The framers of the Havana Charter recognized that monopolistic tendencies were not the sole domain of governments, but they could also result from practices employed by private businesses. It was understood that restrictive business practices could undermine the goal of fair and nondiscriminatory trade. However, Chapter V of the Havana Charter, which listed the obligations with respect to anticompetitive business practices, died together with the ITO. Under GATT only governments would be subject to international regulation, not private businesses. In a similar fashion, GATT would be silent about the application of labor standards and the ability of countries to suspend their obligations to pursue their developmental objectives.

The third major weakness of the provisional GATT related to its lack of specific guidelines concerning decisionmaking procedures. The institutional design of the ITO was quite elaborate and included rules governing the operations of the ITO. The main decisionmaking body was supposed to be a conference consisting of all ITO members with each given one vote, an executive board of eighteen members elected by the conference, and a number of commissions to be formed on a needs (ad hoc) basis. But the ITO never materialized, and due to the provisional nature of GATT, its members were left with no institutional framework to follow. In fact, the countries that signed GATT could not even be called "GATT members" as no formal trade organization existed. Instead, the term "CONTRACTING PARTIES to the GATT"[29] was retained. It would not be until the birth of the WTO in 1995 that the vocabulary changed. With the formal status of the WTO, we can now talk about the members of the WTO.

To summarize, the provisional GATT had no institutional framework to draw on and no procedures to follow. Attached to the agreement were the negotiated tariff concessions, put in the form of schedules, of the twenty-three contracting parties to GATT. The imprecise character of GATT and its obvious limitations, however, were not always detrimental for international trade. To be sure, it was difficult to organize future negotiations or resolve existing disagreements when no rules were in place. On the other hand, the limited nature of GATT forced countries to develop the necessary procedures when they were needed. In a way, the provisional beginnings of the multilateral system provided opportunities for its pragmatic expansion and the emergence of functional institutionalism within GATT. Over the years, the contracting parties developed a set of institutional procedures.

Because they were born in response to specific needs, such procedures also enjoyed a high degree of legitimacy. Some of them—decisionmaking based on consensus is one example—were preserved even after the WTO was established. Another important example of how GATT managed to adapt to the functional needs of trading nations relates to the settling of trade disputes. None of GATT's articles contains any specific reference to the GATT dispute settlement panels. The very limited guidance given in Articles XXII and XXIII on how to approach the issue was gradually expanded by the procedural developments that saw the formation of panels of experts who would adjudicate trade disputes under GATT. This tradition was formalized by a special "understanding" issued at the end of the Tokyo Round of negotiations in 1979.[30]

GATT 1947 begins in Article I with the recognition of the Most-Favored-Nation principle as the foundation of the nondiscriminatory free-trade system; the WTO naturally retains it.

> 1. With respect to customs duties and charges of any kind imposed on or in connection with importation or exportation or imposed on the international transfer of payments for imports or exports, and with respect to the method of levying such duties and charges, and with respect to all rules and formalities in connection with importation and exportation, and with respect to all matters referred to in paragraphs 2 and 4 of Article III, any advantage, favour, privilege or immunity granted by any contracting party to any product originating in or destined for any other country shall be accorded immediately and unconditionally to the like product originating in or destined for the territories of all other CONTRACTING PARTIES.[31]

Unfortunately, GATT provides for exemptions under which countries can continue to discriminate among their trading partners. Therefore, here is a paradox for the GATT/WTO system. On the one hand, the MFN, in the words of Petros Mavroidis, is "the carrot offered to outsiders" to join the system. The MFN principle promises that each country will benefit from nondiscriminatory multilateralism because each country's goods will be automatically awarded the best possible treatment previously granted to such goods by other member countries. On the other hand, the exemptions to its application mean that presently "MFN trade becomes more of an illusion than an actuality."[32]

There are two important exemptions to the MFN. First, Article I includes the grandfathering clause that permitted the contracting parties to GATT to maintain existing regulations even if they were inconsistent with the MFN nondiscrimination principle. However, since the agreement also prohibits the enactment of any new MFN inconsistent trade laws, the significance of this exemption has diminished over time. The second exemption has been far more influential in eroding the application of the MFN principle because it has led to the proliferation of regional trade blocs. Preferential trade blocs are explicitly allowed under GATT Article XXIV and now under the WTO rules. It is widely assumed that this exemption was originally put in place in anticipation of the future European integration process that eventually led to the creation of the European Union.

In addition to the MFN principle, a second principle was set out in Article III of GATT to address discriminatory trade. It is called the National Treatment on Internal Taxation and Regulation principle.

> 4. The products of the territory of any contracting party imported into the territory of any other contracting party shall be accorded treatment no less favourable than that accorded to like products of national origin in respect of all laws, regulations and requirements affecting their internal sale, offering for sale, purchase, transportation, distribution or use. The provisions of this paragraph shall not prevent the application of differential internal transportation charges which are based exclusively on the economic operation of the means of transport and not on the nationality of the product.

The National Treatment principle is meant to prevent a situation in which a country introduces domestic regulations that favor domestic producers and hence discriminate against foreigners. In summary, "what the principle of National Treatment dictates is that once border duties have been paid by foreign exporters, as provided for in a country's tariff schedules, no additional burdens may be imposed through internal sales taxes, differential forms of regulation, etc. on foreign exporters where domestic producers of the same product do not bear the same burden."[33] With time the principle of National Treatment started to play a more prominent role, and the legal interpretation of some of its terms and provisions was the subject of several trade disputes. These trade disputes would become particularly significant under the WTO when the issue of National Treatment gained a special meaning under the new agreement on services, which often applies to the foreign services suppliers that are establishing their commercial presence and expecting nondiscriminatory treatment.

The provisional GATT embodied a set of rules of conduct for international trade that became the basis for its gradual institutional development. GATT's commitment to sponsor future negotiations paved the way for the institutional development of GATT and the gradual expansion of its membership.[34] As more countries joined GATT, the system was further enhanced by the subsequent legal *Understandings* agreed upon by the contracting parties and supported by the functional improvements in the decisionmaking procedures that became part of the GATT tradition. A bureaucracy headquartered in Geneva coordinated GATT. The main obligations it placed on trade policy of the contracting parties were as follows: (1) Export subsidies: Signatories of GATT may not use export subsidies, except for agricultural products; (2) Import quotas: Signatories of GATT may not impose unilateral quotas on imports, except when imports threaten "market disruption" (an undefined phrase usually interpreted to mean surges of imports that threaten to put a domestic sector suddenly out of business); and (3) Tariffs: Any new tariff or increase in a tariff must be offset by reductions in other tariffs to compensate the affected exporting countries.[35]

With more countries wanting to join GATT in the 1960s, the system was faced with a challenge of how to deal with centrally planned economies, which subscribed to an economic system in which no tariffs were used and no private enterprise existed. GATT was primarily conceived for free market economies and not for the emerging communist countries that participated in the negotiations. It was precisely around the time of the Bretton Woods agreements that the growing ideological discord between the two main superpowers became the underlying current of international relations. After the Soviet Union ceased to participate in the Bretton Woods negotiations, it was only a matter of time before the rest of the countries under its sphere of influence would gradually be forced to withdraw. Of course, it was clear from the start that central planning was incompatible with the kind of free market trading rules envisioned by GATT.

With Moscow tightening its knot around Eastern and Central Europe, the countries under the Soviet influence were "encouraged" to make commitments to Soviet-style industrialization and the principles of a planned economy. Institutions were soon established for administering foreign trade relations, but under state communism, such institutions were politically controlled and favored state-run industrialization programs that proudly rejected the Bretton Woods order. Over time the Soviet planners developed the Council for Mutual Economic Assistance (CMEA) organizational network for cooperation among the communist countries. It had its own special trade rules, and pricing and payment schedules that differed significantly from those practiced in free market economies.

The main features of trade relations conducted in the CMEA context, in addition to the above, were "bilateralism, currency and commodity inconvertibility, the monopoly of foreign trade and payments, and special foreign-trade organizations that buffer domestic economic activity against interactions with foreign sectors."[36] The primary political goal behind the CMEA was the achievement of regional self-sufficiency in order to keep interaction with free market economies at a minimum, finally leading to isolation from the rest of the world economy.

The architects of GATT could not predict the full extent of the political and economic divisions that were just beginning to unravel in the late

1940s. Fortunately, they believed that it was still possible to devise a general set of trade regulations that could apply to all. The key was to have provisions in place allowing all countries to join GATT at some point in the future. As Josef M. van Brabant stated, "Near-universal membership was in itself sought as a guarantee for reversing a sharp rise in the degree of intervention of the state in economic affairs since the 1930s. Against that backdrop, compromises had in principle been entertained to accommodate countries with 'another economic system,' if only because it was believed that participation in the global order would persuade those countries in time to bring their system into closer harmony with those of mainstream market economies."[37]

The provisions in Article XVII on state monopolies in the context of market economies provided the basis in GATT for accommodating centrally planned economies.[38] Article XVII:3 of GATT 1947 allowed for "negotiations on a reciprocal and mutually advantageous basis designed to limit or reduce obstacles" to trade resulting from the operation of state trading enterprises.[39] Contracting parties used this provision in the context of GATT accession negotiations by the Soviet-bloc state trading countries.

For example, Poland was a centrally planned economy when it acceded to GATT in 1967. As a result of its accession, it agreed to increase imports from the contracting parties according to a specified formula, and to include in its accession protocol the selective safeguard clause, a provision relating to quantitative restrictions, and special surveillance and consultations provisions.[40] The GATT contracting parties retained discretion to impose selective safeguard measures[41] on imports from Poland. Under the Polish protocol, the right to apply such measures was available only to the market-economy GATT countries, but it was not available to Poland.[42] The right is reciprocal in the protocols of Romania and Hungary. In addition, many contracting parties pushed for keeping the discriminatory quantitative import restrictions on Polish goods during an unspecified transitional period.[43] Romania's accession protocol (1971)[44] contains quantitative import commitments, but the accession protocol of Hungary (1973)[45] does not. In both these cases the GATT contracting parties reserved their right to use selective safeguards and to maintain quotas on Hungarian and Romanian products.

The three nonmarket economies were allowed to join GATT according to a protocol approach where each protocol was different and contained a unique accession formula for each country. For example, Poland's accession protocol stipulated that there were to be annual consultations to oversee the implementation of the obligations, but the Romanian and Hungarian protocols allowed for the reviews to be held every second year. These reviews went on record as meetings full of hostile exchanges over trade policy issues.[46] In fact, Poland's, Romania's, and Hungary's accessions to GATT were often considered only as symbolic gestures. The move, which was intended to bridge the East and West divide, in reality translated to very few tangible economic benefits. Eventually, the special protocol approach used in those accessions became contested as unsatisfactory both by the GATT contracting parties and the Eastern European countries themselves as they claimed that such an approach "provided for their second-class treatment."[47]

GATT was firmly entrenched within the principles of free market economies, and as a vehicle for trade liberalization, it continued to be viewed with apprehension by the Soviet camp. Yet, its original and simple purpose of making the exchange of goods between different countries easier turned out to be the best point of departure for progressive trade liberalization around the world. It has been a remarkable achievement that GATT, which began as a provisional agreement signed by twenty-three countries in 1947, has grown to the position of an important global organization with 152 members as of May 2008.

GATT also provided a forum to conduct new rounds of multilateral trade negotiations. To date, there have been eight major rounds of trade negotiations. The first five of them took the form of "parallel" bilateral negotiations. The sixth round, known as the Kennedy Round, was completed in 1967. The agreement involved an across-the-board 50 percent reduction in tariffs by the major industrial countries. The Kennedy Round represented the first truly multilateral trade agreement because countries were no longer focusing on bilateral reciprocal deals. The Tokyo Round that was concluded in 1979 introduced new nontariff issues such as subsidies, custom-valuations procedures, and antidumping disciplines.[48] Finally, the Uruguay Round (1986–1993) brought some radical changes to the international trade regime, permanently altering the character of GATT and establishing a formal organization, the WTO. In 2001 the Doha Round was initiated. It is the first round of multilateral talks conducted under the umbrella of the WTO, and as such it will be further discussed in later chapters.

The Tokyo Round (1973–1979) deserves some attention here, although I also return to it in subsequent chapters when discussing individual trade issues. The round took place during the time of global economic instability after the fixed monetary exchange of the Bretton Woods system collapsed and the rise in the price of oil for the first time created havoc. Perhaps because of the urgency of the moment, the Tokyo Round was very successful in advancing international cooperation and reducing barriers to trade. During the Tokyo Round, all the institutional developments with respect to the settlement of disputes under GATT were formally adopted as *The Understanding on Notification, Consultation Dispute Settlement and Surveillance of 28 November 1979*. The round also created a differentiated system by allowing separate codes to deal with new issues. The six codes negotiated in the Tokyo Round were (1) an agreement on government procurement, (2) an agreement on customs valuation, (3) an agreement on technical barriers to trade (standards), (4) an antidumping code, (5) a subsidies and countervailing duties code, and (6) an import licensing code.[49] Most developed countries joined all the codes, but developing countries would only join one or two of them, if any. Limited participation of developing countries in the Tokyo Round weakened the system.

In the 1970s, it was becoming painfully obvious that although GATT was remarkably helpful in facilitating prosperity in the developed world, its benefits were not extended to poor developing countries. As the Western countries prospered, international trade remained a source of tension in international relations. While the Tokyo Round reaffirmed the commitment of GATT's contracting parties to the principle of multilateral trade liberalization and international rule making as the response to the monetary and fiscal crises in the world economy, these responses were naturally viewed as one-sided by poorer countries that were unable to play a meaningful role in GATT or outside the system altogether. GATT's rules were designed by the industrial countries and given the provisional nature of GATT's already limited legal framework, the top trading nations could easily dominate GATT's agenda. The Tokyo Round made progress when it came to strengthening rules and expanding the scope of its influence to new trade issues. However, the Tokyo Round also fragmented the system by allowing countries to opt out from its newly negotiated agreements (codes).

Instead of working toward establishing a truly multilateral system for all interested countries, the Tokyo Round institutionalized the "take-it-or-leave-it" approach toward smaller economies with no bargaining power in GATT. It would not be until a decade later during the Uruguay Round when the geopolitical changes would shake international relations and the emerging new economies would demand to be part of the global decisionmaking concerning trade. At the time of the Tokyo Round, however, developing countries that felt marginalized within GATT decided to develop their own alternative world economic order. Building upon the multilateral strategies for global economic reforms first articulated in 1964 with the creation of the United Nations Conference on Trade and Development (UNCTAD), a group of 120 developing countries (originally 77) formulated a list of requests for a new international economic order (NIEO) in 1974. It was hoped the NIEO would ensure a greater participation of poor countries in international economic networks. It called, among other things, for expansion of preferential trade arrangements favoring poor countries, overhaul of the existing international norms of conduct, the significant increase in resource transfers from the industrialized to the developing world (including financial assistance and foreign aid), and the elimination of the third world debt. As part of the NIEO, specific demands were voiced to reform the post–World War

II economic architecture by subordinating the operations of the IMF, the World Bank, and GATT to the authority and supervision of the UN in order to allow poorer countries to influence their decisionmaking processes.[50] The industrialized countries implicitly rejected the NIEO. Just when the industrialized nations were advancing trade liberalization during the Tokyo Round, the vast majority of the less-developed countries felt that their only option to make some meaningful economic progress was to dismantle the existing order.

The Uruguay Round

In contrast to the atmosphere surrounding the Tokyo Round, there were no demands for the establishment of the NIEO during the Uruguay Round. Instead, developing countries decided to work from within the system, although it was not an easy task at the beginning of the round.[51] The ideological divisions during the Cold War hampered any initiatives for economic cooperation among nations, as both sides subscribed to two different and competing visions of an economic model for trade and development. This peculiar Cold War mentality naturally influenced the start of the Uruguay Round in the mid-1980s when the possibility of uniting the economic interests of the West camp and the Eastern bloc under a global trade organization was not yet seriously contemplated. However, it was the end of these divisions that most likely made the biggest impact, leading to the establishment of the WTO. The Uruguay Round marked greater involvement of developing countries. There were no calls for the NIEO because of the renewed hopes for a more fairly integrated global economy. The international geopolitical context surrounding the birth of the WTO provided optimism similar to that experienced at the end of World War II when the Bretton Woods system was put in place and GATT was formed.

As the negotiations commenced, the creation of a formal organization was not even part of the initial agenda of the Uruguay Round.[52] The WTO was proposed for the first time by the Canadian delegation in April 1990,[53] but it would not be until almost two years later when this idea was earnestly pursued. At the outset of the negotiations, the Uruguay Round was expected to fulfill three important tasks: (1) to address those areas of commerce that had been unsuccessfully dealt with under GATT, most notably trade in textiles and clothing and agriculture; (2) to clean up the Tokyo Round codes and create a more unified system; and (3) to expand the GATT rules to new areas of trade, most notably services.[54] The Punta del Este Declaration, which launched the Uruguay Round in 1986, was divided into two parts: Part I, Negotiations on Trade in Goods, and Part II, Negotiations on Trade in Services. Part I included not only most of the Tokyo Round issues like tariffs, quantitative restrictions, safeguards, and subsidies, but also several new ones like intellectual property, agriculture, and investment.[55]

A few years can make a tremendous difference in altering the course of history on the world stage of international economic relations. The Uruguay Round negotiations were in a deep crisis following the unsuccessful ministerial meeting in Montreal in December 1988. In fact, it was at that meeting that the ministers decided to suspend the round for four months to seek agreement on the most contentious issues that were bringing the round to the brink of collapse. The negotiations on agriculture, industrial tariffs, services, and intellectual property were particularly difficult, but problems were reported in almost every negotiating group.[56] After four months had passed, no meeting of the trade negotiations committees was scheduled and the impasse continued. No further meetings at the ministerial level would take place until the end of 1990, the year when the Uruguay Round was first scheduled to be completed.[57]

The Uruguay Round negotiations were eventually resumed and continued until the end of 1993, with the final agreement signed at Marrakesh, Morocco, in April 1994. The outcome of the Uruguay Round went well beyond its initial agenda formulated almost ten years earlier. The round reshaped the world trading system by introducing a number of changes with consequences that would mostly reveal themselves only years later. This chapter will now summarize the main differences that came with the transformation from GATT to the WTO. The scope of the GATT/WTO transformation, however, can only be understood following a careful examination of the most controversial WTO agreements and the positions that different countries took when negotiating them. This will be the task of the remaining chapters.

The Uruguay Round would never have been concluded and signed off by so many countries if it were not for the decision to create a formal WTO. Dissatisfied as they were with many of the WTO agreements, developing countries as a group decided to stay within the system because of the guarantees of equal access to the main decisionmaking bodies of the WTO. In effect, already the road to the Uruguay Round had witnessed a new type of relationship between developing and developed countries fueled by the confidence of the emerging economies. Known as the Café au Lait group, a flexible form of cooperation emerged in 1986 between the so-called G-20[58] group of developing countries and the G9[59] group of the major industrialized countries. This coalition aimed at formulating a shared agenda for the new round of negotiations. The Café au Lait indeed met its objective as the United States, European Communities (EC),[60] and Japan entered the talks with the group to prepare a draft declaration of July 30, 1986, which provided a basis for the Punta del Este Declaration that heralded the launch of the Uruguay Round. The Café au Lait group demonstrated a growing desire of developing countries to be active participants in shaping the international trade agenda.[61]

Despite these early developments, developing countries as a group were not able to achieve what they wanted in the Uruguay Round. They were not able to prevent the inclusion of the agreements on services and on intellectual property, and they were not successful in negotiating a stronger agricultural agreement. Amrita Narlikar, in her research on the subject, observes that ultimately "the consequences of the formation of the Café au Lait were destructive. The coalition had destroyed an old style of diplomacy, without providing developing countries with a viable alternative. Given the dependence of the coalition on external conditions before its strategies could have any effect, the Café au Lait provided an interesting pathway, but not a model."[62] It is an interesting observation. The dependence on external conditions meant, it is believed, that developing countries lacked institutional autonomy in pursuing their own agenda or in changing the agenda as set by others. The provisional power-based GATT system ensured the dominant position of the industrialized countries. This institutional impediment disappeared under the legal framework of the WTO.

In a nutshell, the Uruguay Round achieved the following: (1) it established the WTO as a legal entity that replaced the GATT system and ended its provisional character; (2) it created a legally binding dispute settlement mechanism for the WTO; (3) it introduced new agreements, some of them dealing with new trade issues like services and intellectual property; (4) it initiated multilateral reforms of trade in agricultural products and textiles; (5) it further lowered import duties on industrial products; and (6) it expanded the membership of the WTO with the aim of making it a global organization.

The Uruguay Round created a formal, rules-based organization, the WTO, which brings together a number of trade agreements relating to trade in goods and services, and trade-related aspects of intellectual property rights. The final act of the round also established a unified system of dispute settlement mechanisms for all of the WTO agreements. It includes a formal legal text (rather than just customary practice as it was under GATT) to provide precise guidelines outlining the proper procedures to be followed. The new procedures are based on the concept of compulsory adjudication stipulating measures that prohibit blocking the adoption of the panel. Under GATT, the losing party could block the final stage of the panel proceedings, thus making the GATT dispute settlement mechanism in effect voluntary and nonbinding. This is no longer the case under the WTO. Furthermore, a new appellate body was created to allow WTO members involved in a trade dispute to appeal the decision on a principle of law.

The preamble to the *Marrakesh Agreement Establishing the World Trading Organization* sets out the primary objectives of the WTO: to ensure the reduction in tariffs and other barriers to trade, and the elimination of discriminatory treatment in international trade relations. These goals are intended to facilitate a higher standard of living, full employment, and sustainable development in the member states.[63] After the preamble, the first three articles set out the form, the scope, and the functions of the new organization.[64] These provisions demonstrate the institutional transformation that came with the WTO. The legal language, however, is not able to convey the practical implications that came with the decision to establish such a comprehensive trade organization. This is because the day the WTO was officially initiated, the GATT/WTO transformation process only started. At the time, trade practitioners, scholars, and even the negotiators themselves could not possibly estimate the impact of the WTO on its members. To conclude with Sylvia Ostry's observation made during that period, "None of the models can estimate the full implications of deepening integration or the heart of the new system, the WTO. [Such changes] are not so easily captured by econometric estimates or conventional trade policy analysis."[65]

Another important accomplishment of the Uruguay Round was the expansion of the membership. A move toward such a rule-based system prompted historically vulnerable countries to become involved in the negotiations. The stakes were particularly high for the emerging economies. For most of its history, GATT was considered to be a club of predominantly industrialized nations. Poor and less developed countries were mostly outside its rules, and they tended to express varying degrees of hostility toward multilateral trade liberalization. The first few rounds of talks mainly served to lower trade barriers among the industrialized states, but even during the Tokyo and the Kennedy rounds of negotiations, developing countries played only a small role. The Uruguay Round, however, signaled a major change in this context. The numbers were impressive as 117 countries[66] actively participated in the concluding negotiations and 123 signed the final declaration.

Initially conflicted and unsure about the Uruguay Round and its advanced agenda, the developing countries ended up accepting the WTO. Three main factors were responsible for the support of developing countries for the conclusions of the Uruguay Round: (1) the trade-offs in the final agreement provided various attractive benefits to developing countries; (2) the negotiation process produced negative incentives and positive incentives that on balance encouraged a negotiated outcome; and (3) macroeconomic change and economic reform in developing countries led to new trade policies that were consistent with the liberalizing thrust of GATT multilateral negotiations.[67]

By the end of the 1980s the credibility of GATT had seriously eroded as the process of fragmentation that had begun with the Tokyo Round created growing legal and political difficulties. The Tokyo Round resulted in various codes that applied only to those countries that agreed to sign them. A number of signatories varied from code to code. It was feared that additional codes would lead to even more fragmentation and confusion, which would cause the already overburdened system to become nonoperational. The establishment of the WTO, then, creates order by instituting a legal framework that brings together all the various codes and other arrangements that were negotiated under GATT. Members of the WTO are now obliged to abide by the rules of all WTO agreements as well as the rules of GATT as a "single undertaking."

The changes that came with the completion of the Uruguay Round continue to play a major role in reshaping the world trading system. It has been more than ten years since the WTO was established, and it is finally possible to assess its performance. However, before we begin our analysis, let's summarize the main accomplishments of the Uruguay Round.

Dispute Settlement Mechanism

The legal authority of the WTO infuses it with the power to make the results of trade disputes into legally binding decisions. The essentially voluntary dispute settlement mechanism under GATT has been replaced with a unified and legally binding system. The Uruguay Round produced a new treaty text on dispute settlement, the Dispute Settlement Understanding (DSU).[68] The DSU unifies the previously fragmented assemblage of various GATT dispute settlement procedures, and hence the DSU also increases the predictability and transparency of the overall system. The DSU is understood to be an institutional mechanism for ensuring compliance. It is also intended to clarify provisions of the WTO agreements in accordance with the rules of interpretation under customary international law. Only WTO members can use the WTO dispute settlement mechanism to settle their trade disputes. As a result, the DSU becomes an incentive to join the WTO, since it is the only system for the settlement of disputes among states that has an appellate body and is based on compulsory jurisdiction and binding arbitration.

The General Agreement on Trade in Services (GATS)

From the beginning of the Uruguay Round, the matter of including an agreement on trade in services within the multilateral framework of rules was a source of disagreement among the negotiating parties. The difficult talks produced the GATS,[69] which is the most innovative of all WTO agreements and sets a framework for liberalization of trade in services in the way that restrictions on domestic services can be removed gradually. WTO members are allowed to make liberalizing commitments only in selective sectors—for example, tourism, financial, construction, and telecommunication services. Rooted firmly in the GATT tradition, general exemptions for regional trade arrangements, balance of payments, public order, and health also apply. The GATS brings into the WTO framework provisions dealing with investment, because it contains market access and national treatment guarantees for those foreign service suppliers that want to establish a physical presence in the host country. However, these guarantees are limited to sectors that the countries had decided to liberalize and had made commitments to under the GATS.

Agreement on Trade-Related Aspects of Intellectual Property Rights (TRIPs)

The idea behind TRIPs[70] was to bring intellectual property rights under a multilateral system of international trade rules. The developed countries argued at the outset of the Uruguay Round that the changing patterns of the global economy necessitated an agreement that would set minimum standards of protection for intellectual property rights. Copyrights (and related rights), trademarks, geographical indicators, industrial designs, patents, designs of integrated circuits, and trade secrets are the classifications of intellectual property that are covered under TRIPs.

The inclusion of an agreement on intellectual property rights under the multilateral framework was at the center of much discord throughout the Uruguay Round. The disagreements often reflected the North-South division. The industrialized nations insisted on having such an agreement in order to deal with the challenges of the new knowledge-based economies and to address their complaints about the growing international piracy of new technological inventions and artistic creations. Developing countries, on the other hand, resisted the inclusion of TRIPs into the WTO. They feared that it would create monopolistic tendencies among the industrialized countries, which would make new inventions, technologies, and creations prohibitively expensive and therefore out of reach for poorer countries. Eventually, a compromise was reached, although, as will be shown in the chapter examining TRIPs, many problems remain unresolved even today.

Agriculture

Historically, agriculture has been the most problematic area of international economic relations. Faced with food shortages after World War II, many European countries placed the issue of food security high on their developmental agenda. As country upon country would create programs to provide incentives for farmers to increase production of agricultural products, the governments did not take into account the long-term trade-distorting consequences of such programs. When food security was no longer an issue, however, countries found it difficult to scale down on such practices because of the growing strength of agricultural lobbies.

GATT's rules in principle applied to trade in agricultural products, but various exceptions negotiated by major trading countries allowed trade-restricting measures and subsidies; this left agriculture essentially outside the multilateral system. This is why the primary goal of the Uruguay Round's Agreement on Agriculture was to initiate a set of reforms aimed at introducing fair competition to this traditionally distorted sector of international trade. In terms of the progress made on liberalizing trade in agricultural products, the round did not go far enough.

The Agreement on Agriculture was conceived as a compromise between two objectives: first, to open domestic agricultural markets to foreign competition, and second, to create new predictable rules to govern the agricultural sector on a multilateral level. The Uruguay Round negotiators agreed to introduce a considerable degree of reform in the fundamental rules governing agriculture, but they were unable to reach any substantial deal on liberalizing trade in agricultural products.

An Agreement on Trade-Related Investment Measures (TRIMs)

The increased flows of foreign direct investment around the world have prompted several industrialized countries to advocate the creation of a multilateral investment agreement as part of the world trading system. The Uruguay Round negotiations on this issue, however, revealed the major differences among the participating parties. The resulting WTO Agreement on Trade-Related Investment Measures only explicitly connects with investment the previously existing GATT provisions concerning performance requirements.[71] TRIMs prohibits host countries from imposing certain performance requirements on foreign investors that are inconsistent with basic GATT obligations, such as national treatment and the requirement to avoid quantitative restrictions on trade. Unable to come up with a better outcome, negotiators of the Uruguay Round settled for TRIMs, while they agreed to place investment on a future negotiating agenda of the WTO.

* * *

The above agreements and institutional developments were the important outcomes of the round. Nevertheless, some of these agreements remained unfinished or subject to future negotiations when the round was completed. The negotiators were literally running out of time in December 1993. Because of the complicated US system, most countries believed that if the Uruguay Round was not finalized by January 1994, there was little point in continuing. Participating countries would abandon the talks because of their fear that the US Congress would not ratify the Final Act of the Round as it was negotiated since the special (fast-track) authority given to the administration to negotiate a multilateral deal was about to expire.

Let me explain the dilemma faced by Uruguay Round negotiators in 1993. Under the US system, it is the president and his administration that designates the US trade representative to negotiate international trade deals. But the US Congress has the final say in approving the trade deals made by the administration. In order to negotiate such agreements as final deals—as agreements that will be ratified by the US Congress as negotiated and without possibility that Congress will demand changes or modifications—the US president requires trade promotion authority (TPA) from Congress. Congress can give such (fast-track) authority to the US president for a specified period of time, but it does not have to. To obtain such an authority by the administration is not an easy process. It usually follows heavy bargaining between the administration and Congress that sets parameters of each TPA deal. For example, Congress can demand that each trade deal reached by the administration must contain provisions on labor standards.

Fast-track authority is important for the US negotiating team because it provides them with necessary legitimacy. It also gives countries negotiating with the United States the assurance that Congress will accept any hard-negotiated deals they reach with the US administration without amendments. Historically, without it, countries have been reluctant to negotiate trade agreements with the United States because of the risk that Congress would demand changes and delays. The 1974 Trade Act granted TPA to the president for five years. The Trade Agreements Act of 1979 extended the authority another eight years. The Omnibus Trade and Competitiveness Act of 1988 renewed the fast-track authority until May 1993. The 1988 act was in fact amended to extend TPA for the Uruguay Round agreements reached before April 16, 1994.[72] As there was little hope that the fast-track authority would be renewed again, the Uruguay Round had to be finalized in December 1993. Unfortunately, the frantic mood that surrounded the final months of negotiations did not provide space to reflect and to debate the negotiating deals. Several negotiating groups (telecommunications, financial services, and agriculture) could not even make sufficient progress due to the time constraints, so they agreed to complete the round by making commitments to resume negotiations at a later date.

Conclusion

The 1990s brought immense geopolitical changes that influenced the world economy by creating a climate marked by global cooperation unseen since the end of World War II. The Soviet Union disintegrated into fifteen small independent states. The idea of a communist state with a planned economy was bankrupt. The free market and the policy of economic liberalization gained an instant momentum.

It is my belief that the Uruguay Round would not have resulted in creating the WTO if it were not for the changing climate of the international political economy between 1989 and 1991. Looking back on the decades following World War II and the political and economic hostilities of the Cold War era, it was difficult to ignore the calling of the moment that presented an opportunity for global cooperation. In a world no longer divided between two competing camps, some argue that the WTO "represents an evolutionary adaptation on the part of GATT Members to a new political context, rather than a revolutionary change of direction stemming from a new ideological consensus."[73]

Unlike its predecessor, GATT 1947, the WTO is a formal rule-based intergovernmental organization with its own strengthened dispute settlement mechanism. It is also a member-driven organization, which means that the WTO decisionmaking process relies on the active participation of its member states. The WTO does not have an executive committee; every member state has, in principle, identical judicial power of one voice, one vote. Furthermore, and in contrast to GATT, the WTO scope is vastly enlarged to include such new issues as investment, services, and intellectual property.

The WTO is also about globalization, which sees the world being more integrated than ever before. It is a different world than the one GATT was born into. GATT was a club of a few trading nations that largely ignored the needs of less-developed countries. The WTO gives all its 152 members equal legal voice. Both the need to cooperate multilaterally and a requirement to design a comprehensive and predictable organization have led governments to create the WTO. However, if the WTO truly aims to promote prosperity and equality in global economic transactions, it must take into consideration the impact its rules are having with respect to socioeconomic development around the world. As Ernst-Ulrich Petersmann has commented: "The non-economic values of WTO law are no less important for the human rights and welfare of citizens than the economic welfare effects of liberal trade."[74] In order to achieve these goals, the organization must also operate effectively and fairly to meet the expectations of the participating countries. The next chapter will show how WTO's principles, structures, and practices can sometimes constrain some of its members while empowering others and how these contradictory pressures influence the operation of the WTO.

Notes

1. Deborah Z. Cass, *The Constitutionalization of the World Trade Organization—Legitimacy, Democracy, and Community in the International Trading System* (Oxford: Oxford University Press, 2005), pp. 5–6.

2. Judith Goldstein, Miles Kahler, Robert O. Keohane, and Anne-Marie Slaughter, "Introduction: Legalization and World Politics," in "Legalization and World Politics," a special issue of *International Organization* 54, no. 3 (Summer 2000): 385–399.

3. Robert Hudec, *Enforcing International Trade Law: The Evolution of the Modern GATT Legal System* (Salem, NH: Butterworth Legal Publishers, 1993).

4. John Croome, *Reshaping the World Trading System—A History of the Uruguay Round* (Geneva: World Trade Organization, 1995).

5. Michael M. Kostecki, *East-West Trade and the GATT System* (New York: St. Martin's Press, 1978).

6. Peter B. Kenen, *Managing the World Economy; Fifty Years After Bretton Woods* (Washington, DC: Institute for International Economics, 1994), p. 11.

7. John G. Ruggie, "International Regimes, Transactions and Change: Embedded Liberalism in the Postwar Economic Order," *International Organization* 36 (Spring 1982): 379–415.

8. Forty-five countries signed the final agreement on July 22, 1944. For more details about the organization, the Articles of Agreement of the IMF, and its history, see www.imf.org.

9. Andrew Moravcsik, "New Statecraft? Supranational Entrepreneurs and International Cooperation," *International Organization* 53, no. 2 (1999): 267–306.

10. James M. Boughton, "Harry Dexter White and the International Monetary Fund," *Finance and Development* 35, no. 3 (1998).

11. Louis W. Pauly, *Who Elected the Bankers? Surveillance and Control in the World Economy* (Ithaca, NY: Cornell University Press, 1997), pp. 82–86.

12. The current formula uses special drawing rights (SDRs) in its calculation. Each country receives 250 basic votes plus a quota of 1 voter per 100,000 SDRs. (The largest, the United States [17.11 percent], has 371,743 votes, while the smallest, Palau, has 281 votes).

13. Robert S. Walters and David H. Blake, *The Politics of Global Economic Relations* (Englewood Cliffs, NJ: Prentice Hall, 1992), pp. 78–79.

14. Kenen, *Managing the World Economy*, p. 14.

15. Sylvia Ostry, *The Post–Cold War Trading System: Who's on First?* (Chicago: University of Chicago Press, 1997), p. 61.

16. Clair Wilcox, *A Charter for World Trade* (New York: Macmillan, 1949), pp. 14–21.

17. A tariff is a tax on imported goods that is charged by customs officials before such imported goods are allowed to cross the border and enter a destination country.

18. Ostry, *The Post–Cold War Trading System*, pp. 63–65.

19. Wilcox, *A Charter for World Trade*, p. 53.

20. Kenen, *Managing the World Economy*, p. 14.

21. Petros C. Mavroidis, *The General Agreement on Tariffs and Trade—A Commentary* (Oxford: Oxford University Press, 2005), p. 3.

22. John S. Odell, *Negotiating the World Economy* (Ithaca, NY: Cornell University Press, 2000), p. 162.

23. Rorden Wilkinson, *The WTO—Crisis and the Governance of Global Trade* (London: Routledge, 2006), pp. 30–32.

24. Wilcox, *A Charter for World Trade*, p. 42.

25. John Jackson, *The World Trading System: Law and Policy of International Economic Relations* (Oxford: Oxford University Press, 1997), pp. 94–103.

26. Wilcox, *A Charter for World Trade*, pp. 223–327.

27. Ibid., pp. 246–247.

28. John H. Barton, Judith L. Goldstein, et al., *The Evolution of the Trade*

Regime: Politics, Law, and Economics of the GATT and the WTO (Princeton, NJ: Princeton University Press, 2006), p. 40.

29. The term "CONTRACTING PARTIES to the GATT" was always capitalized. This indicated that the entire GATT membership was the top decisionmaking organ in the GATT.

30. Mavroidis, *General Agreement on Tariffs and Trade*, p. 6.

31. Article I of GATT 1947.

32. Mavroidis, *General Agreement on Tariffs and Trade*, p. 112.

33. Michael J. Trebilcock and Robert Howse, *The Regulation of International Trade*, 2nd ed. (London and New York: Routledge, 1999), p. 29.

34. Please see Article XXVIII bis in Appendix 1.

35. Paul R. Krugman and Maurice Obstfeld, *International Economics—Theory and Policy* (Boston: Addison-Wesley Longman, 1997), pp. 238–239.

36. Josef M. van Brabant, *The Political Economy of Transition: Coming to Grips with History and Methodology* (London: Routledge, 1998), pp. 51–52.

37. Josef M. van Brabant, "Eastern Europe and the World Trade Organization: The Present Position and Prospects for Accession," in Iliana Zloch-Christy (ed.), *Eastern Europe and the World Economy—Challenges of Transition and Globalization* (London: Edward Elgar Publishing, 1998), p. 155.

38. Please see Article XVII of GATT 1947 listed in Appendix 1.

39. Ernst-Ulrich Petersmann, "GATT Law on State Trading Enterprises: Critical Evaluation of Article XVII and Proposals for Reforms," in Thomas Cottier and Petros C. Mavroidis (eds.), *State Trading in the Twenty-First Century* (Ann Arbor: University of Michigan Press, 1998), p. 76.

40. GATT, *Protocol for the Accession of Poland,* Basic Instruments and Selected Documents (BISD) Fifteenth Supplement (1968), pp. 46 and 52.

41. The measures were referred to as *selective* safeguard measures to distinguish them from safeguard measures permitted under Article XIX of GATT. Article XIX permits measures that are applied on an MFN basis, namely, against all imports of the product in question, regardless of the source.

42. GATT, *Protocol for the Accession of Poland,* Paragraph 4, pp. 48–49.

43. Jan Woznowski, *Polska w GATT (Poland and the GATT)* (Warsaw: PWE, 1974).

44. GATT, *Protocol for the Accession of Romania,* Basic Instruments and Selected Documents (BISD) Eighteenth Supplement (1972), pp. 5–10.

45. GATT, *Protocol for the Accession of Hungary,* Basic Instruments and Selected Documents (BISD) Twentieth Supplement (1974), pp. 3–8.

46. Leah A. Haus, *Globalizing the GATT—The Soviet Union's Successor States, Eastern Europe, and the International Trading System* (Washington, DC: Brookings Institution, 1992), p. 53.

47. Vassil Breskovski, "Bulgaria and the GATT—A Case Study for Accession," *World Competition* 17, no. 2 (1993): 46; Eliza R. Patterson, "Improving GATT Rules for Nonmarket Economies," *Journal of World Trade Law* 20, no. 2 (1986): 186.

48. Gilbert R. Winham, *International Trade and the Tokyo Round Negotiation* (Princeton, NJ: Princeton University Press, 1986).

49. Ibid., pp. 417–424.

50. Walters and Blake, *The Politics of Global Economic Relations,* pp. 217–221.

51. See Chapter 8, which deals with the politics of the Uruguay Round in this context.

52. See "Ministerial Declaration on the Uruguay Round" in Croome; *Reshaping the World Trading System*, pp. 382–392.

53. Ostry, *The Post–Cold War Trading System*, p. 193.

54. Barton et al., *The Evolution of the Trade Regime*, pp. 92–94.

55. Croome, *Reshaping the World Trading System*, pp. 382–392.

56. Terence P. Steward, *The GATT Uruguay Round—A Negotiating History (1986–1992)*, vol. 1 (Deventer, Netherlands: Kluwer Law and Taxation Publishers, 1993), pp. 1–33.

57. Croome, *Reshaping the World Trading System*, pp. 168–174.

58. The G-20 group included Bangladesh, Chile, Colombia, Hong Kong, Indonesia, Ivory Coast, Jamaica, Malaysia, Mexico, Pakistan, Philippines, Romania, Singapore, Sri Lanka, South Korea, Thailand, Turkey, Uruguay, Zambia, and Zaire.

59. The G9 group included Austria, Australia, Canada, Finland, Iceland, New Zealand, Norway, Sweden, and Switzerland.

60. European Communities is a legal term used in the WTO when talking about the European Union (EU). This tradition goes back to the EC Treaty of Rome of 1957. Subject to ratification by the EU member states, the Treaty of Lisbon negotiated in 2007 would rename the EC Treaty the "Treaty on the Functioning of the European Union" and replace references to the European Communities with references to the European Union.

61. Amrita Narlikar, *International Trade and Developing Countries: Bargaining Together in GATT & WTO* (London and New York: Routledge, 2003), chap. 5.

62. Ibid., p. 171.

63. "The Preamble," in *The Results of the Uruguay Round of Multilateral Trade Negotiations. The Legal Texts* (Geneva: WTO, 1995).

64. See Articles I–III in Appendix 2.

65. Ostry, *The Post–Cold War Trading System*, p. 177.

66. Ibid., p. 175.

67. Gilbert R. Winham, "Explanations of Developing Country Behaviour in the GATT Round Negotiation," *The World Economy* 21, no. 3 (1998): 116–117.

68. "Annex 2: Understanding on Rules and Procedures Governing the Settlement of Disputes," in *The Results of the Uruguay Round of Multilateral Trade Negotiations*.

69. "Annex 1B: General Agreement on Trade in Services," in *The Results of the Uruguay Round of Multilateral Trade Negotiations*.

70. "Annex 1C: Agreement on Trade-Related Aspects of Intellectual Property Rights," in *The Results of the Uruguay Round of Multilateral Trade Negotiations*.

71. See Article III and Article XI of GATT 1994.

72. Ostry, *The Post–Cold War Trading System*, pp. 118–119, 196.

73. Kendall Stiles, "Negotiating Institutional Reform: The Uruguay Round, the GATT, and the WTO," *Global Governance* 2, no. 1 (1996): 119.

74. Ernst-Ulrich Petersmann, "The WTO Constitution and Human Rights," *Journal of International Economic Law* 3, no. 1 (2000): 19.

CHAPTER 3

Establishment of the World Trade Organization: Principles, Structures, and Practices

Throughout the second part of the twentieth century, trade remained a source of international tensions. Subsequent rounds of negotiations conducted within the GATT framework enlarged its scope and its membership but did very little to calm the criticism pointing to the growing divide between the industrialized core and the developing world.

Since one of the tasks of the Uruguay Round was to create a more coherent and unified system, the negotiators faced multiple pressures to produce a deal that would be perceived as fair and just. In the eyes of the law, all are equal. This legal equality under unified rules remains a noble idea behind the WTO. However, it is not enough for an organization and its members to formulate principles based on legal rules; rules need to be embedded within a proper institutional structure, and they must follow practices that are seen as both legitimate and fair. As will be shown in this chapter, the WTO is a paradox. The organization does offer opportunities for equal participation, yet once its members have engaged in competitive participatory processes, its decisionmaking process has become paralyzed by struggles, with no institutional mechanism in place to successfully resolve them.

Much has been said about the move toward legalization of world politics over the past two decades. The formalization of the world trading system has prompted us to speculate whether the WTO will ever move toward becoming a new constitution for the global economic order. At the minimum, the WTO is seen as an advanced, but still predominantly technical, monitoring and compliance mechanism—an institutional tool for managing trade relations. Those who favor this view of the WTO believe that to be effective such an organization should stay away from questions about distributive fairness, socioeconomic development, or democratic governance. Instead, the WTO should only concentrate on the objective interpretation and application of the existing rules, dispute resolution, and on monitoring whether the commitments made by its members are fulfilled according to these rules. On the other side of the spectrum, however, there are those who consider the WTO to be the first elusive step toward global economic governance. This perspective rests upon the recognition that several of the WTO agreements—for example, on services and intellectual property—already either get in the way or complement domestic trade policies of WTO member states. In line with this perspective, it becomes necessary to include in the discussion about the future of the WTO a wide range of issues such as sustainable development, environmental standards, corporate responsibility, labor standards, equal access, democratic processes, and even human rights.

There is a problem with the two conflicting views presented above, because the debate about the WTO becomes polarized between two uncompromising positions. The organization is seen either in narrowly technical terms as an abstract self-contained entity or is seen broadly as an all-encompassing global body with a potential of running the world economy of the future. In reality both views are misleading. Certainly, the WTO is more than a technical tool for managing international trade flows. With its strengthened dispute settlement mechanism and a range of agreements that deal with issues that previously fell under the sole domain of the nation-states, the WTO does enter the realm of domestic policy making of its member states. At the same time, however, the WTO is far from being a global economic government. Its institutional arrangement is still quite limited, and most of the issue areas it covers relate back to the decisions undertaken by individual members.

Therefore, after explaining the main principles, operational structures, and practices of the WTO, this chapter suggests taking a different view when thinking about the WTO: a view that shifts the focus of the debate toward examining the power relations inside the organization. The idea is to look at the decisionmaking processes inside the WTO and consider the WTO as a microcosm of the changes taking place on the stage of international economic relations. In taking such an internal view of the WTO, the chapter further investigates practical as well as theoretical dilemmas posed by the legalization of world trade. In particular, it is argued that the changes initiated by the legalization of the world trade system under the WTO revealed the changing dynamics in the global economy: the reduced domination of the industrialized North and its inability to shape the agenda of the multilateral trade system. The historically asymmetrical world economy has been undergoing a shift in power relations, and the main benefactors of this transformation are developing countries, with China, India, and Brazil leading the way.

Armed with the opportunities provided to them by the legal framework, developing countries as a group have started to assert their autonomy when it comes to the decisionmaking within the WTO. A critical moment on this path was reached at the 1999 WTO ministerial meeting in Seattle. This meeting was the first where the developed nations proved to be ineffectual both as leaders and as agenda-setting players, while developing countries maintained their unified opposition. It was a peculiar stage in the life of the WTO, since it was at this very meeting that the organization also became a target of criticism by many disillusioned nongovernmental organizations (NGOs) and individuals who considered it to be part of the destructive forces of globalization. In this chapter, we are particularly interested in one of the main indictments against the WTO: that it is undemocratic.

When used in the context of the internal power relations inside the WTO, the term "undemocratic" needs to be carefully inspected given a significant, and largely unexpected, turn that the organization has taken under the influence of developing countries. To study the new developments inside the WTO, we consider the Schumpeterian model of competitive democracy. In the context of the WTO, this model focuses on the new principles of the WTO that provided for the enhanced autonomy of individual member states as it examines opportunities and limitations that exist for dealing with the challenges posed by domination embedded in the trading system.

The Promise of a Global WTO and Judicial Equality

Power relations shape the world economy. The system of international economic transactions has been persistently asymmetrical as it consists of highly industrialized states as well as many poorer countries at different levels of economic development. The dominant position of the rich developed countries cannot be simply assumed away, even when it comes to the rules-based WTO guided by the principles of nondiscrimination.

Nevertheless, the legal turn that came with the GATT/WTO transformation made many experts believe that the WTO would create a predictable and transparent, level playing field for all trading nations. This is because of the status of the WTO as a formal institution consisting of legal agreements and guarded by its dispute settlement mechanism based on the principle of compulsory adjudication. Despite its promises, however, from the beginning not all the actors involved enthusiastically embraced the birth of the WTO.

Like never before, the disagreements over justice and fairness influenced the negotiations of the Uruguay Round. The main issues were related to the structure and content of the talks, definition of reciprocity, evaluation of costs and benefits for individual countries, and so on. Still, the final outcome was presented as a potentially balanced solution.[1] The developed countries were pleased to have agreements on trade in services (GATS) and intellectual property (TRIPs) included within the WTO, while developing countries were hopeful about (1) an agricultural agreement, which offered a promise of reforming this traditionally distorted area of trade; (2) a new agreement on trade in textiles and clothing, which promised to eliminate the quota restrictions of the Multi Fibre Agreement;[2] and (3) the new legal form of the organization, which offered a promise of equitable rules. Even so, the WTO remained an unfinished project when it was officially inaugurated in January 1995. There were several agreements and issue areas where the fate of the new organization was left either to legal interpretations or future negotiations. Most important, the implementation of the new agreements presented a difficult-to-measure task, which would slowly turn into one of the crucial tests for the WTO.

It would take a few years before the implementation of the existing commitments would be recognized as posing a considerable "development challenge" for developing and transitioning economies.[3] Many impending problems were not apparent when the frantic negotiations stopped in December 1993. The enthusiasm over the final far-reaching deal tended to mask the uncertainties about the unresolved issues. However, by 1999 the outcome of the round would increasingly be considered a "bad deal" by developing countries.[4] While the Uruguay Round created a sea change in the world trade system, "the implications of the transformation of the system were not well understood by either side."[5] Nonetheless, one of the main achievements of the Uruguay Round was the enlargement of membership and the inclusion of developing countries in the newly established and legally strengthened organization on equal terms.

The round was long and difficult. The insistence of the developed countries, most notably the United States and the EC, to include agreements on services and intellectual property created a sea of hostility between them and the developing world.[6] By the same token, many issues that were high on developing countries' agendas were not resolved to their satisfaction: the agreement in agriculture was far weaker than what the developing countries had hoped, the agreement dealing with trade in textiles was conditioned upon its implementation, the antidumping issues were not resolved, and the market access and preferential treatment issues were left in a state of uncertainty. Most of the persistent conflicts were over what kind of special treatment and exemptions could be justified for developing countries and how to ensure fair reciprocity among vastly different economies.[7] The negotiators were eventually able to quiet these conflicts by transforming GATT into the WTO, which was a significant institutional overhaul of the system. The guarantees embedded within the WTO's legal framework not only solidified the transparency of the new organization, but also offered opportunities for developing countries to play an active role in the newly created governing bodies of the WTO: the General Council and the Ministerial Conference.[8]

There are three main principles—institutional guarantees—meant to ensure the legal equality of the WTO members. First, the WTO is a formal member organization with the status of an international legal entity, it consists of a number of legal agreements, and every WTO member has equal standing under these legal instruments. This means that to become a WTO member, a country has to accept all WTO agreements as a single package—a single undertaking.

Second, the Uruguay Round produced a new unified treaty text on dispute settlement, the WTO Dispute Settlement Understanding. The legal authority of the WTO infuses it with the power to make the results of trade disputes into legally binding decisions. The crucial aspect of the DSU is the automatic acceptance of decisions reached by a dispute settlement panel and, if appealed, the appellate panel. Every WTO member has equal access to the DSU under the same rules and procedures.

Third, the WTO is a member-driven intergovernmental organization where all its members reach decisions regarding the operation of the organization, and its future goals, by consensus. The consensus principle, together with the institutional and legal guarantees of the WTO, ensure that even the weakest WTO members have equal access in the General Council and the Ministerial Conference. The consensus principle has been inherited from GATT.[9] In practice, it means that a decision is considered to be taken by consensus if no WTO member objects to it.

The judicial equality of all WTO members is derived from the above three institutional guarantees. The legal provisions included in Articles IV, VIII, and IX of *The Marrakesh Agreement Establishing the World Trade Organization* specifically ensure the judicial equality of all WTO members, which can be defined as the legally embedded assurance for all WTO members that they have equal access to the decisionmaking bodies of the WTO, the General Council and the Ministerial Conference, and its dispute settlement mechanism, while being bounded by the same set of legal instruments.[10]

The idea of *single undertaking* is further meant to reinforce predictability and unity of the rules-based WTO system. It first emerged as a response to calls for cleaning up the confusing post–Tokyo Round assembly of codes that individual countries could pick and choose to sign. As a rule, most developed countries joined all the codes, whereas developing countries would only join one or two of them, if any. This situation was in fact consistent with the overall rationale of the round: "The Tokyo Round negotiations took place on the understanding that participation in the negotiations was optional and consequently each GATT Contracting Party was free to choose if and when it acceded to any of the negotiated Codes."[11] This kind of rationale also meant that developing countries considered the round to be primarily for the benefit of the industrialized world and accordingly felt that any extra liberalizing commitments were outside their responsibilities.

A growing dissatisfaction with the codes after the Tokyo Round resulted in an understanding that this kind of optional participation in various agreements was indeed fragmenting, and hence weakening, GATT and should be avoided in the future. In an attempt to remedy the mistakes of the past, it was agreed at the beginning of the Uruguay Round that all negotiations concerning trade in goods would be conducted under the principle of single undertaking. However, since a group of developed nations was insisting on negotiating a new agreement on trade in services, the round was to be conducted along two separate paths.

In order to separate the issues that would be negotiated under single undertaking from those that were not, the Punta del Este Declaration launching the Uruguay Round in 1986 was divided into two parts: Part I, Negotiations on Trade in Goods, and Part II, Negotiations on Trade in Services.[12] A curious move was to include under the first part not only most of the Tokyo Round issues but also several new ones like intellectual property, agriculture, and investment. As we will see later in the book, the different issues under negotiation would evolve to a degree that was not anticipated at the beginning of the round, expanding well beyond the Punta del Este Declaration.

For example, one of the most politically charged issues had to do with including an agreement on intellectual property in the WTO. Even though, the Punta del Este Declaration only mentions trade in counterfeit goods, TRIPs is the most comprehensive multilateral agreement on intellectual property ever negotiated. The push to include TRIPs would lead to sustained complaints by many developing countries that they never anticipated such a far-reaching agreement at the start of the round.

The Punta del Este Declaration contained also a provision that stressed the importance of reciprocity. Conflicting interpretations of what that reciprocity should entail would never be successfully resolved during the Uruguay Round. While the position taken by the major trading partners was that reciprocity should mean greater concessions made by the developing countries, especially with respect to new agreements, developing countries would insist that special exemptions and privileges were necessary to rebalance the system.[13] Different interpretations of initial expectations about the outcome of negotiations led to many conflicts and some surprise developments, like the one concerning the principle of single undertaking. Although at the beginning of the Uruguay Round negotiating parties accepted the premise of single undertaking with respect to trade in goods, very few of them would initially consider that it could entail the establishment of a comprehensive and unified legal WTO framework on all issues for all countries. However, this would be its eventual role in the new organization.

The decisive moment in interpreting single undertaking as an all-encompassing approach to agreements under negotiations took place following the presentation of the Dunkel Text. This document extended single undertaking to all outcomes of all negotiations to all participating countries. The text was a key initiative of Arthur Dunkel, the then–GATT director-general, and it arguably rescued the Uruguay Round in December 1991.[14] This lengthy document coherently put together the results of the different negotiating groups. In doing so it sent a positive signal by pointing out where progress was made and where improvement was necessary. It also sent a clear signal that all the progress made so far could be wasted because no separate codes would be allowed on limited issues and for selective countries. Its opening paragraphs included a bold statement that: "No single element of the Draft Final Act can be considered as agreed till the total package is agreed." The negotiating parties understood that the final agreement would be based on single undertaking.

The Dunkel Text apart from resuscitating the talks by bringing together various achievements of the fading Uruguay Round, also reinforced the idea that the negotiations were about introducing unity and predictability to the world trading system. It was an objective that raised expectations about the future organization. The notion of single undertaking was understood as a necessary step to make the WTO universal, effective, and transparent. Yet, as we will see later in the book, the "take it all or leave it" rationality behind the single undertaking can be perceived as limiting the overall flexibility of the WTO, especially during multilateral negotiations.

The second important aspect of judicial equality of all WTO members is enshrined in the DSU. The fundamental feature of the DSU is its goal to uphold trade rules and fair and equal treatment for all its members, no matter what the size of their economy. The crucial achievement of the DSU relates to the automatic acceptance of decisions reached by a dispute settlement panel (and the appellate panel), which becomes legally binding. In addition, the new procedures stipulate requirements for timely conduct, adoption, possible compensation, or retaliatory-type actions.

The DSU, often called the WTO's "crown jewel," was negotiated at the end of the Uruguay Round after countries agreed about creating a formal organization. Many legal scholars consider the DSU to be at the heart of the system, as they point out that "[t]he dispute settlement process of the WTO has been remarkable in respect of the volume of cases, the relative efficiency of the process, the diversity of issues, and the generally high quality of decisions."[15]

There are four important characteristics of the DSU that make it into such a central part of the WTO. First, WTO agreements are brought under the DSU, which ensures that each trade dispute is addressed by the same unified set of procedures. This is consistent with the principle of single undertaking, which, by extension, also allows cross-retaliation across different agreements. Under the principle of single undertaking, in case of a proven breach of obligations under one specific agreement, the subsequent refusal to implement the required changes means that retaliatory measures can be authorized under the DSU in such a way that they cross over to other agreements.

Second, the Appellate Body was created to provide a forum in which appeals can be made. The Appellate Body is a permanent seven-member body, three of whom may serve on any one panel assembled to reexamine the outcome of a WTO trade dispute resolution panel. Article 17 of the Understanding on Rules and Procedures Governing the Settlement of Disputes (Annex 2 of the WTO Legal Texts) specifies the procedures that apply to the Appellate Body and its mandate.

In the words of the former director of the Appellate Body Division, which administers the work of the Appellate Body, the objective behind its establishment was to provide a security blanket to ensure that no mistakes are made during the DSU panels. This was particularly important given the fact that the DSU panel reports under the WTO were to be automatically adopted as legally binding.[16] It should be noted that legal provisions governing both the dispute settlement panels as well as the Appellate Body strive to guarantee the neutrality of the panels. The DSU has been enormously successful judging by the number of disputes initiated by various WTO members. In March 2008 dispute number 373 was recorded when the United States contested China's measures affecting financial information services and foreign financial information suppliers.[17]

Third, once a decision is made, by either a DSU panel or the WTO Appellate Body, the "reverse-consensus" rule applies, which means that in order for the decision not to be adopted, all members would have to voice their preference to the contrary. This is in sharp contrast to the GATT system, which permitted the blocking of a panel resolution if only one country decided not to adopt the outcome, including the losing party of the dispute itself. In short, this means the automatic adoption of a WTO regular panel report and an Appellate Body report unless there is a consensus among WTO membership not to adopt it.

The fourth major change brought on by the DSU is the procedural clarity and the power vested in the organization to impose trade sanctions when the losing party refuses to comply with the outcome of the WTO-adjudicated dispute. When satisfactory compliance does not occur, the winning party to the dispute is permitted options to enforce proper compliance. Some prominent scholars have maintained, however, that there should be no such option offered to a losing party.[18] They argue that once either the DSU panel or the Appellate Body reaches the decision, the country that lost the dispute must immediately comply with this decision, as it is a legally binding order. This means that a country, which was found in violation of its WTO obligations, must immediately remedy the situation by bringing its trade measures into conformity.

There is, however, another group of scholars and trade practitioners[19] who believe that each WTO member has in fact three options upon losing a trade dispute: (1) they could agree with the binding recommendation and bring its trade measures into conformity with its WTO obligations; (2) they could compensate the winner in order to settle the dispute without necessarily complying with the binding recommendation of the DSU; and (3) they could ignore the decision and the winning country altogether and suffer the wrath of retaliation as the DSU authorizes the relevant measures to compensate the winning state.

The issue of compliance is at the heart of the WTO judicial preoccupation with ensuring that every WTO member is treated in equal terms subject to a predictable and transparent set of rules. Those who argue that a losing country has no choice but to comply with its WTO obligations point out the danger of trying to remedy the violations by other means; any compensation and retaliation can in principle distort the world trade system by providing a WTO member with a way out of its obligations. This dilemma also touches upon the issue of fairness and the limited ability of small economies to obtain satisfactory results when winning a dispute with a powerful trading nation that still refuses to change its trade policy even if it violates WTO obligations.

The third aspect of judicial equality, namely the consensus-based decisionmaking in the two main WTO governing bodies, interests us most, however. This is because the most important initiatives about the future of the WTO are undertaken during the monthly meetings of the General Council and the semi-annual ministerial meetings. Furthermore, the first two guarantees are necessary for the third to offer some concrete opportunities to all its members to shape the agenda of the WTO. The third guarantee builds upon the previous ones by giving all members equal voice over all aspects of the system. The rest of the chapter will closely probe the implications that the judicial equality of WTO members has on the power relations inside the organization.

The Fairness Principle and Its Limitations

Let us begin by summarizing three immediate challenges faced by the WTO in the context of the fairness debate. The first challenge comes from the inherently asymmetrical nature of the world economy. Simply put, the wide discrepancy between the North and the South when it comes to wealth and the level of economic development inevitably allows some WTO members to be more influential economic players than others. The major trading nations not only embody large volumes of trade flows but their governments also have at their disposal enormous resources that allow them to bring together the best experts skilled in every possible area of international economic activity. The negotiating teams, as well as permanent delegations to the WTO that represent the rich nations, are routinely large and well paid. This is in sharp contrast to the delegations representing poor countries. They often consist of fewer than five people who are stretched to the limits in trying to attend multiple meetings on vastly diverse issues. The similar problem of costs and resources applies in the case of the WTO dispute settlement mechanism. In principle every WTO member has equal access to it, and yet the huge costs of such proceedings often prevent poorer states from considering it. The idea of judicial equality may be a right step toward creating a level playing field, but the challenge remains to meaningfully integrate the poor and the less developed countries into a system where the biggest part of world trade transactions still evolves around a handful of industrialized countries. From the point of view of poor countries, judicial equality becomes then the necessary first step toward equal participation in the system that nevertheless still requires substantial reforms.

Second, the WTO is based on the universal principles of equal rules for all. Yet, the numerous exemptions for special and differential treatment and provisions maintaining the pre-GATT discriminatory practices have always existed within the GATT/WTO system.[20] This fact forces a serious debate over reciprocity and nondiscriminatory, equal access for all WTO members. For example, Part II of GATT 1947 allowed the existing legislation to be kept (grandfather rights) even if it was inconsistent with the GATT principles of nondiscrimination. Part II was to be suspended with the establishment of the ITO. Since the Havana Charter establishing the ITO was never ratified, under the resulting provisional agreement a number of countries continued to use GATT-inconsistent legislation. The most notorious example was the US Countervailing Duty Law, which permitted the United States to impose antidumping duties on steel imports from a number of developing countries.[21] With time, many nations considered this law to be grossly unfair. In a similar fashion, a number of waivers and special exemptions were authorized by GATT that suspended a full range of obligations and permitted a number of countries (most notably the United States and the EC[22]) to heavily subsidize their agricultural sector while limiting foreign access to it.[23] On the other hand, the General System of Preferences legitimized a preferential set of arrangements and exemptions for developing countries under GATT. And it would be difficult to suddenly reject such an approach to developing countries given the fact that the developed countries were champions of many exemptions. The right to preferential trade arrangements was possible under Article XXIV of GATT, despite the fact that it undermined the fundamental principle of the postwar system: nondiscrimination.[24] These issues were never successfully dealt with in the Uruguay Round, and GATT Article XXIV has remained in place under the WTO. Therefore, the legal universalism of the WTO agreements is a myth not only because of the asymmetrical nature of the world trading system but also because of somehow distorted application of the principle of nondiscrimination.

Third, the WTO is said to be a member-driven organization, which compels self-identification of an individual state's needs, interests, and demands. But under a multilateral system, an arbitrary unilateral action by individual members is discouraged. The WTO promotes the outcomes that are supposed to benefit all WTO members in the name of a more integrated global economy. However, to protect their national interests, countries present demands that often conflict with those of their trading partners. Moreover, it is practically impossible for economically weak countries to advance their interests if they are at odds with the position expressed by the powerful trading states.

From its beginning, GATT implicitly highlighted the systemic asymmetry, because "GATT emerged as precisely the kind of trade institution best suited to the satisfaction of industrial (largely US) interests and evolved thereafter in a tightly path-dependent fashion."[25] However, with the completion of the Uruguay Round, that ostensibly deterministic path of the world trading system's institutional development was broken. The changes reflected the geopolitical transformation of the world economy that saw the emergence of new trading giants like China, India, and Brazil. Most important, in parallel to this transformation, the new legal environment within the WTO facilitated a break from the past dominated by North American and European leadership. What is fundamentally different is the fact that the group of influential states in the WTO today includes not only the original designers of GATT, but also countries that used to play a marginal role in the system. China, India, and Brazil are skillful at using the WTO rules for their advantage in shaping the agenda of the WTO with or without entering into issue-based coalitions with other developing countries.

For those who believe in multilateralism, one definitely positive result of the WTO is the formal space it created where the agenda-setting processes are open to competition and where the powerful can be contested and their unreasonable demands ignored. Consequently, in recognizing the limitations of the asymmetrical world economy, on the one hand, and the opportunities offered by the multilateral legal rules of the WTO, on the other, I suggest thinking about fairness in terms of the minimization of domination in the world trade system. Reducing domination means creating a more competitive global trade environment where the traditionally powerful nations of the West are not able to unilaterally impose their preferences on smaller economies but must instead negotiate the terms of trade.

Clearly, the WTO has become a platform that provides historically marginalized poor and developing countries with a legal framework to effectively contest domination by the industrialized countries. The major trading states have become constrained in making arbitrary decisions by the framework of legal rules that they themselves have helped to create. These constraints have developed into a two-level game where WTO members struggle to advance their interests. It is a two-level game because, while WTO members must operate within the structures determined by the principles of the system, they are trying to go beyond and expand the boundaries of the system by developing new practices grounded in these principles. The game then becomes a relentless struggle to control the agenda setting within the WTO. The first level of the game relates to the institutional changes brought about by the transformation from GATT to the WTO. On this level, a powerful bureaucratic machine delineates the parameters of permissible practices in the WTO. Under its authority, the WTO is compelled to operate within the self-imposed legal and operational structures that are supposed to reduce the ability of its members to act in an arbitrary fashion. These bureaucratic constraints are mainly derived from the principle of single undertaking but also relate to the principle of decisionmaking by consensus. The second level of the game allows WTO members to take advantage of the principle of judicial equality and shape the processes within the WTO decisionmaking bodies.

In one important work examining international organizations as bureaucracies, the authors observe how rules and standardized practices that are designed to tell actors what action is appropriate can actually lead to pathology-creating cultures that produce dysfunctional dynamics within the organization.[26] Indeed, there is a creeping bureaucratic aspect to the way the first level struggles to unfold within the WTO. What is different about the WTO is the fact that it is the first global organization that by offering judicial equality to all its members creates the second level of access to decisionmaking. The second level of the game offers opportunity for change, as WTO members can use it to assault the first level of bureaucratic constraints. This opportunity is particularly important for small and developing countries.

The equal legal rules greatly matter for smaller and emerging economies that used to be outside the system, because they constitute "their best defence against the use of power to settle trade disputes,"[27] and during the Uruguay Round the weaker countries "recognized that the alternative to a rule-based system would be a power-based system and, lacking power, they had most to lose."[28] This is why the search for fairness should be considered in the context of using the legal rules of the WTO to reduce domination embedded within the world trade system.

In view of that, one must look inside the WTO and try to determine the patterns of interaction among WTO members. It is also useful to examine the relationship between the WTO decisionmaking processes and the WTO trade negotiation processes. Although both sets of processes are linked together, they also differ to some extent. The WTO decisionmaking process mainly refers to the normal and ongoing operation of the organization centered on two of its governing bodies, the WTO General Council and the WTO Ministerial Conference. Then again, the trade negotiations conducted within the WTO framework represent special types of processes that are institutionally subordinated to the decisionmaking processes in the WTO. It is one of the functions of the WTO to provide the forum for negotiations.

Trade negotiations conducted within the framework of the WTO are either issue-driven negotiations (negotiations on liberalization of trade in services that commenced in 2000) or they are round-driven negotiations. The Doha Round of negotiations formally initiated in 2001 by a special ministerial declaration is the best example here. All WTO round-driven negotiations are multilateral, which means that they are open to all interested WTO members and, following the principle of single undertaking, their results will become part of the WTO's set of legal instruments. There is also the special case of the WTO accession negotiations. They take place when a country wants to join the WTO and has to negotiate terms of accession.[29] The accession type of negotiations can become quite controversial because the existing members often push new demands, so-called WTO-plus commitments, on the acceding country.[30]

Inevitably connected with the trade negotiation processes is the WTO decisionmaking process, in which trade negotiations are proposed, initiated, and officially completed. Decisionmaking centers on the two governing bodies of the WTO, the General Council and the Ministerial Conference, where decisions are made by consensus. The principle of consensus was developed under GATT when the membership was much smaller and the process was dominated by the industrialized nations. As membership grew under the WTO, the management of the decisionmaking process slowly became too difficult to handle.[31] However, it would be hard to imagine that the principle of consensus would be abandoned, because of its ostensibly democratic nature.

The tradition of consensus is considered to be deeply democratic because it assumes that a decision can be made only when all interested parties agree. In fact, some theorists of liberal democracy have supported extending the principle of consensus into the realm of international organizations precisely for ensuring their democratic character. John Rawls, for example, introduced the idea of an *overlapping consensus*—or agreement on *justice as fairness*—between citizens who hold different religious, political, and philosophical views. Justice, for Rawls, can occur when those with conflicting views and backgrounds reach a consensus on how to cooperate.[32] In one of his last works, Rawls tried to formulate the Law of Peoples, which once completed "would also include guidelines for forming organizations for cooperation among peoples and for specifying various duties and obligations."[33] What's more, out of the three organizations that he had in mind, one was "framed to ensure fair trade among peoples."[34]

However, the idea of transplanting the theory about justice as fairness from the domestic into the international level of analysis must be viewed with caution. Despite its reliance on the principle of consensus, its critics regard the WTO as ineffective and hence unfair because of skepticism over whether consensus can truly be achieved given the multiplicity of conflicting interests expressed by vastly diverse countries. In other words, one can wonder whether the idea of consensus may not lead to silencing dissent by quietly pressuring economically weak countries into acceptance of adverse outcomes. Still, in principle, decisionmaking by consensus is closely associated with the sought-after idea of fairness.

The plea for fairness in international trade was vigorously expressed by Joseph E. Stiglitz who, following the failed Seattle Ministerial Conference, noted that "[t]here are two basic principles that should govern the next set of trade negotiations: fairness, and especially fairness to the developing countries, and comprehensiveness (the need to include issues that are important to developing countries)."[35] However, after empirically stating a number of steps that need to be taken in order for these two principles to materialize, Stiglitz never defines the notion of fairness. The question remains of what criteria to use to assess fairness, especially given the large number of diverse actors involved. As another author states, "indeed, philosophical abstractions and normative theories about justice and fairness aside, what one regards as a fair bargain depends on several factors: who the actor is, who the other negotiating parties are, and the forum in which negotiations are taking place. Parties can apply different criteria in defining fairness, resulting in claims that are mutually contradictory and yet equally legitimate."[36]

The questions of fairness asked in the context of the WTO may be impossible to answer, even if one concentrates only on outcomes of negotiations that benefit most of the negotiating parities, including poor developing countries. In reality, the task of measuring the benefits can present a number of challenges given the diverse nature of the so-called developing countries camp.[37] Overall, the notion of fairness fails to provide a specific pathway for reforming the WTO because it implies the need to examine the WTO via moral considerations.

We suggest a different set of criteria in assessing the way the WTO—

and most specifically its decisionmaking processes—is evaluated. First, it is argued that many critics overlook the view from inside the organization. Second, they are partial in their understanding of democracy. The criticisms are routinely grounded either in the aggregative or deliberative traditions of democratic theory. The first tradition favors *majority prevails* constitutional solutions, while the latter tradition favors a pluralist process based on referenda and debates. According to Ian Shapiro, both traditions "overestimate the importance of the idea of the common good for democracy. Instead, democracy is better thought of as a means of managing power-relations so as to minimize domination."[38] It makes sense to rethink the fairness principle when it comes to international trade as the attempt to minimize domination by historically powerful countries in the WTO-managed system.

Reducing Domination in the World Trade System

Those who consider the WTO as undemocratic often concentrate on the relationship that exists between the organization and the societies that are impacted by the WTO agreements signed by their governments without any consultation with their own societies. This external view of the WTO, however, neglects the progressively democratic internal dynamics of the WTO. The omission can be partially attributed to the level-of-analysis problem that arises when we evaluate the performance of international organizations. Our expectations appear to treat international organizations as if they were mere extensions of our own countries. Then again, international organizations are entities that, although they are inseparably connected to the domestic sphere of their member states, nevertheless have their own *agoras* where members (*demos*) gather to engage in the decisionmaking processes. These processes, as examined from within the organization, provide an alternative view of what it means for an international organization to be democratic.

To address the fundamental criticism directed toward the WTO, we begin with the critical question of who decides that an international organization is illegitimate and undemocratic. Should only the members and their governments make this assessment? Still, the WTO—and international trade issues in general—influences many aspects of economic activities taking place inside the territory of its members and hence indirectly touches the lives of countless people and communities. Should then the citizens in the countries and territories that belong to the WTO be the ultimate judges of the WTO?

Being faced with the above dilemma, we make one important distinction before we begin to test the democratic qualities of an international organization. The distinction relates to the delineation of the demos. After all, democracy is a form of governance under which the power to govern lies with the people, the demos. The demos constitutes a community that makes governing decisions and is, in turn, influenced by these decisions. It is difficult to talk about how democratic or undemocratic a particular system is without demarcating its demos. Fritz Scharpf identified a similar tension concerning the decisionmaking in the European Union. He thought it was important to make a distinction between input-oriented and output-oriented democratic legitimacy and between the domestically formulated preferences and the EU institutional-level collectively binding decisions.[39]

For that reason, in order to formulate questions concerning the WTO demos we must differentiate between what we call the *internal* versus the *external* democracy of an international intergovernmental organization. This distinction serves to further problematize discussions concerning international organizations. By making a distinction between internal versus external democracy, it is observed that there are multiple communities that have different stakes in the decisionmaking processes of any particular international organization, including the WTO.

The following are two working definitions of the terms. First, the *internal democracy* of an international organization has to do with the processes and structures of interaction between the members of the organization. The questions concerning the internal democracy should only be asked in the context of the rules and procedures developed by and for the members of such an organization and their representatives. Second, the *external democracy* of an international organization, in contrast, has to do with the perceived impact that the same organization is having on the constituencies and the stakeholders of the individual members. The questions concerning the external democracy should only be asked in the contexts of domestic decisionmaking processes of the individual members.

The relationship between the internal and external democracy of an international intergovernmental organization is complicated and context-specific. In fact, it is possible that an intergovernmental organization can meet all the criteria of one, while failing the test of the other. The simple example would be an international organization where member states enjoy a fully competitive decisionmaking environment under the system of optimally designed rules that equally apply to all members, with no possibility of any of the members permanently dominating the system. Here the criteria of internal democracy are met.

Although such an organization may be perfectly democratic internally, it may not be externally. Consider, for example, a scenario in which member states of this fictitious organization are dictatorial and authoritarian regimes whose domestic decisionmaking processes are conducted on the level of the governmental elites who dominate their own societies by force. What view would the majority of disenfranchised citizens have about such an international organization when it is operated in isolation by a group of dictatorial leaders that may or may not be their own?

It is also true that "democratic legitimacy in the international system, and in international institutions in particular, cannot be guaranteed only through legitimate and democratic decision-making within each participating state."[40] Why should the WTO members be guided or restrained in their intergovernmental negotiations by the political processes taking place elsewhere, in the domestic space of other members, even if such members are established democracies?

Keeping in mind these problems, we are mainly concerned here with the notion of the internal democracy of an international organization. The task is to probe the internal processes of the WTO, while leaving aside any doubts relating to the external democracy of the WTO. Questions about how the individual members' preferences and positions within the WTO are shaped by the domestic stage are extremely important; however, they contribute little to the discussions about decisionmaking processes that take place inside the WTO.

When assessing the merits of the WTO as an international organization, it is suggested that to be considered internally democratic, such an organization has to allow for competitive processes to exist in such a way as to prevent the systemic domination by any of its members or a group of members. This view is grounded in Schumpeter's theory of competitive democracy, which favors a situation characterized by unstable power relations where "power is acquired only through competition and held for a limited duration."[41] It is argued that the principles of legal equality of the WTO allow for such democratic competition to take place.

Critics of the WTO who view the organization as *undemocratic* tend to ignore the value of competitive democracy in the WTO because they are grounded in the aggregative or deliberative traditions of democratic theory. Shapiro, who criticizes both traditions for not addressing the persistence of power relations, made this distinction. The aggregative tradition strives toward arriving at the common good via institutional mechanisms (constitution). The deliberative tradition, on the other hand, displays "a touching faith in deliberation's capacity to get people to converge on the common good."[42] Both traditions are unhelpful when dealing with international institutions, because they are not focusing on reducing domination within the system but instead place emphasis on the hazy concept of the common good.

Let me explain what is meant by these traditions. Both traditions have their roots in Jean-Jacques Rousseau's concept of the general will that allegedly directs society toward the common good. In the aggregative tradition the aim is to arrive at the outcome by consensus that is generally acceptable and seen as legitimate due to the observance of the rules that govern the process. Power here is divided among different branches of government (*Federalist Papers*, 1788). If we were to take this tradition seriously in the context of an international organization, we would propose a constitution for the WTO with the assumption that a constitution would enhance legitimacy of the WTO system as a whole. Scholars who support this position tend to believe that justice and human rights could also be advanced this way.[43]

Others remind us, however, that a constitutional drive may actually exacerbate the legitimacy difficulties of the WTO.

> Constitutionalization driven by the judicial branch of the WTO, could be recommended as a strategy for building up pressure for formal institutional change, i.e. the creation of an explicit level of federal governance at the WTO, with the regulatory powers required for positive integration. Why this is unlikely to happen, or more precisely the legitimacy difficulties that would arise if it were to happen, is illuminated by developments in the European Union once Europeans became widely conscious that the Community institutions were indeed behaving as an autonomous federal order of governance, acting directly on the citizens of Member states. These developments show the danger of, in Weiler's words, *adopting constitutional practices without any underlying legitimizing constitutionalism*.[44]

Given recent developments in the EU, namely first the rejection of the European Constitution by French and Dutch voters in June 2005 and then retreat from a formal constitution in the 2007 Treaty of Lisbon, it seems that the future of the aggregative ideal of democracy is not the best option for international organizations. This is consistent with the findings of international relations theory, which still sees the state not only as the primary actor on the international stage, but also as an actor that values its sovereignty. External treaties and constitutions tend to lock in certain arrangements, making it difficult to opt out or to contest the existing order. In the context of the WTO, a constitution could in fact preserve whatever domination is embedded in the system and narrow the space for contestation.

Theorists of deliberative democracy, in contrast, believe that we can establish democratic institutions if they are agreed upon under perfect deliberative conditions. In some ways this proposition is a reaction to the drawbacks of constitutionalism. Deliberative democracy theorists are skeptical of the constitutional arrangements that are said to favor inertia and the status quo; they believe that an essential prerequisite of a working democracy is deliberation.[45] Shapiro's critique of deliberative democracy starts with the question of who decides which issues should be presented for discussions and negotiations.[46]

The efforts of democratizing the WTO in this tradition propose increasing participation of the maximum number of relevant participants to take part in the WTO decisionmaking process. But the following dilemmas remain unresolved: How is the relevant participant established, and who decides when the discussion is over and the optimum outcome of deliberation is reached? If we were to take this tradition seriously, we would see the demos of an international organization enlarged indefinitely. Since deliberation should involve all who are concerned, an open door policy, under which everybody is welcomed, would have to be maintained. Yet, to recall the concept of the internal democracy of an international organization, this kind of open policy would upset democratic competitive processes taking place inside an organization by giving voice to the outsiders (nonmembers). It would not be democratic, from the members' point of view, if these self-identified relevant actors, but in effect outsiders, would influence the internal decisionmaking processes without being accountable for it. This is precisely why developing countries reject the proposition of increasing participation by NGOs in the WTO decisionmaking processes, especially since a disproportional number of NGOs are based in the industrialized countries.[47]

It seems that both aggregative and deliberative democratic traditions are unsatisfactory when trying to determine whether or not the WTO is a democratic organization. As an alternative, a test of a fair and democratic international institution could be that it minimizes domination by enhancing the autonomy of its members. This formulation is based on the Schumpeterian competitive democratic method that sees power in a political system acquired in an ongoing competitive process.[48] According to the principles of judicial equality that underline the WTO, it can be argued that the WTO is the only global organization with the institutional arrangement that allows for its members to formulate decisions in which member states gain their influence and power by engaging in a competitive struggle for shaping the agenda of the WTO.

Only under the multilateral system of equal rules, in which small and big countries are given identical legal recognition, can one observe the surfacing of a competitive democratic zone of intergovernmental participation where equal voice of every member becomes a decisionmaking right. Under such a competitive democratic environment, power relations are constantly negotiated and domination is henceforth minimized. In short, the democratic competitive behavior then aims not toward establishing some kind of common good, but rather toward reducing the power previously held unchallenged by the industrialized countries.

If we accept the premise that the central task of a democratic intergovernmental organization is to manage power relations in order to minimize domination, we can observe some interesting changes taking place in the world trading system. In particular, we can observe the emergence of a new competitive behavior within the WTO championed by a number of developing countries. The historically vulnerable developing members of the WTO have been increasingly autonomous in influencing the agenda of the WTO by taking advantage of the available institutional mechanisms. Their behavior in the WTO decisionmaking bodies is vigilant, activist, and unbending, such that power relations are constantly contested, even at the cost of bringing the organization to a standstill.

Developing Countries Take Advantage of Equal Rules

The turning point for developing countries as influential actors contesting the dominant position of the industrialized countries in the WTO took place on the occasion of the 1999 Seattle meeting. The following ten events are chosen to illustrate the increasingly significant role played by developing countries as a group in the WTO decisionmaking bodies since that momentous year: (1) the preparation of an agenda for the Seattle ministerial meeting, (2) the highly antagonistic 1999 election of the new director general, (3) the breakdown of the Seattle ministerial meeting, (4) the placing of implementation concerns on the WTO agenda, (5) the placing of TRIPs-related concerns on the WTO (and global) agenda, (6) the creative cross-retaliation by Ecuador using TRIPs, (7) the Doha Declaration, (8) the collapse of the Cancun ministerial meeting, (9) the failure of the negotiations on liberalization of trade in services, and (10) the collapse of the Doha talks.

As of the early months of 1999, developing countries became exceptionally active in submitting a large number of proposals (220) to be included in the agenda of the WTO ministerial meeting scheduled to take place at the end of that year. Needless to say, these proposals were being routinely ignored.[49] What was peculiar about this situation was the inability of the developed countries to override the concerns of the developing countries and forge a workable document. The degree of hostility reached high levels during the General Council meetings, with the developed countries pushing for inclusion of new issues (especially investment and competition policy) and the unwavering developing countries rejecting them while insisting on focusing on problems resulting from the implementation of the WTO agreements. This situation ultimately made it impossible to put forward an organized agenda.[50]

Following the departure of Renato Ruggiero, the General Council started a process of electing a new director-general of the WTO. What was initially expected to be a short event grew into a prolonged and contentious dispute. Leading developed countries supported their own candidate, Mike Moore of New Zealand. Developing countries, however, wanted Supachai Panitchpakdi of Thailand. When the impasse appeared to be impossible to solve, WTO members agreed that the normal term of six years would be divided between the two.[51] This awkward compromise symbolized the growing divisions in the WTO and the uncompromising position of developing countries. The compromise also weakened the position of the director-general and created bureaucratic havoc during what was a crucial period for the WTO.[52] Mike Moore took over the office too late to help prepare for the Seattle meeting, and Supachai became director-general on September 1, 2002, just one year before the failed Cancun meeting.

While the Seattle meeting provoked strong reactions on the streets, the mood inside the conference rooms was also very hostile.[53] The meeting exposed many problems within the organization.[54] First, the cost of implementing the new agreements was becoming a serious issue for many poor WTO members. Second, the attempt by the developed countries to talk only with a selective few developing countries as the arbitrary chosen representatives of the developing world (the so-called Green Room option) was flatly rejected. Third, developing countries refused to include any new issues on the WTO agenda and became particularly upset when the US president publicly insisted on including labor standards within the WTO framework. The Seattle Ministerial Conference ended with an ironic show of unity as virtually all developing countries walked out from the meeting.[55]

Developing countries came to Seattle unified to demand their place at the steering wheel of the WTO or, alternatively, ready to stall the talks altogether. In fact, since Seattle, developing countries started to utilize their legal rights to contest the developed countries' proposals and to formulate their own initiatives. It took almost twelve months of confrontation and forceful behavior by a number of developing countries during the post-Seattle meetings of the WTO General Council for developed countries to finally recognize the position of developing countries. Many proposals were submitted. Eventually these sustained efforts succeeded. At the momentous meeting of the General Council in December 2000, WTO members adopted a resolution firmly acknowledging the demands of developing countries with respect to the implementation process.[56]

Developing countries have traditionally focused their attention on the TRIPs. Many developing WTO members have experienced difficulties with implementing the agreement due to the high costs involved, their lack of previous experience in this legislative area, and the impact of TRIPs on the prices of new technology and inventions (including life-saving medications). The sustained campaign of developing countries resulted in making it one of the top issues for the WTO and for the public global agenda. The final result, the 2001 Doha Declaration on the TRIPs Agreement and Public Health, was an example of how a broad coalition of developing countries was able not only to reframe the issue—which only a few years back was considered a closed subject by the industrialized nations—but also had many of their demands met: "A coalition lacking obvious power achieved significant, unexpected gains despite careful opposition from powerful transnational corporate firms and their home governments."[57]

In preparation for the Seattle Ministerial Conference, developing countries started to question the effectiveness of the WTO dispute settlement system, not only because of the issue of sanctions, but also because of its cost. Many developing countries would not become engaged in a trade dispute because the favorable outcome of a DSU decision could be practically and politically difficult to implement when the losing party is a large industrial state and the winner is an economically vulnerable country. In November 1999 (when the discussions about TRIPs in the General Council were getting frequent), Ecuador decided to use TRIPs as an instrument for enforcement. It meant that Ecuador asked for authorization to suspend some of its concessions and its obligations under TRIPs (as well as GATS) as a way of "cross-retaliation" in one of the most prolonged trade disputes.[58] This very creative move unsettled the developed countries, which have championed the strong protection of intellectual property under the enforcement of the WTO. After Ecuador was authorized to proceed with its request, the EU, the losing party in the dispute, agreed to reach a settlement. This outcome demonstrated how a skillful legal maneuver by a relatively economically weak country could force an economic giant to pay attention to its needs.

Indeed, countries that traditionally have been unable to influence the working of international economic organizations continued to be very successful in shaping the agenda of the WTO. Once the initial turn was made, the need for even more formal recognition of the developing countries' position at the WTO ministerial meeting was becoming urgent. This necessity materialized in the unprecedented Doha Declaration, which firmly links the issues of trade and development. In contrast to the GATT system, which put emphasis on the technical side of trade negotiations, the Doha Declaration calls for the refocusing of the multilateral trade agenda by stressing the developmental dimension of trade issues. The Doha Declaration was adopted in November 2001 at the WTO fourth ministerial meeting in Qatar.[59] It was an important breakthrough that confirmed the growing autonomy of developing countries inside the WTO. Most important, the declaration initiated a new round of trade negotiations that were supposed to focus on the needs of developing countries.

The breakdown of the Doha Round talks during the fifth WTO meeting in Cancun in September 2003 has been widely attributed to the strong stance taken by developing members of the WTO on a number of issues of vital importance to them. When, as was expected, the industrialized nations refused to deal with these issues, delegations from the developing world walked out of the negotiations. The commentaries issued by various trade practitioners from the developing world stressed the shift in the position of developing countries within the WTO. The Brazilian foreign minister wrote, "I am convinced that Cancun will be remembered as the conference that signaled the emergence of a less autocratic multilateral trading system." Meanwhile, the South African minister congratulated the developing world and said, "This is the first time we have experienced a situation where, by combining our technical expertise we can sit as equals at the table. This is a change in the quality of negotiations between developing and developed countries." And the minister from Ecuador described the Cancun meeting as historic, as "the beginning of a better future for everyone."[60]

Still, the road to the Sixth WTO Ministerial Conference in Hong Kong had been rough. The eventual Hong Kong compromise in December 2005 was an indication of more troubles to come. First of all, the elimination of export subsidies in agriculture, as demanded by developing countries, was dependent upon the completion of the modalities by the end of April 2006. In addition, WTO members were to submit comprehensive draft schedules of commitments based on these modalities by July 31, 2006. The text also required WTO members to develop modalities on food aid, export credit programs, and the practices of exporting state trading enterprises by the end of April 2006, a deadline perceived by many observers as unrealistic. These deadlines were not met, and the Doha Round talks were suspended in August 2006.

The meeting in Hong Kong demonstrated the strength of developing countries in shaping the agenda of services negotiations. The Agreement of Trade in Services has long reflected the North-South divide in the WTO. To advance the Uruguay Round commitments under the GATS, new negotiations commenced in 2000. Under the Doha Declaration, WTO members were to submit their services request lists by June 30, 2002, and their initial offers of service market access by March 31, 2003. Only a limited number of developing countries had done so, because the implementation costs were too large and the benefits too uncertain for many developing countries.

Because of the insistence of industrialized nations, the initial draft of the Hong Kong Declaration contained provisions (in particular Annex C) requiring that all WTO members enter into plurilateral negotiations with a goal of meeting some clearly stated qualitative objectives. As a result of the fierce resistance given by developing countries, the language of Annex C has been considerably weakened in stressing the unique position of developing countries. Overall, the Hong Kong Declaration asserts that negotiations are nevertheless to be conducted "with appropriate flexibility for individual developing countries as provided for in Article XIX of the GATS."[61] Developing countries were hence able to significantly limit the scope of the services negotiations. Given the fact that very little progress has been made, negotiations in services are now cautiously considered a failure.

The Doha Round talks were frozen again in August 2006, leaving the WTO in a state of uncertainty. During the acrimonious meeting of the WTO General Council meeting when the talks collapsed, it became clear that the developed countries were no longer the dominant players in the WTO. The frustration expressed by the negotiators from the countries that used to control the GATT decisionmaking processes could, however, signal troubles for the multilateral trade system. It appears that the internal democracy of the WTO does not sit well with the traditionally powerful industrialized countries, which used to be unchallenged when making decisions that often impacted other countries. An additional blow to the democratic principles of judicial equality came in the spring of 2007 when the Doha Round deteriorated to the level of ambiguous talks between the representatives of the EU's European Commission, India, the United States, and Brazil. These talks eventually collapsed, but the very fact they took place without the rest of WTO membership signaled troubles for the democratic decisionmaking process in the WTO.

Conclusion

The WTO was established with a promise to uphold the principle of nondiscrimination and also to advance the principle of fairness in international trade. Through the institutional transformation from GATT to the WTO, some new structures were established to ensure the applications of new WTO rules and practices. However, the WTO retained many practices from the GATT era and remained structurally constrained by some of the rules and procedures it operates under. On the positive side, the judicial equality offered by the WTO to all its members opened a zone for democratic competition within the WTO.

The starting point of this analysis recognizes that we are dealing with a historically asymmetrical system of international trade. Given this reality, it is suggested that an international organization that operates within such a system can be considered internally democratic if it offers opportunity to weak and vulnerable players to become autonomous by providing them with equal judicial rights. Such equal judicial recognition allows them to resist domination and to influence the decisionmaking processes within an institutional framework of an organization, alone or in concert with other disadvantaged members.

Upon a closer examination, the WTO is the only international organization that currently offers judicial guarantees of equality, and hence it allows for a competitive zone of democratic interaction among its members. The competitive dynamics inside the WTO diffuses power relations within the system by making it permanently unstable and hence difficult to dominate. Because of the gains derived from the judicial equality of all WTO members, a number of developing countries have been able to contest the dominant position of the industrialized countries via democratic competition in the decisionmaking bodies of the WTO.

The internal democracy of the WTO has curtailed the ability of the industrialized nations to shape the agenda of the organization. However, because of these developments, the traditionally dominant actors in the world economy have not enthusiastically embraced the increased participation of developing countries in the WTO. Even if developing countries feel more able than ever to pursue their own objectives within the WTO, they must engage in a relentless struggle to secure their autonomy. This constant struggle creates a potentially detrimental condition for all WTO members by breaking down the decisionmaking process in the WTO.

This is very problematic and reveals that the WTO is indeed an unfinished project from the institutional point of view. It still operates on principles and practices derived from the GATT era. The present conundrum in the WTO can only be resolved if the second-level game played by the empowered developing countries can be brought to a conclusion in new institutional structures of the WTO. New institutional reforms should limit the continuing struggles inside the WTO. One option would be to turn away from the principle of consensus and allow voting to take place in order to determine the outcomes of talks. Second, the principle of single undertaking should be revisited, since it has become a legal straitjacket restricting flexibility of countries to opt out of new agreements that they could never be able to implement to their benefit anyway.

Notes

1. Cecilia Albin, *Justice and Fairness in International Negotiation* (Cambridge, UK: Cambridge University Press, 2001), pp. 108–109, 137–138.

2. The Multi Fibre Agreement (MFA), introduced in 1974 by a group of the industrialized countries, unilaterally imposed quotas restricting the amount that developing countries could export. Under the Uruguay Round deal, the MFA was to be eliminated by 2005.

3. Michael J. Finger and Philip Schuler, "Implementation of Uruguay Round Commitments: The Development Challenge," in Bernard Hoekman and Will Martin (eds.), *Developing Countries and the WTO: A Pro-active Agenda* (Malden, MA: Blackwell Publishing, 2001).

4. Sylvia Ostry, "World Trade Organization: Institutional Design for Better Governance," in Roger B. Porter et al. (eds.), *Efficiency, Equity, Legitimacy* (Washington, DC: The Center for Business and Government at Harvard University and Brookings Institution Press, 2001), p. 364; also see Asoke Mukerji, "Developing Countries and the WTO—Issues of Implementation," *Journal of World Trade* 34, no. 6 (2000): 39–40.

5. Sylvia Ostry, "The Uruguay Round North-South Bargain: Implications for Future Negotiations," in Daniel L. M. Kennedy and James. D. Southwick (eds.), *The Political Economy of International Trade Law* (Cambridge, UK: Cambridge University Press, 2002), p. 288.

6. Sylvia Ostry, *The Post–Cold War Trading System: Who's on First?* (Chicago: University of Chicago Press, 1997), pp. 184–185.

7. Albin, *Justice and Fairness in International Negotiation*, pp. 108–109.

8. Mitsuo Matsushita, Thomas J. Schoenbaum, and Petros C. Mavroidis, *The World Trade Organization: Law, Practice and Policy* (Oxford, UK: Oxford University Press, 2003), pp. 9–11.

9. Friedl Weiss, "WTO Decision-Making: Is It Reformable?" in Daniel L. M. Kennedy and James D. Southwick (eds.), *The Political Economy of International Trade Law* (Cambridge, UK: Cambridge University Press, 2002), p. 74.

10. Please see relevant provisions of Articles IV, VIII, and IX in Appendix 2.

11. Chandrakant Patel, "Single Undertaking: A Straitjacket or Variable Geometry?" T.R.A.D.E. Working Paper No.15 (2003), p. 6.

12. John Croome, *Reshaping the World Trading System.* (Geneva: World Trade Organization, 1995), pp. 382–392.

13. Albin, *Justice and Fairness in International Negotiation,* pp. 137–139.

14. WTO/GATT, *Draft Final Act Embodying the Results of the Uruguay Round of Multilateral Trade Negotiations* (MTN.TNC/W/FA), GATT Secretariat (December 20, 1991).

15. Donald McRae, "The WTO in International Law: Tradition Continued or New Frontier?" *Journal of International Economic Law* 3, no. 1 (2000): 38.

16. Debra P. Steger, *Peace Through Trade: Building the WTO* (London: Cameron May, 2004), p. 154.

17. WTO, *China—Measures Affecting Financial Information Services and Foreign Financial Information Suppliers (Complaint by the US)* (DS373) (March 3, 2008).

18. Most notably: John J. Jackson, Robert E. Hudec, and Debra P. Steger. See Steger, *Peace Through Trade*, pp. 245–246.

19. Judith Hippler Bello, Rufus Yerxa, Tim Reif, and Alan Sykes. These trade pundits believe that the main binding WTO obligation is to maintain a balance of concessions. See ibid.

20. Peter-Tobias Stoll and Frank Schorkopf, *WTO—World Economic Order, World Trade Law* (Leiden, Netherlands: Martinus Nijhoff Publishers, 2006), pp. 12–13, 39–41.

21. Ostry, *The Post–Cold War Trading System*, pp. 68–69.

22. Ibid.

23. Melaku Geboye Desta, "The Integration of Agriculture into WTO Disciplines," in Bernard O'Connor (ed.), *Agriculture in WTO Law* (London: Cameron May Ltd., 2005), pp. 18–19.

24. Ostry, *The Post–Cold War Trading System*, p. 83.

25. Rorden Wilkinson, *The WTO—Crisis and the Governance of Global Trade* (London: Routledge, 2006), p. 44.

26. Michael Barnett and Martha Finnemore, *Rules for the World: International Organizations in Global Politics* (Ithaca, NY: Cornell University Press, 2004), pp. 34–39.

27. John F. Helliwell, *Globalization and Well-Being* (Vancouver, BC: UBC Press, 2002), p. 16.

28. Ostry, *The Post–Cold War Trading System*, p. 193.

29. Anna Lanoszka, "The WTO Accession Process—Negotiating Participation in a Globalizing Economy," *Journal of World Trade* 35, no. 4 (2001).

30. Chapter 7 will deal with accession negotiations in some detail.

31. As of May 2008, the WTO had 152 members.

32. John Rawls, *Political Liberalism* (New York: Columbia University Press, 1996).

33. John Rawls, *The Law of Peoples* (Cambridge, MA: Harvard University Press, 1999), p. 86.

34. Ibid., p. 42.

35. Joseph E. Stiglitz, "Two Principles for the Next Round or, How to Bring Developing Countries in from the Cold," in Bernard Hoekman and Will Martin (eds.), *Developing Countries and the WTO: A Pro-active Agenda* (Malden, MA: Blackwell Publishing, 2001), p. 11.

36. Amrita Narlikar, "Fairness in International Trade Negotiations," *World Economy* (August 2006): 1005.

37. Under the label of developing countries, many scholars bring together such economically diverse countries as Bangladesh, Brazil, Cambodia, China, Guatemala, Indonesia, India, Kenya, Madagascar, Morocco, and South Korea, just to name a few. Over 100 countries (developing, less developed, and least developed) are often brought together for analytical purposes when discussing the developing countries in the WTO.

38. Ian Shapiro, *The State of Democratic Theory* (Princeton, NJ: Princeton University Press, 2003), p. 3.

39. Fritz Scharpf, *Governing in Europe—Effective and Democratic?* (Oxford, UK: Oxford University Press, 1999), pp. 6–13.

40. Americo B. Zampetti, "Democratic Legitimacy in the World Trade Organization; The Justice Dimension," *Journal of World Trade* 37, no. 1 (2003): 110.

41. Shapiro, *The State of Democratic Theory*, p. 57.

42. Ibid., p. 10.

43. Ernst-Ulrich Petersmann, "From the Hobbesian International Law of Coexistence to Modern Integration Law: The WTO Dispute Settlement System," *Journal of International Economic Law* 1, no. 2 (1998): 175–178.

44. Robert Howse and Kalypso Nicolaidis, "Legitimacy and Global Governance: Why Constitutionalizing the WTO Is a Step Too Far," in Roger B. Porter, Pierre Sauve, Arvind Subramanian, and Americo Beviglia Zampetti (eds.), *Efficiency, Equity, Legitimacy: The Multilateral Trading System at the Millennium* (Washington, DC: Center for Business and Government at Harvard University, and Brookings Institution Press, 2001), p. 241 (emphasis in original).

45. Jürgen Habermas, *Between Facts and Norms: Contributions to a Discourse Theory of Law and Democracy* (Cambridge, MA: MIT Press, 1996).

46. Shapiro, *The State of Democratic Theory*, p. 33.

47. Miles Kahler, "Defining Accountability Up: The Global Economic Multilaterals," in David Held and Mathias Koenig-Archibugi (eds.), *Global Governance and Public Accountability* (London: Blackwell Publishing, 2005), p. 33.

48. Joseph A. Schumpeter, *Capitalism, Socialism and Democracy* (New York: Harper Perennial, 1976), p. 269.

49. Dilip K. Das, "Debacle at Seattle—The Way the Cookie Crumbled," *Journal of World Trade* 34, no. 5 (2000): 186.

50. WTO, *Preparation for the 1999 Ministerial Conference* (JOB[99]5868 and 6223) (October 1999).

51. WTO, *Minutes of October 06, 1999 General Council Meeting* (WT/GC/M/48) (October 27, 1999), pp. 7–16.

52. Once the General Council elects a new director-general of the WTO, what follows is a difficult process of electing four deputy-directors and other auxiliary staff.

53. John S. Odell, "The Seattle Impasse and Its Implications for the World Trade Organization," in Daniel L. M. Kennedy and James D. Southwick (eds.), *The Political Economy of International Trade Law* (Cambridge, UK: Cambridge University Press, 2002), pp. 400–401.

54. Das, "Debacle at Seattle."

55. Ostry, "World Trade Organization," p. 364.

56. WTO, *General Council: Implementation-Related Issues and Concerns* (WT/L/384) (December 19, 2000).

57. John S. Odell and Susan K. Sell, "Reframing the Issue: The WTO Coalition on Intellectual Property and Public Health, 2001," in John S. Odell (ed.), *Negotiating Trade—Developing Countries in the WTO and NAFTA* (Cambridge, UK: Cambridge University Press, 2006), p. 85.

58. Naboth van den Broek, "Power Paradoxes in Enforcement and Implementation of World Trade Organization Dispute Settlement Reports," *Journal of World Trade* 37, no. 1 (2003): 146.

59. WTO, *Ministerial Declaration* (WT/MIN/[01]/DEC/W/1); *Declaration on the TRIPS Agreement and Public Health* (WT/MIN/[01]/DEC/W/2); *Implementation-Related Issues and Concerns* (WT/MIN/[01]/DEC/W/10), (November 14, 2001).

60. As cited in Fatoumata Jawara and Aileen Kwa, *Behind the Scenes at the WTO—The Real World of International Negotiations; The Lessons of Cancun* (London and New York: Zed Books, 2004), pp. xxii–xxiii.

61. WTO, *Hong Kong Ministerial Declaration—Doha Work Programme,* Para 26 (WT/MIN/[05]/W/3/Rev.2) (December 18, 2005).

PART 2

The Three Pillars of the World Trade Organization

CHAPTER 4

Trade in Goods

The history of GATT serves as an example of how a small and essentially unfinished treaty can slowly develop into a complex international organization. It was a modest beginning of the trade system not only because of the absence of an institutional base, but also because GATT was signed by a small group of countries and only covered a limited range of goods. Almost fifty years after GATT was put in place, its clublike setting became permanently changed by the formalized WTO and its ambitious new agreements that would cover a wide range of economic activities.

Starting with this chapter, my task is to examine the new WTO agreements, the controversies surrounding them, and the emerging trade dilemmas caused by the transformations taking place in the world economy. The scope of several WTO agreements is unprecedented and hence many disagreements follow their implementation. This only makes the analysis more interesting, however, since the contemporary trade agenda has become closely linked with the sociopolitical and developmental contexts of many societies.

For most of its postwar history, GATT did serve as an agreement only concerned with traditional trade in goods. Even as additional codes were added and lists of tradable products were getting longer, GATT remained preoccupied with the exchange of goods. It mainly guarded the application of tariff concessions made by the contracting parties and provided a forum for new rounds of multilateral talks on further reduction of tariffs. Consequently, GATT's influence went only as far as tariffs and border issues were concerned.

The decisive step toward extending the influence of GATT beyond the merchandise trade, and consequently beyond the border measures, was made during the Uruguay Round. At its conclusion, the newly established WTO was described as consisting of three pillars: agreements relating to trade in goods, trade in services (GATS), and trade-related aspects of intellectual property rights (TRIPs). While the second and the third pillars are essentially two single agreements, the first pillar is an assembly of thirteen agreements, including GATT.

This chapter concentrates on trade in goods. Considered to be a traditional domain of GATT, trade in goods acquired an extended reach under the WTO with the new agreements that were added. The chapter first provides a brief overview of tariff concessions and reductions during the postwar era, and then it examines, in the historical context, the issues surrounding the three newest agreements belonging to the first pillar of the WTO: an agreement on agriculture, an agreement on textiles and clothing, as well as an agreement that deals with antidumping measures. Because agricultural trade for decades has been the most contentious area of the world economy, special attention is paid to the WTO Agreement on Agriculture. To a certain extent the hostilities that have characterized the negotiations on agriculture, as well as the peculiar treatment of textiles and clothing sectors, have long reflected the North-South divide that has not been fully resolved within the WTO.

The remaining nine agreements that constitute the first pillar of the WTO are not addressed here. This is not because they are of lesser importance. At least two of them are examined in the later chapters of this book. However, it would be beyond the scope of this book to examine them all. Some of them are technical agreements that relate to complicated border issues or determination of proper standards of imported goods. Because these agreements are highly technical and narrow in scope, their sociopolitical and developmental implications are relatively minimal, especially in comparison with the major agreements, which are at the center of this book, and which interest us most precisely because of the gravity of their influence. The first pillar of the WTO agreements on trade in goods are as follows.

GATT 1947 and Agreements on

- Agriculture
- Application of sanitary and physosanitary (SPS) measures
- Textiles and clothing
- Technical barriers to trade
- Trade-related investment measures
- Antidumping
- Customs valuation
- Preshipment inspection
- Rules of origin
- Import licensing procedures
- Subsidies and countervailing measures
- Agreement on safeguards

History of Tariff Concessions on Manufacturing Goods

Tariff reductions have come a long way since the onset of GATT. The declared aims of reducing barriers to international trade were carried out in a steady but uneven progression of rounds that saw countries negotiate tariff concessions and removals. When GATT came into force in 1947, the average tariff level for industrial products was high, about 40 percent.[1] Twenty-three countries, which then made up about 80 percent of international trade, had agreed to reduce their tariffs. The United States, at its peak position in the postwar years of unparalleled economic preponderance, cut its tariffs by about a third. But in the next decade there would be a much slower pace governing the removal of tariffs. The Annecy (1949) and Torquay (1950–1951) rounds, as one historian remarked, are more notable for the expansion of GATT's membership than for the rather lukewarm tariff removals that were negotiated in them.[2] Thankfully, despite the loss of optimism that clouded GATT's travails in the 1950s, there was no serious movement that would reverse the earlier progress made in 1947 and after due to the pledge of countries not to invoke an article in the general agreement that would permit the revocation of tariff concessions.

The 1960s, however, would see a greater willingness of countries to cut their tariffs. The Dillon Round, negotiated among the United States, the European Economic Community (now known as the European Union), eleven other developed countries, and six less developed countries, ended with an agreement for tariffs to be reduced by a fifth on 20 percent of dutiable imports.[3] In all, US$4.9 billion of tariffs were cut.[4] More impressive was the subsequent Kennedy Round, concluded in 1967, in which tariffs were further reduced by a fifth on 55 percent of dutiable imports.[5] More tariffs were to be phased out over an eight-year implementation period following the Tokyo Round negotiations, which saw all countries that participated reduce their tariffs by an average of approximately 26 percent. Once again the United States took the initiative here and had cut its tariffs by over a third.[6] The average industrial tariff level in the United States was 60 percent in 1934 and 25 percent in 1945, but only 4.3 percent in 1979 following the Tokyo Round of GATT negotiations.[7] With these gradual steps, which had by that point accumulated to the successes of the Tokyo Round, the average tariff level for industrial goods had now fallen from the postwar high of 40 percent to 6 percent by the end of the 1970s.[8]

Whatever the major achievements these rounds accomplished, they would be dwarfed by the outcome of the Uruguay Round. To examine the tariff reductions made in this round, it may be appropriate to review the tariff reductions in the imports of industrial products. After all, given the amount of investment in industrial products that developing countries had allocated, industrial exports accounted for over seven-tenths of total exports for more than forty developing countries. The United States and the EU reduced tariffs on industrial goods produced in developing countries by 23 percent and 22 percent, respectively. Japan was more generous in that the country's tariffs were cut by 30 percent. Developing countries also benefited each other by reducing their tariff levels by an average of 21 percent. All economies, industrial and developing, agreed to tariff cuts that were on average 28 percent of pre-round rates.[9]

The tariff rates of industrial products imposed by the United States fell from an average of 5.4 percent to 3.5 percent. It is important to note that the reduction in tariff rates still was not uniform among the various product categories. For example, textiles and clothing only saw modest reductions in tariffs as they fell from 16.7 percent to 14.6 percent, or almost 13 percent. Tariffs for fish and fish products similarly fell a little over 14 percent of pre–Uruguay Round rates. Tariff reductions were more drastic in other categories. The average tariffs for metals, nonelectric machinery, and wood products fell 62 percent, 72 percent, and 83 percent, respectively.[10] The EU also significantly cut its average tariffs from 5.7 percent to 3.6 percent. But like the United States, its reductions in the tariffs for textiles and clothing were also comparatively tepid, as they only fell to 9.1 percent from 11 percent, or 17.3 percent. The most drastic cuts that the EU made were not too dissimilar to the United States, in nonelectric machinery, wood products, and metals.[11] Japan, to say nothing of its prohibitively high tariffs in agriculture and other industries it recognizes as strategic, was more liberal in cutting its manufacturing tariffs in comparison to both the United States and the EU. In fact, Japan eliminated all tariffs in transport equipment and nonelectric machinery and reduced the average tariffs on electric machinery by almost 97 percent. Even in textiles and clothing, Japan was relatively more generous by cutting tariffs from an average rate of 11.3 percent to 7.6 percent. Overall, the average tariff rate in Japan fell from 3.9 percent to 1.7 percent.

In aggregate terms, the agreement reached at the Uruguay Round specified a target for tariff reductions in the amount of 36 percent for industrial countries and 24 percent for developing countries.[12] Indeed, the countries that continue to have the highest tariff rates are those belonging to the developing world. In fact, the tariff rates from these countries tend to discriminate against industrial countries, for imported goods from industrial countries faced on average higher tariffs than those from other developing countries. Moreover, because their economic growth strategies had placed a higher premium on industrial goods, manufacturing industries in the economies of developing countries enjoy greater protectionist measures than producers of primary products. The most egregious users of tariffs tend to be found in South Asia, where tariffs average from 10 percent to 60 percent. The poorer parts of the world, meaning the developing countries in

Latin America, Africa, and the Middle East, range from 10 percent to 25 percent. Tariffs in most industries in developed countries tend to be less than 5 percent. Such are the new tariff rates following the tariff negotiations in the Uruguay Round.[13]

Why Multilateral Talks Are Difficult When It Comes to Agriculture

It is no doubt a truism that agriculture remains the most contentious sector in international trade. It is customary to hear of obstinate governments unwilling to open their agricultural sectors to the world markets. Indeed, what has made the Uruguay Round of trade negotiations such a prolonged affair, and set the Doha Round adrift, has been the inability to arrive at a comprehensive multilateral agreement dealing with trade in agriculture. The problem is multifold. On the one hand, there is the defiance of the EU and the United States to reduce their agricultural subsidies and to open their markets to agricultural products from the developing world. On the other hand, there is the steadfast insistence of many developing countries to maintain their own protectionist policies even amidst a liberalization of the agricultural sectors of developed countries. The difficulty to arrive at a mutually beneficial compromise is further complicated by the fact that the respective positions of the negotiating parties are well entrenched for reasons that are political, economic, and even cultural.

In reality there is no one country in the world that is not employing some sort of protectionist agricultural measures. No government can easily ignore powerful agricultural interest groups that lobby for sustaining various barriers to foreign agricultural products, even if the costs of maintaining such barriers, while subsidizing local farmers, do not make any economic sense.

The factors that engender the difficulties of obtaining multilateral agreements in agriculture are firmly rooted in the past. It was the Great Depression starting in 1929 and the widely adverse effects it caused in the United States with respect to farmers' incomes, price fluctuations, and even food shortages that helped initiate protectionism in the agricultural sector. Government subsidies and support programs have since been designed to provide stability for the industry and curtail the sort of economic volatility that characterized the industry's experience in the Depression-era United States.[14] Although Europe too was affected negatively by the collapse of the global economy in the interwar years, it was the colossal destruction of World War II that further impressed upon the Europeans the need for food security.[15] In part, the traumatic memory of postwar food shortages gave impetus to the creation of the Common Agriculture Policy, which was originally proposed in 1960 to ensure adequate food production within the European Economic Community.

It may be simply said then that the United States and the countries of Western Europe aspired to obtain self-sufficiency in food production in order not to be reliant on other countries, be they friends or possible adversaries, for such essential goods. One enduring line of thought regarding agricultural protection in the late nineteenth century was that it also related to the military strength of the country:

> The purpose of the new tariffs in the later nineteenth century was often expressed in traditional terms, as not so much social as national defense. In public discussion, most attention focused on grain tariffs. Higher food prices for the consumer might be justified if the result of food protection was to increase the cultivated area, and thus raise the capacity of the state to defend itself in longer struggles against others in the competition of nations. But this argument then shaded into a social variant. Only an army based on a rural population, it was argued, could be effective; and so the farmer had to be preserved as a mainstay of military as well as of social order.[16]

As well reasoned as these arguments for self-sufficiency and food security may be, such policies nevertheless have had perverse consequences. The fixing of prices at a level above market-clearing prices in the Common Agricultural Policy has not only helped farmers obtain stability in their incomes but has also induced them to produce as much as they can to maximize their revenue. Because agricultural technology has made considerable advances in the past fifty years that have helped boost productivity and minimize production costs, the problem of oversupply and the difficulties of reforming the policy have become increasingly acute.[17] It is small wonder that maintaining the Common Agricultural Policy has cost the EU a significant majority share of its budget until recently.

The US agricultural industry has the same unfortunate incentives for overproduction, and the vested industry interests there are likewise so powerful that any meaningful reform designed to considerably reduce these subsidies would be politically unpopular and difficult to legislate. Such subsidy systems nevertheless create losers out of many groups of people. While consumers in the developed world are enjoying stable subsidized prices of their basic food products, the farmers in the developing world are not able to compete on the agricultural world markets because of the high production costs. Still, consumers in the developed world are affected because governments pay for the subsidies at the behest of taxpayers, and the market is further distorted by the rents producers pay to exert lobbying pressure on behalf of their interests. Moreover, the subsidies tend to favor large and more efficient farms, which are able to cut costs through the use of the newest technological innovations in agriculture. This means that small farms are being pushed out of the market even in the developed world, thus leaving many farmers unemployed, while big farms are getting bigger with the help of subsidies. These big farms also contribute to the destruction of the environment through the use of chemical fertilizers to increase their production.

Protectionism in agriculture, although the motives for it may largely be construed as strictly economic and political, is also linked with a broader set of arguments aimed at protecting cultural traditions of some nations. In an age of globalization where technology advances rapidly and cities grow larger and become more alienating, rural life and the idealized simplicities of farming can play a significant role in discussions concerning national identity. Those who believe that a rural way of life constitutes part of a national heritage see agricultural subsidies as a means of protecting the veritable character of a nation by supplying farmers their incomes and ensuring their survival. But if it is not the rustic images that stir public sympathy for farmers asking for continuing subsidization, then it is the believed worth of ensuring that certain agricultural goods, which are also understood as cultural, will be made. Several European states have repeatedly made such a cultural connection when arguing for a special treatment of an agricultural sector or insisting on the recognition of intellectual property rights in, for example, various types of cheese and wine.

The political, economic, and cultural reasons described above allow one not only an understanding of the interests governments have in granting special protections to their agricultural industries, but also an appreciation for the difficulties faced by trade negotiators trying to reform such a politically sensitive sector of the world's economy. After all, many governments are reluctant to alienate the potential rural vote by slashing subsidies and allowing a free-trade regime to take hold of their countries' agricultural sectors whereby the law of comparative advantage may rule uncompromisingly and the vagaries of the market may run roughshod over certain farms, businesses, and communities. Nor would governments like to forgo self-sufficiency by entrusting food production to foreign suppliers whose reliability and quality can never be taken for granted.

The European Common Agricultural Policy is arguably the most widely known system of agricultural subsidies and assistance programs in the developed world. Its political importance cannot be overestimated since it was one of the essential parts of the 1957 Treaty of Rome, which was the founding treaty of the European Economic Community. While initially mandated in the Treaty of Rome to provide food security and also stability to farmers' incomes by guaranteeing a minimum price set above market clearing prices and paying farmers direct subsidies for crops planted, the Common Agricultural Policy has become a system of inefficiencies in which farmers overproduce to better their incomes. In fact, the direct payment of subsidies to farmers had at one point become such a central part of the EU that over three-quarters of its budget was devoted to the Common Agricultural Policy. While the European arrangement is seen as the most egregious example of agricultural protection run amok, US protectionism in agriculture, whose existence in its various forms is longer than that of the Common Agricultural Policy, is also a system from which farmers are guaranteed a price higher than the market level. Nevertheless there are restrictions put in place on how much can be produced. Certain commodities are not even guaranteed an artificially high price. Rather, the United States refunds farmers based on a formula to ensure that their costs do not exceed their revenues.[18]

Agricultural subsidies are also used in Canada to protect the grain and dairy industries. It is through the Canadian Wheat Board, which was in fact established in 1935, that farmers in western Canada have their incomes ensured by a stable and predictable flow of cash should production expectations go unfulfilled or market conditions become too adverse. Then, in the early 1970s when market prices for daily products became unstable, Canada adopted a system of supply management. The Canadian Dairy Commission Act is the backbone behind the federal regulatory authority (normally delegated to provinces) and is responsible for marketing of milk and dairy products.

Lastly, the Japanese domestic market in meat, dairy, wheat, and rice is especially protected by a combination of tariffs, a price support system, import quotas, and state monopolies. Some of Japan's high agricultural tariffs are legendary (800 percent for rice, 250 percent for wheat) and they effectively shield domestic producers from foreign markets. It appears that in 2004 alone, the Japanese government spent some Y5.283 trillion (5.283 trillion yen; US$47 billion) in support of the farming sector.[19] Such costs are becoming increasingly indefensible given the overall difficult economic situation in Japan, resulting in necessary reduction of public expenditures in other areas and higher taxes. A 2001 comparative study examining the average agricultural tariffs of Japan, the EU, and the United States arrived at the following results: 12 percent in the United States, 30 percent in the EU, and 58 percent in Japan.[20] The high level of tariffs of these three trading powers only magnifies the scope of agricultural protectionism with domestic subsidies and other protective measures that already cost a great deal.

The countries enumerated above are all developed with sufficient economies to produce enough for themselves and others, but what of the developing countries? In what ways are they affected by the massive subsidization programs awarded to the agricultural sectors of the countries of the North? At first, it should be noted that throughout the latter part of the twentieth century, the import-substitution strategies adopted by many poorer countries to improve their economies tended to neglect agriculture by placing a greater emphasis on industrialization and the manufacturing sector. In Argentina, such policies forced many farmers to close their farms and move to the cities in search of manufacturing jobs that often never materialized. This focus on industrialization was supported by particular monetary policies and resulted not only in underinvestment in agriculture, but as G. Edward Schuh points out, in growing reliance on food imports. Developing countries

> tended to over-value their currencies, and in some cases by very large amounts. This over-valuation constituted an implicit export tax and an implicit subsidy on imports. If and when domestic food prices rose as a consequence of this discrimination, they imposed explicit export taxes and embargoes on exports, supported by licensing agreements. If the disincentives to agriculture were especially severe from so strongly shifting the domestic terms of trade against that sector, the over-valued currency eventually came into play as an import subsidy, and food imports would begin to flow in.[21]

Such monetary policies eventually proved unsustainable. The US dollar ceased being fixed after President Nixon floated it in August 1971, and petrodollars inundated banks and were eventually "recycled" in the form of low interest loans to developing countries.[22] By the 1980s, US monetary policy, under the direction of Federal Reserve chairman Paul Volcker, necessarily had to change course to reverse the dollar's depreciation. The crisis that ensued not only had major ramifications for the US economy, but also for the developing countries that now had to service their debts with an increasingly expensive US dollar and higher interest rates.[23] The crisis that unfolded was particularly difficult to handle by countries that were having problems with food security. Some developing countries had to rely more on food imports than necessary; sometimes this was due to their own policies and sometimes it was because of an unfavorable geographic location, poor climate, and overall weakness of their agricultural sector.

Some of the weaknesses of the agricultural sectors in the developing world, most notably in Africa, had their roots in the colonial era. The European empires expected the colonies to serve as cheap sources of single products, which led to the creation of export-oriented mono-crop economies. The European colonizers would offer incentives to the domestic farmers in a form of cheap food products to have them replace their domestic diversified food production with one special crop. For example, when the British came to Ghana, they turned the country into a cocoa-producing colony. Another famous case was Senegal, a country that became a center for peanut production in the French colonial empire. Such policies resulted in the overall decline of food production relative to growing populations in a number of African countries even after they became independent.[24]

Diminished food security resulted in chronic malnutrition, sustained food shortages, and in time many African countries' dependence on cheap (subsidized) imports from the former colonial powers. Paradoxically, by the 1990s, the agricultural subsidies in the industrialized countries benefited some former colonies, because they created an oversupply of agricultural products, and to deal with the problem of oversupply, the industrial countries would end up sending agricultural products, either in the form of food aid or in the form of below-cost discounted products, to the doorsteps of poor nations.

While some benefited, other countries with a large agricultural base of their own voiced a more pertinent allegation concerning the consequences of the policies of the developed countries. In regard to the protectionist policies that encourage the overproduction of food supplies, traditionally agricultural nations became concerned about dumping. Dumping is the trade practice of selling goods in another market at below-cost prices and has several potential effects on the targeted economy into which the goods are being dumped that are worth considering. First, flooding a market with below-cost goods could potentially drive local firms out of business, for they may be unable to sell their own goods at such low levels. Second, dumping also gives disincentives for local firms to enter the market because they are not able to compete with a flow of cheaper foreign products. Dumping can, therefore, stymie the performance of a national economy by discouraging growth in certain sectors. This was indeed the perverse effect of the large supplies of food offered benignly by the United States in the form of foreign aid to a number of African countries. Such assistance proved helpful in the short term but harmful in the longer run as it deterred local food production. In the end, the unemployment created as a result of local farmers being unable to sell their products gave rise to more long-term social problems in some African communities.

Because the overproduction of food in the developed world may be traced to the distorting effects of subsidization programs, the crux of the matter for the developing world is that they are simply unable to compete. While they may liberalize their own economies and allow foreign firms to set up shop locally, developing countries feel, not without reason, that they have little means of penetrating the well-established agricultural markets of North America and Europe in turn. Agricultural trade has been not quite free but instead rather unfair.

Under GATT, there was never any legal distinction between agricultural products and other merchandise goods. The United States, with its economic preeminence in the immediate postwar era, was the first country to push for special treatment with regard to agriculture in GATT.[25] The memory of the Great Depression's effects on the agricultural industry, described above in small detail, moved US trade negotiators to seek allowances for protectionist measures for the agricultural sector. Already, of course, US farmers did enjoy the subsidies and benefits of the US farm program. As far back as 1929, the government implemented the Agricultural Marketing Act that created the Federal Farm Board. Since 1933, when it was compelled to deal with the economic depression and volatility in the agricultural sector, Congress has passed a number of laws intended to stabilize prices and provide adjustment support for farmers. We should mention here the notable 1937 Sugar Act, which introduced direct benefit payment to US sugar producers, effectively separating prices for sugar in the United States from those on the world's markets. A series of prewar Agricultural Adjustment Acts were followed by far-reaching wartime measures that saw the supports extended to a vast number of agricultural items. In fact, it would be difficult to list agricultural products or farm animals that were not covered: even peanuts were added to the list in 1941. Shortly after the war, the discussion in Congress began over the extension of high agricultural subsidies. The Agricultural Act of 1948 lowered some of the support and introduced some degree of flexibility to the US support programs, but it nevertheless reinforced the general attitude that agriculture is different and should be protected.

The context of postwar policy initiatives potentially pitted agricultural concerns against the idea of trade liberalization. After all, the freshly initiated GATT advocated free trade and was in principle hostile toward any protectionist measures. Still, it was felt, GATT should not place any restrictions that may hinder the ability to safeguard the agricultural industry from potentially volatile market forces. Article XI of GATT, for example, proscribes the use of quantitative restrictions on trade unless the exporting countries experience food shortages or domestic substitute goods face similar restrictions.[26] Export subsidies are also essentially prohibited, as outlined in Article XVI of the General Agreement, unless the goods are primary products, which are "any product of farm, forest, or fishery at an early stage of processing," and the exporting country does not acquire "more than an equitable share of world export trade in that product."[27] In general, under GATT, subsidies or other protective measures were expected to be temporary and introduced only under rare circumstances.

The United States early on recognized that Article XI would not be sufficient in itself to allow a lawful continuation of its protectionist policies in agriculture and thus asked for a special waiver to keep them. Further exemptions were sought in order to ensure the passage of GATT in the US Senate such that Article XI would not be applied to such goods as sugar, peanuts, dairy products, and other agricultural items. Indeed, although these domestic goods did not similarly face restrictions as their substitute imports, per Article XI, the demands for a non-time-limited waiver from the strictures of Article XI with respect to agricultural products were met with US threats to withdraw from GATT. This development set an uneasy precedent.

As Michael J. Trebilcock and Robert Howse alert us, "this exemption for the United States may well have had the effect of dampening efforts to enforce strictly Article XI against other CONTRACTING PARTIES," although later GATT dispute settlement panel decisions would adopt a narrower view of how the provisions of Article XI should be interpreted.[28]

The prohibition of export subsidies in Article XVI has also been problematic interpretatively because of the methodological difficulties of ascertaining the definition of an "equitable share" of the world market in the subsidized exported good. Let me quote the relevant part of Article XVI to illustrate the problem:

> Accordingly, CONTRACTING PARTIES should seek to avoid the use of subsidies on the export of primary products. If, however, a contracting party grants directly or indirectly any form of subsidy which operates to increase the export of any primary product from its territory, such subsidy shall not be applied in a manner which results in that contracting party having more than an equitable share of world export trade in that product, account being taken of the shares of the CONTRACTING PARTIES in such trade in the product during a previous representative period, and any special factors which may have affected or may be affecting such trade in the product.

Indeed, for a legal document, one cannot help but be puzzled over its lack of precision. Similarly, the GATT panels had problems with resolving disputes over this issue. The problem was not only the definition of equitable share, but also the way of measuring the effect of the subsidy in question. While one might assume that a drastic increase in the volume of exports of one country following the implementation of certain subsidies and a concomitant decline in the export of another country's could potentially be a reasonable means of determining the impact of the export subsidies, panel decisions have not consistently adopted such reasoning. Although French export subsidies on wheat flour were judged as producing an inequitable share of the world market in a 1958 ruling by the GATT panel, the EU's subsidies on the same product were deemed fair in a subsequent ruling made more recently, despite how the supranational organization's share of the world market in wheat flour went from 29 percent to 75 percent between 1962 and 1981.[29] After all, the panel understood that one cannot be so mono-causal with regard to export subsidies and world market share, and, as a result, there ought to be unambiguous evidence that demonstrates the impact of export subsidies on enlarging the market share of a country's good(s). Still, even if we agreed that Article XI was too restrictive, resulting in countries seeking exemptions, while Article XVI was too cumbersome, resulting in conflicting interpretations, the blame should not be placed on the weakness of GATT but rather on the lack of political will to enforce multilateral disciplines as they related to agriculture.[30]

It should be kept in mind that although Western Europe, and also Japan, maintained their protectionist policies much to the chagrin of US agriculturalists, they were nevertheless tolerated due in large part to the Cold War and the fear emanating from the Soviet Union. A strong, self-reliant European Economic Community was in the interests of US policymakers, for it could provide a bulwark against the possible spread of communism. These concerns over transatlantic security eventually came to be mitigated, whereas there was growing awareness that the next round of trade negotiations should address more sufficiently the contentious issue of agriculture. One economic impetus was the seemingly paradoxical need of the Soviet Union for food imports during the Leonid Brezhnev era.[31] While exporters in the developed world greeted with alacrity the appearance of a new consumer with a potentially large appetite for grain, other countries that relied on food imports were concerned that they would soon face significant food shortages.[32] These fresh concerns over food security, and a provocative US embargo announced on soybeans, prompted negotiators in the Tokyo Round of GATT negotiations in the 1970s to address the tariff and nontariff barriers on the trade of agricultural goods. Already in the Tokyo Round agricultural talks were separated from other matters and had then only covered meat, dairy, and grain. Most agricultural concessions, although still quite limited, were reached through bilateral talks between the United States and the European Communities and respectively with Japan and Canada. These four constituted the Quad group that was at the forefront of the Tokyo Round. The only two multilateral agreements negotiated during the Tokyo Round—the bovine meat and the international dairy agreements—were largely symbolic, as they were designed mainly to facilitate the flow of information among the signatories.[33]

Clearly any serious efforts during the Tokyo Round to liberalize the agricultural trade proved to be fruitless, due in part to the European Economic Community's own maneuvering to leave agriculture out of the agenda, growing trade deficits in the global economy, and the US agricultural industry's own troubles in the 1980s. This nevertheless compelled policymakers to engage in greater debates over protectionist farm policies.[34] Still, outside of the United States, and Europe for that matter, there were sustained calls for agricultural trade reform. A group of fourteen countries—Argentina, Australia, Brazil, Canada, Chile, Colombia, Fiji, Hungary, Indonesia, Malaysia, New Zealand, the Philippines, Uruguay, and Venezuela—formed the Cairns Group in April 1986 to push for the elimination of agricultural export subsidies and for more general reforms of this sector. Having found agricultural protectionism totally at odds with the economically liberalizing spirit of GATT, members of the Cairns Group would succeed in forcing agriculture on the agenda for the next trade round that would begin in earnest in Punta del Este, Uruguay, in September 1986.

The WTO Agreement on Agriculture

Although the final result was modest, the area of agriculture nevertheless became a significant feature of the Uruguay Round. At first, the submission of proposals by a number of countries helped to articulate those countries' position and also to provide a suggested outline of the trajectory that negotiations over agriculture and their scope ought to follow. The US position was particularly audacious in that it supported the "phase-out of all trade distortive production and export subsidies within 10 years, the conversion of all non-tariff measures, and dramatic improvements in market access."[35] The response from other countries was a combination of bewilderment and skepticism, as it was unclear whether such a proposal was genuine or merely an aggressive negotiating strategy. Yet, as Clayton Yeutter pointed out, notwithstanding the practical impossibilities of obtaining these high-minded objectives, it was congruent with the principles and spirit advocated by GATT since its inception in the immediate postwar era.[36] The purpose of the US position was to roll back the apparent tendency in the 1980s of states increasingly adopting more restrictive protectionist measures in agriculture by negotiating "a specific, definitive, precise agreement, not one that might be subject to varied interpretations."[37] In short, as the Uruguay Round commenced, the United States became an official ally of the Cairns Group in advocating the total elimination of agricultural export subsidies, a significant reduction of domestic subsidies (price support, guaranteed income schemes, etc.), total conversion of all quantitative restrictions into predictable tariffs, and better market access for foreign agricultural products.

This position was far reaching and was immediately contested by Europe and Japan, although for different reasons. While Europeans were willing to improve market access, they nevertheless insisted on maintaining their export subsidies. However, Japan was interested in introducing strict rules prohibiting export subsidies but vigorously rejected the proposal for the elimination of quantitative restrictions as well as the proposal advocating better market access for foreign products. The lines of conflict were drawn and would persist to the end of the round, especially between Europe and the United States.

This does not mean to say that the United States was unappreciative of the position of the Europeans, whose Common Agricultural Policy seemed all too impervious to meaningful reforms should policymakers have desired them. They understood that any negotiated agreement would necessarily be sensitive to the interests of the European Economic Community. While the European Economic Community did agree that there should be some loosening of domestic support measures, there was still reluctance to budge on the issue of export subsidies. For the most part, the European Economic

Community sought to safeguard a number of protectionist measures. Income support was still deemed necessary; in fact, the Europeans did not perceive it to distort trade even if the United States begged to differ given the proclivity of income support to induce overproduction.[38] Furthermore, the Europeans' desired adjustment measures that would likely include domestic support would need to be implemented to mitigate the effects of liberalization.

Although the positions of the United States and the European Economic Community were divergent but not wholly irreconcilable, there was little that broke the deadlock between them over agriculture. The Mid-Term Review hosted in Montreal, Canada, in 1990 did not have the effect of bringing delegations closer to any agreement other than agreeing to negotiate "substantial progressive reductions in agricultural support and protection sustained over an agreed period of time."[39] And yet.the delegations appeared to have become more adamant following Montreal about breaking the impasse, as if all the disappointments of the Mid-Term Review had a galvanizing effect. Also, as we remember from an earlier chapter, this was the time when the Cold War was coming to an end and there was a feeling that the world was moving toward greater economic cooperation. The sense of unifying global values was at odds with the lack of progress of the Uruguay Round. The director-general of GATT, Arthur Dunkel, requested each negotiating group's chairman to draft for submission outline agreements. The outline submitted by the Negotiating Group on Agriculture's chairman, Aart de Zeeuw, used the four-tiered approach espoused by the United States and the European Economic Community of making reform and headway in four areas: export subsidies, production subsidies, import access, and food safety measures.[40] While the Europeans remained wary about the objectives set forth in the outline concerning production and export subsidies, they nonetheless soon showed greater willingness in the new decade to pursue reforms in the Common Agricultural Policy.

Indeed, a proposal regarding reform in the Common Agricultural Policy was brought forward by the European Economic Community's commissioner for agriculture, Ray MacSherry, that advocated the cessation and gradual reversal of the widening of agricultural subsidies.[41] While one may view these reforms as being too lukewarm, they were nonetheless a step in the right direction as they were more congruent with the goals set forth by the United States and the Cairns Group. The December 1991 Draft Final Text (the Dunkel Text) produced by GATT's director-general to help inject greater confidence over the efficacy and pace of negotiations became a benchmark for the resolution of existing disagreements. The Dunkel Text was radical in some respects because it proposed universal tariffication by which complete elimination of quantitative restrictions can be attained and it called for a significant 36 percent reduction in spending on export subsidies as well as a reduction of 24 percent in the volume of export subsidies and a 20 percent reduction in domestic subsidies. Furthermore, the Dunkel Text proposed substantially different treatment for poorer countries by allowing them to maintain various subsidies programs or extending the period during which other supportive measures would have to be eliminated.[42]

Throughout 1992 intense talks between the European Economic Community and the United States and its Cairns Group partners continued. Eventually, when a contemporaneous trade dispute over oilseed policy in Europe was resolved and the November 1992 Blair House agreement between the United States and the European Economic Community was signed, it appeared at last that a new era of cooperation over agricultural trade had finally arrived. The Blair House agreement promised to reduce export subsidies by 21 percent and domestic subsidies by 20 percent but on an aggregate basis.[43] The agreement did raise the ire of France, which felt that, among other things, the requirements for reducing export subsidies were still excessive. France also demanded a special waiver for the European Common Agricultural Policy to permanently shield it from being challenged by the GATT trade disputes panels, despite the six-year exemption period guaranteed by the Blair House agreement.[44] Just when the final deal completing the Uruguay Round seemed to be within reach, the French government threatened to reject the proposal. However, France was soon to be satisfied with concessions regarding the methods allocating the base year for the calculations of the subsidies reductions. Another concession was negotiated at the request of Japan and Korea allowing them to postpone the tariffication process, the negotiations were completed in December 1993, and the Uruguay Agreement was eventually signed on April 15, 1994, in Marrakesh, Morocco.

So what did the Uruguay Agreement do then for agriculture? To begin, it had finally brought the long-controversial sector into the international trading regime now managed by the WTO agreements. The Uruguay Round, in a word, sought to deny agriculture the special exemptions it had received throughout the postwar period. Other than the partial victory for the principle of equal rules for all countries, the WTO Agreement on Agriculture did accomplish several items:

- The agreement specifies the disciplines for *domestic support* (subsidies) and calls for a reduction of 20 percent in the Aggregate Measure of Support from 1986–1988 base years levels in industrialized countries in six years. For developing countries this reduction is to be 13 percent in ten years, while the least-developed countries would be completely exempted. The subsidies to be reduced in accordance to these disciplines are those that are recognized as trade distorting—domestic support programs are known as the Amber Box. Subsidies in environmental programs, research programs, food aid, and other areas are exempted (known as the Green Box) while direct payments to food that are tied to production-limiting programs are permitted (known as the Blue Box).

• With respect to *export subsidies*, developed countries are required to make a 36 percent reduction in the value of expenditures in this category from the 1986–1990 base period or a 21 percent reduction in volume over six years. Developing countries face looser requirements, for they have to make instead 24 percent or 14 percent reductions in expenditures and volume respectively.[45] This means that the WTO Agreement on Agriculture still permits export subsidies. Interestingly enough, only about twenty-five of all the members of the WTO (counting the EU as one) have agricultural export subsidies and they are all developed countries, thus demonstrating the double standards that exist within the organization. For most of the members of the WTO there is no distinction between agricultural and nonagricultural exports subsidies and since export subsidies are prohibited under the WTO, one of the Doha Round demands as expressed by developing countries is the total elimination of agricultural export subsidies by the developed world.[46]

• With respect to *market access*, a significant achievement of the WTO Agreement on Agriculture has been *tariffication*, whereby quantitative restrictions (restrictive quotas that indicate the allowable maximum imports of foreign products) are to be converted into their tariff equivalents. Newer quantitative restrictions and other nontariff barriers cannot be introduced anymore as instruments of protection. Tariff-rate quotas are acceptable. Tariff reductions are to be bound (i.e., not subject to an increase). Moreover, the agreement calls for a reduction in the level of tariffs, which have to be reduced by an average of 36 percent over a six-year period by the industrialized countries and by an average of 24 percent by developing countries over a ten-year period. The least-developed countries are again exempted from these provisions.

Although the WTO Agreement on Agriculture was a great achievement given the past history of this sector, the exemptions it allowed from its provisions left additional reforms of the sector in the hands of future negotiations.

The most politically charged exemptions concern the reduction of domestic support measures, which have been classified as various boxes according to the level of trade distortions they were causing. The most distortive measures like direct price support for farmers are classified as "Amber Box," but countries have been allowed to exempt up to 5 percent of total agricultural production from the disciplines of the WTO agreement and hence continue to use domestic subsidies, often on the most strategically important products. "Green Box" subsidies can be given to farmers in the form of income support with no specific product and production target in mind. These subsidies are not given any limits under the WTO Agreement on Agriculture. With time, the "Green Box" subsidies could become a problem because of the growing tendency to divert other forms of domestic subsidies under this category to ascertain the same result through these more "legitimate" means. The recent argument in support of biofuels, for example, means that farmers in Europe and North America are granted massive research assistance funds that are perfectly legal under the WTO agreement, but which nevertheless amount to subsidies, putting farmers in the developing world into further disadvantage.

Another disappointing shortcoming of the agreement is its silence with respect to the use of government agencies as agricultural monopolies that either resell imported agricultural products at below-market prices, set the amounts of imported products, or designate domestic agents to purchase them often at preferable prices. In the end, one can conclude that the final outcome of the Uruguay Round on agriculture meant an important step on the path to reforming the multilateral rules that manage agricultural trade. Still, the round achieved very little in terms of making trade in agricultural products more open and less distorted.[47]

Article 14 of the agriculture agreement makes a specific connection with the WTO Agreement on the Application of Sanitary and Phytosanitary Measures (SPS). It calls for international standards regarding food safety to be harmonized with oversight of such organizations as the International Plant Protection Organization, the International Office of Epizootics, and the Codex Alimentarius. The specific aim of the SPS agreement as stated in Article 2 is to guarantee that every WTO member has a right "to take sanitary and phytosanitary measures necessary for the protection of human, animal or plant life or health" provided that such measures are consistent with the provisions of the agreement. Any claim set forth by governments that imports should meet certain standards and regulations must show that science supplies ample evidence for the reasoning of those standards and regulations. Otherwise, countries can make their challenge at the WTO. But at a time when the science of genetics and biotechnology is constantly evolving and producing new inventions, it often becomes difficult to come up with some conclusive criteria for assessing their safety and the depth of government regulations required.

Indeed, at the heart of any trade dispute initiated under the SPS agreement is "the question of the legitimacy of a WTO Member's health and safety regulations."[48] For example, the EU has consistently adopted a precautionary-principle approach to restrict imports of GMOs (genetically modified organisms). The precautionary principle works on the assumption that because today's science cannot completely ensure the long-term safety of certain products, the health and safety regulations should reflect precaution and restrict the usage and imports of such products. The United States, however, has traditionally been skeptical about the precautionary approach to new products, and as a result, its regulatory system supports production and international trade of genetically modified products.

The application of the precautionary principle provoked several trade disputes between the EU and the United States, with both sides arguing that their broadly divergent regulations are scientifically applied and consistent with the WTO agreement.[49] However, if the two top trading partners cannot agree on the criteria assessing the legitimacy of implemented safety regulations, one can only sympathize with developing countries, many of which have expressed concerns that the application of the SPS agreement can effectively be used as a means for enacting protectionist measures that restrict market access for their agricultural products.

It needs to be emphasized that despite the inclusion of agriculture in the multilateral architecture of the WTO, there is still much that needs to be done. Tariffication was a welcomed start, but the tariffs that remain in agriculture are still high. For example, in comparison with average tariffs on manufacturing goods, which can range from 0 percent to 15 percent among WTO members, tariffs on agricultural products range from 50 percent to 150 percent. And if these tariffs continue to be reduced at the rate applied in the past, it would take decades to reduce them to the level of manufacturing tariffs.[50] Moreover, access to markets in the developed countries remains limited for developing countries because of the sometimes restrictively high food standards and regulations. These issues were supposed to be addressed during the Doha Round. However, as the Doha Round missed its realistic deadline in June 2007, the agricultural talks continued to be unsuccessful. The chapter examining the growing role of developing countries in the WTO pays closer attention to the recent developments in the WTO negotiations.

Multilateral Negotiations over Textiles and Clothing

While certainly less overtly controversial than agriculture, the seeming lack of controversy over the trade of textiles and clothing should not be mistaken to mean facility in reaching a truly meaningful multilateral accord. In fact, it was not until the Uruguay Round that the textiles and clothing sectors lost their special case status as being outside GATT and were finally disciplined according to the rules and regulations of the WTO. A perennial economic fear that has long bedeviled developed countries following the signing of GATT and throughout the mid-twentieth century was that freer trade in textiles and clothing would mean those industries would lose out to firms operating in the developing world.

This was a particularly salient issue given how the largest industries in a number of developed countries, such as the United States, were in fact in textiles.[51] Because textiles and clothing can be made through labor-intensive processes, such goods produced in countries where labor is relatively much cheaper could prove very competitive for items made in richer countries, where unskilled and semiskilled labor is guaranteed better incomes and even protected through unions. Indeed, it is the developing countries like China, India, Indonesia, the Philippines, Malaysia, and Mexico, just to name a few, that enjoy comparative advantage in labor. In short, the global economic liberalization of the textiles and clothing industries was a perceptible danger to jobs, and, by extension, the economic well-being of countries of the developed world. In the meantime, however, the gains of economic liberalization here were calculated to be quite significant for developing countries, for textiles accounted for a very large proportion of imports shipped from the developing countries to countries in the Organization for Economic Cooperation and Development (OECD).[52] As Trebilcock and Howse reported, "It has been further estimated that if all import restrictions were removed, developing country textiles exports would increase by about 50% and clothing exports by 128.9%."[53]

These concerns gave rise to a reason to place textiles and clothing outside the disciplines of GATT. This curious exclusion was possible given the prolonged domination of the GATT trading system by a group of industrialized nations that effectively resisted any meaningful opening of their markets on a competitive basis to textile and clothing products from the developing world. Over the years, the international trade in textiles and clothing became managed in a separate way by being granted special exemptions from the principles of free trade and economic liberalization that GATT advocated. Already the Short-Term Cotton Arrangement and the Long-Term Cotton Arrangement saw the negotiating of special rules for these products, the latter of which lasted until 1973. But the most relevant agreement, in terms of endorsing protectionist attitudes in spite of the spirit of free trade contained in the general agreement, was the Multi-Fibre Arrangement (MFA). Implemented in 1974, the MFA was conceived out of fears that the textile and clothing industries in the developing world would overtake those in developed countries and was brought into existence by the efforts of the latter who were keen in mitigating the threats posed by cheap imports of cotton, manmade textiles, and wool.[54]

The divergent and contradictory interests of the negotiating parties is reflected well in the MFA's own preamble:

> The basic objectives shall be to achieve the expansion of trade, the reduction of barriers to such trade and the progressive liberalization of world trade in textile products, while at the same time ensuring the orderly and equitable development of this trade and avoidance of disruptive effects in individual markets and on individual lines of production in both importing and exporting countries.[55]

How to achieve these seemingly opposing goals was no small matter for the developing countries affected by the MFA. While Article 2 called for the reduction and eventual removal of existing trade restraints in textiles, unless such barriers were justifiable according to GATT, an importing country could nevertheless impose trade restrictions upon the exports of another country should it perceive serious market disruptions, provided that consultations with that country prove fruitless within sixty days. Restraints in this regard, however, were only allowed to be temporary, but that is not to say that renewals of the restraints were difficult to acquire.[56] Furthermore, under Article 4, voluntary export restraints were also allowed, even if there were no threats, real or perceived, emanating from market disruption. The believed *risk* thereof was an adequate excuse for any such import restrictions, which amounted to lowering the existing import quotas in an arbitrary fashion and hence creating many economic problems for exporting developing countries, which found the system to be unfair and unpredictable. To quote Marcelo Raffaelli, "the MFA apparently had never been intended by developed CONTRACTING PARTIES as a tool for liberalization, but rather as a waiver for the imposition of restrictions of a kind forbidden by the General Agreement."[57] If not that, it was to provide a very flexible means for the adjustment of developed countries to the less expensive imports from developing countries.

Despite its extensions in 1977 and 1981, the MFA was soon recognized to do little to spur economic liberalization in textiles and clothing. GATT's director-general, Arthur Dunkel, who also was the chairman of the Textiles Committee of the Multi-Fibre Arrangement, increasingly believed that the aforementioned sectors should bear witness to more "meaningful liberalization" despite its seeming impossibility with the acrimony that permeated the negotiations between developed and developing countries throughout the MFA extensions and the beginnings of the Uruguay Round.[58] Yet, as Raffaelli shows, the structure of international trade in textiles had undergone several fundamental shifts that would gradually facilitate greater willingness to discipline textiles.[59] First, there were new entrants to the export market such as China, whose market was hitherto closed, while erstwhile exporters, namely Japan, gradually became net importers. Second, firms in the developed world began outsourcing their manufacturing operations in the developing world to take advantage of the relatively lower wage rates.[60] Arguably the most widely known example of this trend was the outward processing achieved by US businesses in Latin America, although businesses located in the European Economic Community would also adopt similar practices in Eastern Europe and North Africa. Third, a global restructuring of the economy occurred whereby inflation wracked some of the economies of the developing world. At the turn of the decade, world trade was actually decreasing because of a global recession, and world manufacturing production grew at a tepid 1 percent.[61]

Amidst all these processes, the application of the MFA by the developed world, which was varied and never uniform, was lessened by the end of the 1980s. Initially highly restrictive, the European Economic Community eventually became more relaxed toward the latter part of the decade, and the United States began to import more and more from the developing world despite the implementation of policies that were ostensibly more restrictive. Thanks to a number of political reasons that motivated greater US willingness to accommodate China, the import quotas set by the United States in its negotiations with China were in fact quite sizable.[62] Canada, however, saw its policies become even more restrictive as the decade passed due to recurrent fears that cheap imports from the developing world would wreak havoc on the large domestic textiles industry.

Yet, the protectionism employed by the industrialized world would give way with the partial successes that the Uruguay Round achieved over textiles. The Agreement on Textiles and Clothing was thereby negotiated multilaterally to do away with the bilateral quotas that were negotiated under the purview of the MFA. Indeed, the Agreement on Textiles and Clothing essentially mandated the expiration of the MFA by January 1, 2005. Through its application to all members of the WTO, the Agreement on Textiles and Clothing seeks to reverse protectionism in the industry and end its special case status that has long excluded it from the rules and disciplines that govern the international trade of other industrial products. In four phases the WTO members were required to reduce their quantitative restrictions on textiles such that by the conclusion of the third phase in 2002, 51 percent of their restrictions would be eliminated.[63] This entailed, not without controversy, that the bulk of the reductions in quantitative restrictions would take place in the last three years of the four-phase process. By leaving the opportunity of the bulk of quantitative restrictions to be eliminated at the last possible time, the potential remains for those protectionist measures to be extended if sympathetic politicians seek to appeal to those who have the most to lose from their removal.[64]

The Agreement on Textiles and Clothing is not without its problems. For example, if importing countries fear that their markets are being disrupted by the exports of another country, they still may be able to engage in bilateral consultations with the exporting country with possible recourse to unilateral action, subject to the Textiles Monitoring Body (the supervisory body of the agreement's implementation). But whatever the restrictive measures (safeguards) that may be imposed unilaterally, their uppermost longevity is three years with no possibility of renewal.[65] Still, even after the significant reduction in tariffs called for by the agreement, the tariffs that will continue to exist post facto will remain normally higher than the average tariffs placed on other industrial goods.[66] Consumers in the industrial countries and producers in the developing world nevertheless are expected to win with the widened range of choice and the cheaper goods on store shelves, while the other economic costs associated with maintaining quotas are done away with. Then again, critics of economic globalization believe that this new global division of labor overall hurts both sides. While in the developed world factories close as they cannot compete with the cheaply produced textile products imported from the developing world, the workers in the poorer countries of the globe are being exploited to keep costs of production as low as possible. These arguments, which assume that governments are either negligent or have no role to play in formulating and monitoring trade policies, oversimplify the situation, which varies from country to country.

In addition, one single state, China, a major low-cost producer, is capable of influencing international trade in textiles and clothing. After all, in accordance to the laws of comparative advantage, the free trade of textile products would essentially award the efficient producer who enjoys the relative availability of the cheapest labor and materials. The safeguards that may be put in place to mitigate the effects of China's imports can still only exist for three years. A special restrictive measure was negotiated by the United States with China, the product-specific safeguard, which came into effect with China's accession to the WTO in December 2001 and would last until 2013, to protect the US economy from any disruptions ascribed to Chinese imports.[67] These safeguards would help extenuate somewhat the large growth forecasted for Chinese textile exports in the post-accession era.

WTO Agreement on Antidumping Measures

Dumping is the economic practice where firms sell their exported goods in a secondary market either below cost or below the price that other firms sell within that market. It is a form of price discrimination because the "offending" firm exports their product at a different price than in its domestic market. For firms to be able to dump, they must be located in imperfectly competitive industries whereby they are able to set the prices and not take what is given in the market. Further, there has to be a segmentation of the market by which domestic consumers are unable to purchase the cheaper goods that are sold in foreign markets.[68] Yet, it is debatable whether this is an economic practice that is so egregious to warrant protectionist measures. The concerns of developing countries that the dumping of agricultural products potentially stifles the development of critical industries such as those in food production and impedes their own economic development may be justified. But it is arguably less clear if the United States, and other developed countries with large and robust economies, can sufficiently rationalize the usage of antidumping measures to protect its industries from alleged incidents of dumping. After all, the supposed crime of dumping is based on perception. It is in the eyes of the beholder.

Antidumping legislation has long existed in the United States before the signing of GATT. The Antidumping Act of 1916 and Title VII of the Tariff Act of 1930 have provided US lawmakers with the legal guidelines on how to pursue cases and implement measures to protect domestic firms and industries against dumping practices.[69] The United States is not the only country that has tried to curtail alleged instances of dumping. For much of the mid-century, the other countries to exercise antidumping have included, by and large, the EU, Canada, and Australia. Toward the end of the 1980s, the group of countries that employed antidumping measures has become less exclusive. Thanks to training, developed technical expertise, and other capacity-building efforts, developing countries have shown greater willingness to use antidumping measures such that between 1985 and 2002 almost two-thirds of all antidumping petitions were initiated by developing countries. Interestingly enough, nearly three-quarters of those same investigations were made against other developing economies. The growth in the number of countries seeking to apply antidumping measures has also entailed the stellar increase in the number of antidumping cases heard worldwide. The average number of antidumping cases that were made each year between 1980 and 1985 was 144. Between 2000 and 2001 the average spiked to 318 cases.[70]

Both GATT and the WTO view dumping as a condemnatory act that cannot yet be prohibited, for it is recognized as a practice not initiated by governments themselves but rather businesses.[71] Nevertheless, guidelines are provided, in Article VI of GATT, on how incidences of dumping can be determined to have occurred and how antidumping measures, should they be pursued by governments, ought to be implemented in order to minimize the risks for protectionism and make trade further equitable.[72] But the aforementioned article does acknowledge the difficulties in credibly ascertaining whether or not dumping is being practiced, especially if a product was made in a nonmarket economy where subsidies already distort its normal price. However, regardless of this possible problem with respect to goods produced in nonmarket economies, a significant difference between the normal price and the export price is one way to determine dumping. If there is no normal or domestic price, it necessarily has to be "constructed" using data on production costs and its export price sold in a third country's markets with allowances made for taxes, currency conversions, quantities, and profits.[73] In short, it is very difficult to demonstrate with certainty that an export price of a product in one faraway country is in fact superficially below the costs price in order to validly allege dumping. Repeatedly, countries accused of dumping have argued that such low prices are the natural outcome of their economic conditions and are simply dangerously competitive for their trading partners that would use antidumping measures as an excuse for protectionism.

As a growing number of countries have been unhappy about the use of antidumping measures, the negotiators pushed for a new agreement on this issue. The outcome again was not quite what many governments wanted. It is even hard to call it a new agreement since it is based on GATT Article VI previously mentioned. Still, the agreement makes important clarifications. For antidumping action to be justified, there has to be evidence that shows clearly that injury has been inflicted by dumping onto a domestic industry. According to the WTO Antidumping Agreement, the evidence must show that the alleged injury can be proved by "both (a) the volume of the dumped imports and the effect of the dumped imports on prices in the domestic market for like products, and (b) the consequent impact of these imports on domestic producers of such products."[74] If an antidumping measure is enacted proactively, as if to deter or mitigate the threat of material injury, then a causal link has to be convincingly demonstrated to exist "between the dumping and the material injury caused to domestic industry [which is recognized to produce like products]."[75] Should a national government choose to pursue antidumping measures and if it meets the minimum requirement that more than 3 percent of comparable imports are in fact the dumped imports, the antidumping measure can only last five years.[76]

It is the United States that has used antidumping measures most frequently to protect certain sectors of its economy from perceived instances of injury. There is in fact a process through which aggrieving firms that perceive dumping by foreign firms can make their appeals for assistance. First, firms file a petition claiming material injury by foreign imports to the United States International Trade Commission, which verifies the charge of injury, and the Department of Commerce, which is the agency responsible for determining whether or not dumping has occurred. When either agency reaches a negative decision on these areas, then the case is dismissed. Sometimes, however, the case is terminated should a settlement be reached between the aggrieving firms and the industry accused of dumping. Other times, and indeed most regularly, antidumping measures are imposed when the decisions of the International Trade Commission and the Department of Commerce affirm the petitioning businesses' complaints. Between 1979 and 1998 two-thirds of determinations of injury by the International Trade Commission were positive and close to half of these cases saw the average tariff rate imposed by the Department of Commerce.[77] A study conducted by Chad P. Brown, Bernard Hoekman, and Caglar Ozden found that the most common target of US antidumping investigations are developing countries, particularly the poorer bracket among them, with those investigations being less likely to be terminated before the final injury decision than those made on developed countries.[78] The bias against developing countries is further compounded by the fact that developing countries face higher import duties than developed countries should a positive injury decision be acted upon. The authors of the study ascribe the bias to the "differences in capacity across countries to defend their interests and their WTO rights."[79] Developing countries, in short, may have neither the technical expertise nor the incentive, for the costs of fighting antidumping action far outweigh the perceived benefits.

Conclusion

The functional need that propelled it into existence meant that GATT was used initially only as far as the contracting parties needed it to manage their reciprocal concessions. And these concessions largely meant tariff reductions on selective goods. This would not have been the case had the ITO project survived. The ambitious scope of the proposed organization went well beyond the simple technical arrangements aimed at managing tariff reductions. The failure of the ITO then meant that the bulk of the decisions concerning various trade-related issues reverted back to the sovereign domain of individual states and away from the international level. The obvious consequences of this would be more flexibility retained by trading nations with respect to their trade policies, but it would also mean more incentives for countries to stay outside GATT rules or seek exemptions from these rules in order to meet domestic trade policy objectives.

Such tendencies would become especially pronounced with respect to agriculture, the use of antidumping measures, and trade quotas on textile and clothing products from the developing world. The restrictive measures used by GATT contracting parties to protect their industries from foreign competition using antidumping regulations or other nontariff restrictions in agricultural and textile trade came under increased scrutiny and criticism by a number of developing countries. The system of restrictive quotas that prevailed under the MFA was long considered discriminatory by all parties involved, while protectionism in agriculture was becoming too costly for the EU and the United States and was limiting access for other producers, with detrimental effects on overall agricultural production worldwide.

The three new WTO agreements discussed in this chapter came into existence after years of keeping the issues they cover mostly outside GATT, at the disadvantage of developing countries. From the beginning of the Uruguay Round, developing countries insisted on bringing these issues under multilateral rules. In the end, agreements on agriculture and textiles and clothing became a bargaining chip in the hands of the negotiators. Developing countries were persuaded to accept the new controversial WTO agreements on services and intellectual property in exchange for new agreements on agriculture and textiles and clothing.

The original GATT did not distinguish between merchandise goods and agricultural products. This legal uniformity, however, did not stop countries from treating agricultural sectors in a quite exceptional way. This happened because of the historical problems governments had with ensuring adequate food supplies in times of economic crises and armed conflicts. Over the years, agriculture became the most distorted area of international trade. But following decades of relative prosperity and new technological advances, which led to more predictable and sustained food production around the world, a growing number of countries called for reforms of the international rules pertaining to trade in agricultural products as the Uruguay Round was to be launched. The resulting agreement was crucial to the conclusion of the round, but it fell short of expectations and was criticized on all sides as incomplete.

It is important to remember that agricultural and textile and clothing sectors are the most strategic sectors from the developing world's point of view. It is then in the interest of many developing members of the WTO to ensure that predictable and fair multilateral rules govern these sectors. Furthermore, the arbitrary use of antidumping actions must be curtailed if the world trade system is to be more equitable. The legal principles on which the WTO is based can only work if there are no exemptions given to the industrialized countries, as happened under GATT at the time when it was mainly a club of such countries.

Current trade talks should strive to remedy the historical asymmetries that still persist within the system, but they must do so in such a way that no special exemptions are allowed for those countries that have sufficient bargaining power and are capable of extracting such exemptions. Or, alternatively, a broad range of exemptions should be allowed and given to poor developing countries to remedy the inequalities of the system. In short, WTO members must decide whether they want to build a truly universal organization with equal rules for all, or they would rather legitimize the existing exemptions and work toward a system where exemptions are evenly allowed among all WTO members.

Notes

1. Organization for Economic Cooperation and Development, "The Doha Development Agenda: Tariffs and Trade" (August 23, 2003), www.oecd.org (accessed July 6, 2007), p. 2.

2. Douglas A. Irwin, "The GATT in Historical Perspective," *American Economic Review* 85, no. 2 (1995): 325.

3. J. Michael Finger, "GATT Tariff Concessions and the Exports of

Developing Countries—United States Concessions at the Dillon Round," *Economic Journal* 84, no. 335 (1974): 566.

4. "General Agreement on Tariffs and Trade," *International Organization* 16, no. 4 (1962): 889.

5. Finger, "GATT Tariff Concessions," p. 566.

6. Alan V. Deardoff and Robert M. Stern, "Economic Effects of the Tokyo Round," *Southern Economic Journal* 49, no. 3 (1983): 606.

7. Robert S. Walters and David H. Blake, *The Politics of Global Economic Relations* (Englewood Cliffs, NJ: Prentice Hall, 1992), p. 16.

8. Organization for Economic Cooperation and Development, "The Doha Development Agenda," p. 2.

9. Marcelo de Paiva Abreu, "Trade in Manufactures: The Outcome of the Uruguay Round and Developing Country Interests," in Will Martin and L. Alan Winters (eds.), *The Uruguay Round and the Developing Countries* (Cambridge, UK: Cambridge University Press, 1996), pp. 62–63.

10. Richard Blackhurst, Alice Enders, and Joseph F. Francois, "The Uruguay Round and Market Access: Opportunities and Challenges for Developing Countries," in Martin and Winters, *The Uruguay Round and the Developing Countries*, p. 131.

11. Ibid., p. 132.

12. Joseph F. Francois, Bradley McDonald, and Hakan Nordstrom, "The Uruguay Round: A Numerically Based Qualitative Assessment," in Martin and Winters, *The Uruguay Round and the Developing Countries*, p. 255.

13. Ibid.

14. Antonio P. Salazar Brandao, Eugenio Diaz-Bonilla, Bruce L. Gardner, Devinder Sharma, and Alan Swinbank, "A Dialogue: Trade Liberalization in Agriculture," *SAIS Review* 23, no. 1 (2003): 87.

15. Ibid.

16. Harold James, *The End of Globalization: Lessons from the Great Depression* (Cambridge, MA, and London: Harvard University Press, 2003), p. 14.

17. Michael J. Trebilcock and Robert Howse, *The Regulation of International Trade*, 2nd ed. (London and New York: Routledge, 1999), pp. 255–256.

18. Ibid., p. 255.

19. Bennett Richardson, "Sticky Situation for Japan's Rice Policy," *Asia Times*, July 28, 2005.

20. Paul Gibson, John Wainio, Daniel Whitley, and Mary Bohman, "Profiles of Tariffs in Global Agricultural Markets" (AER-796) Economic Research Service USDA (January 2001), pp. 24–29.

21. G. Edward Schuh, "Developing Country Interests in WTO Agricultural Policy," in Daniel L. M. Kennedy and James D. Southwick (eds.), *The Political Economy of International Trade Law* (Cambridge: Cambridge University Press, 2002), p. 437.

22. Ibid., p. 438.

23. Ibid., p. 439.

24. Peter J. Schraeder, *African Politics and Society—A Mosaic in Transformation*, 2nd ed. (Belmont, CA: Thomson & Wadsworth, 2004), pp. 70–71.

25. Trebilcock and Howse, *The Regulation of International Trade*, p. 247.

26. Ibid., p. 247.

27. Ibid., p. 249.

28. Ibid., p. 248.

29. Ibid.

30. Stefan Tangermann, "Agriculture on the Way to Firm International Trading Rules," in Kennedy and Southwick, *The Political Economy*, pp. 256–257.

31. Clayton Yeutter, "Bringing Agriculture into the Multilateral Trading System," in Jagdish Bhagwati and Mathia Hirsch (eds.), *The Uruguay Round and Beyond: Essays in Honour of Arthur Dunkel* (Berlin and Heidelberg, Germany: Springer-Verlag, 1998), p. 62.

32. Ibid.

33. Gilbert R. Winham, *International Trade and the Tokyo Round of Negotiation* (Princeton, NJ: Princeton University Press, 1986), pp. 248–253.

34. Yeutter, "Bringing Agriculture," p. 64.

35. Ibid., p. 67.

36. Ibid., p. 67.

37. Ibid., p. 68.

38. Trebilcock and Howse, *The Regulation of International Trade*, p. 260.

39. Yeutter, "Bringing Agriculture," p. 69.

40. Ibid., pp. 68, 70.

41. Ibid., p. 71.

42. Dale H. Hathaway and Merlinda D. Ingco, "Agricultural Liberalization and the Uruguay Round," in Martin and Winters, *The Uruguay Round and the Developing Countries*, pp. 32–39.

43. The Dunkel Text proposed the cuts to domestic subsidies be implemented on a commodity-by-commodity basis, which would ensure fair distribution of the cuts. It was not possible, however, to negotiate this. The outcome agreed in the Blair House accord meant that some potentially irrelevant subsidies (from the trade point of view) could see deeper cuts than subsidies affecting strategically important commodities.

44. This so-called Peace Clause expired on January 1, 2004.

45. Yeutter, "Bringing Agriculture," pp. 72–73.

46. Melaku Geboye Desta, "The Integration of Agriculture into WTO Disciplines," in Bernard O'Connor (ed.), *Agriculture in WTO Law* (London: Cameron May, 2005), p. 23.

47. Hathaway and Ingco, "Agricultural Liberalization," pp. 39–49.

48. Michael Trebilcock and Julie Soloway, "International Trade Policy and Domestic Food Safety," in Kennedy and Southwick, *The Political Economy of International Trade Law*, p. 541.

49. Lee A. Jackson and Kym Anderson, "What's Behind GM's Trade Disputes?" *World Trade Review* 4, no. 2 (2005): 203–228.

50. Schuh, "Developing Country Interests," p. 442.

51. Gary H. Perlow, "The Multilateral Supervision of International Trade: Has the Textiles Experiment Worked?" *American Journal of International Law* 75, no. 1 (1981): 93–133.

52. Bernard M. Hoekman and Michel M. Kostecki, *The Political Economy of the World Trading System: The WTO and Beyond*, 2nd ed. (New York and Oxford: Oxford University Press, 2001), p. 226.

53. Trebilcock and Howse, *The Regulation of International Trade*, p. 376.

54. Perlow, "The Multilateral Supervision of International Trade," p. 101.

55. Multi-Fibre Arrangement quoted in ibid., pp. 100–101.

56. Ibid., p. 102.

57. Marcelo Raffaelli, "Bringing Textiles and Clothing into the Multilateral Trading System." in Martin and Winters, *The Uruguay Round and Beyond*, p. 51.

58. Ibid., p. 52.

59. Ibid., p. 53.
60. Ibid.
61. Ibid., p. 55.
62. Ibid., p. 54.
63. Ibid., p. 58.
64. Ibid.
65. Trebilcock and Howse, *The Regulation of International Trade,* p. 390.
66. Ibid., p. 390.
67. Mark Williams, Kong Yuk-Choi, and Shen Yan, "Bonanza or Mirage?: Textiles and China's Accession to the WTO," *Journal of World Trade* 36, no. 3 (2002): 581.
68. Paul Krugman and Maurice Obstfeld, *International Economics: Theory and Policy,* 7th ed. (Boston: Pearson-Addison Wesley, 2006), p. 131.
69. Peter-Tobias Stoll and Frank Schorkopf, *WTO—World Economic Order, World Trade Law* (Leiden, Netherlands: Martinus Nijhoff Publishers, 2006), p. 162.
70. Chad P. Brown, Bernard Hoekman, and Caglar Ozden, "The Pattern of US Antidumping," *World Trade Review* 2, no. 5 (2003): 352.
71. Stoll and Schorkopf, *WTO*, p. 151.
72. Ibid., p. 152.
73. Ibid., pp. 154–155.
74. Ibid., p. 156.
75. Ibid., p. 156.
76. Ibid., pp. 158–159.
77. Brown, Hoekman, and Ozden, "The Pattern of US Antidumping," p. 361.
78. Ibid., p. 369.
79. Ibid.

CHAPTER 5

The Global Services Economy

The services economy has been enjoying spectacular growth over the past twenty years with little sign of slowing down. To begin with, technological advances in the field of telecommunication now have allowed speedy delivery of various financial, educational, business, entertainment, and information services across borders and oceans. Furthermore, improved transportation services have helped to make tourism, distribution, and construction services into powerful global industries. To promote more efficient allocation of resources, many countries have decided to either privatize or allow greater foreign competition in those industries that were hitherto both largely regulated by the state and dominated by state-owned enterprises. These developments have provided an impetus to initiate negotiations under the GATT framework on designing the first multilateral agreement to cover global trade in services. The General Agreement on Trade in Services (GATS) was one of the key results of the Uruguay Round and now constitutes the second pillar of the WTO.[1]

The GATS was strongly advanced by the industrialized countries, specifically by the United States and the European Economic Community, although, as we recall from the previous chapter, the declaration launching the Uruguay Round separated services negotiations from other single-undertaking issues.[2] This happened at the insistence of developing countries.[3] Many of them were not ready to broaden the scope of the multilateral agenda. By resentfully agreeing to keep services outside the main stream of negotiations, developing countries perhaps hoped that if an agreement on services were to be negotiated, they would not have to sign it because it would become an optional plurilateral code. However, as was discussed before, the Uruguay Round took a few unexpected turns. Persuaded by the trade-offs in agriculture and textiles and clothing, developing countries eventually accepted the GATS, which became an integral part of the WTO single undertaking.

Still, developing countries as a group continue to be apprehensive about the GATS, despite the fact that it allows a considerable degree of flexibility in designing each country's own services liberalization schedule. Some of the reasons include difficulties in deciding which sectors should be open to foreign competition and problems in estimating costs and benefits of liberalization. Decisions about what to liberalize are complicated and should be grounded in practical experience. But in the past, most of the countries with underdeveloped economies did not have very well developed service sectors. This is not surprising when one bears in mind that poverty and underdevelopment often went hand-in-hand with authoritarianism and a centrally planned command economy where even the most fundamental basic services such as retailing, banking, publishing, construction, and transportation were managed by state monopolies. Generally speaking, under interventionist economic systems, resources, if there were any, would be allocated to the production of manufacturing goods. This would in turn result in limited and outmoded service sectors.

However, establishing a viable services economy requires an enormous amount of regulatory activity. Many developing countries have only rudimentary laws regulating their services economy. Regrettably, their governments often lack the expertise and resources needed to design competent regulatory regimes. Such governments would rather resist liberalization than risk leaving service sectors unregulated to face foreign competition. Consequently, the controversies that accompany the GATS often fall along the lines dividing the industrialized and the developing members of the WTO.

This chapter explains the main provisions of the GATS and takes a look at a few selective service sectors in the context of the WTO negotiations. It also identifies some of the more pronounced problems with the GATS that may be the outcome of its design, such as scheduling problems and issues related to interpretation of commitments made under its framework. A cautionary note must be given at this point. Trade in services includes many diverse activities. Hardly any generalization can be made that can apply to all service industries, and it is precisely because of this diversity that we can only concentrate on a few selective sectors, which perhaps best reflect a wide range of issues brought about by opening services to foreign competition.

The overall assessment of the GATS is guarded. The agreement does have the potential to become a tool not only for advancing liberalization of services but also for assisting countries in designing adequate and relevant regulatory regimes. However, vast disparities among WTO members' approaches to regulatory activities, conflicting priorities, and differences in the level of economic and institutional development among WTO members all require a special degree of attention to be paid to individual members' needs as they relate to services, but it would be an impossible task to follow. Besides, the WTO cannot be responsible for the preparatory work done on behalf of its individual members. This is not its mandate, and it should not be. It is a matter of sovereign responsibility for each country to make decisions that would concern their own economies. However, confronted by an overwhelming task of preparing an optimum negotiating position that would satisfy all domestic players, many countries opt for the status quo and refrain from negotiations. In a way, the GATS becomes sabotaged by its own flexibility. The services negotiations stumbled during the Doha Round, thus indicating that the GATS is truly a work in progress.

Services Liberalization and the GATS

The GATS is a unique agreement because of its scope and peculiar architecture. The agreement's design is intended to permit WTO members to take charge of their services liberalization. Notwithstanding the political and economic pressures faced by countries during negotiations, WTO members can carefully decide which service sectors they want to open to foreign competition and on what terms. The GATS allows countries to liberalize only selected sectors, and in addition, the agreement contains provisions listing the limitations that can be used to restrict the degree of their liberalization. The impact of the GATS on individual WTO members can be very small if a country decides to liberalize very few of its service sectors. However, it can be significant if substantial commitments are made under the GATS.

Because of its distinctive structure, the GATS constitutes a peculiar anchorage of flexibility within the highly legalized WTO framework. While other agreements have to be fully adopted as they are by each WTO member, the GATS acts more like a negotiating tool, with basic rules that guide the process of services liberalization. It also contains instructions and schedules allowing countries to record their liberalizing commitments in services. Ironically, however, its inherent flexibility makes the GATS a highly complex negotiating tool. Because countries have at their disposal a wide range of liberalizing options, an exceptional level of expertise is required to confidently choose the most advantageous of them. In addition to the technical knowledge about the GATS itself, negotiating teams should learn as much as possible about the performance and shortcomings of their domestic service sectors in order to formulate a well-informed negotiating agenda. The biggest challenge is to coordinate the preparations of a negotiating position among various ministries and interested private business groups. It is well known that even the industrialized countries lack comprehensive statistical data that monitor and assess the performance of various domestic service industries.

The GATS is structured in two parts. The first part is the actual legal text of the agreement, which consists of its articles and annexes. The second part is composed of the schedules of country-specific commitments undertaken by WTO members. The first part contains general obligations, which apply automatically to all WTO members and all sectors they decided to liberalize. The second part contains country-specific commitments, which include the detailed schedules listing those service sectors that became unlocked to foreign competition, together with any limitations placed on their level of openness.

The first part of the GATS outlines the rules that should guide the liberalization process. The GATS still has a strong connection with the fundamental principles of GATT, namely the MFN principle. Under Article II of the GATS, WTO members are obliged to immediately and unconditionally extend to services or service suppliers of all other members "treatment no less favorable than that accorded to like services and service suppliers of any other country." The only possible derogation from the MFN principle exists in the form of the so-called Article II–Exemption. Members were allowed to take such exemptions at the time of acceptance of the GATS. Furthermore, exemptions may be granted either at the time of a country's accession or, for current members, through the negotiating of a waiver under Article IX of the Marrakesh Agreement Establishing the WTO. Any such exemption is subject to review and should only last for a decade. Another important principle of the GATS concerns transparency (Article III of the GATS) that obliges all WTO members to publish all regulatory measures that influence the operation of the liberalized, or partially liberalized, sectors.

With respect to country-specific commitments, even in those sectors for which the liberalizing commitments are made, WTO members still can add a number of legally permissible limitations to restrict the way a particular service sector is being opened to foreign competition. General exemptions for regional trade arrangements, balance of payments, public order, and health also apply.[4] In short, every WTO member can design its own schedule of liberalizing commitments according to its level of development and economic needs, provided such a WTO member has an expert knowledge of the agreement and of its own service sectors.

For example, when a country decides to liberalize, or, in WTO jargon, grant market access to a certain service sector, it may do so subject to one or more limitations enumerated in Article XVI (2) of the GATS. Limitations may be imposed on the number of service suppliers, service operations or employees in a sector, the value of transactions, the legal form of the service supplier, or the participation of foreign capital.

However, in any sector that a WTO member decides to liberalize, a member is obliged to grant foreign service suppliers treatment no less favorable than that extended to its own like services and service suppliers (the principle of *national treatment*). However, such treatment does not need to be identical to that which is applied to domestic firms.[5] This means that the foreign firm cannot be treated less favorably than domestic firms. They can, however, be granted some special status or more favorable conditions than the domestic firms receive.

When negotiators were first contemplating the design of the agreement, they were facing several major challenges. Because the barriers to trade in services mainly come in the form of domestic regulations, and cross-border service flows are mostly invisible, the first challenge was to decide how to define the trade in services and how to record to what extent a particular sector is being liberalized. This latter challenge was particularly daunting. For example, it is not enough to say that a tourism sector in a country called Acadia will be partially liberalized. Acadia should be able to convey to its trading partners whether such partial liberalization means that only a limited number of foreign companies will be able to build hotels in the territory of Acadia. Or whether it means that in fact every foreign company can build a hotel in Acadia; however, such a company has to enter into a special joint venture agreement with the government of Acadia. In addition, every foreign company must employ only citizens of Acadia as managers of these new hotels. These are just basic examples of possible limitations that can be put in place while liberalizing tourism services in Acadia. The challenge facing the designers of the GATS was not only how to enable countries to negotiate, but also how to record the final outcome of services negotiations.

The next challenge was to understand the impact of some domestic regulations that protect existing firms from competition by new entrants, both foreign and domestic. Another challenge had to do with a multiplicity of economic activities that services comprise. For example, an individual firm providing a particular service, such as insurance, can involve the issue of cross-border trade via the Internet or regular mail, the establishment of a commercial facility in a foreign country (investment), the selling to foreign clients at the domestic location, and the dispatch of professional representatives to other countries.[6]

In order to address these challenges, the designers of the agreement decided to focus on the way the services are delivered, or more precisely, supplied. The negotiators agreed that the GATS would contain a definition of trade in services based on the four possible modes of how services can be supplied. Paragraph 2 of Article I defines trade in services as the supply of a service through any of four modes: (1) cross-border supply, (2) consumption abroad of a service, (3) supply through commercial presence, and (4) supply through the presence of individuals (natural persons).

Cross-border supply of a service happens from the territory of one country into the territory of another: for example, distribution of educational services via mail, performing accounting services via the Internet in India for firms in Canada, or providing credit-card support services via telephone from India to the United States. *Consumption abroad* happens when the consumer moves to the territory of another country and buys services there: for example, if a Canadian citizen opens a bank account in Switzerland. Consumption abroad also happens when the property of a consumer is sent abroad for servicing, as in the case of car repair. *Supply through commercial presence* involves direct investment in the export market through the establishment of a business there for the purpose of supplying a service. *Supply through the presence of natural persons* means the temporary presence in the export market of an individual for the purpose of supplying a service. A professor from Mexico traveling to Spain to give a series of lectures for which she gets paid would be such an instance in this respect. Such a person could be the service supplier herself or an employee of the service supplier. In both cases, the GATS definition covers only the temporary stay of such persons.

The four modes of supplying services expand the way we now think about international trade. Trade is no longer only about shipping and receiving goods from faraway countries; trade now surrounds us in many unexpected ways, such as when we receive a credit application from a foreign bank that has recently opened a branch in our country or when we buy a design plan for our summer house from an overseas architect via the Internet or when we shop at a new Wal-Mart outlet around the corner.

Moreover, in order to respond to the challenge of identifying the restrictions that apply only to foreigners and those restrictions that apply domestically to whatever firm is already operating in the country, the negotiators of the GATS separated the way the liberalizing commitments can be made into market access and national treatment. This of course also means that the GATS agreement, and more generally the WTO, can have an impact on a far wider range of domestic policy and regulation than GATT. For example, the national treatment obligation in the GATS concerns not only the treatment of the service (that is, the product), but also the right of establishing a commercial presence in the host country and treatment of the foreign business investors supplying the service. Mode 3, or supply through commercial presence, acquires a special meaning under the GATS since it deals with foreign direct investment. This is very significant because a multilateral investment agreement does not yet exist. And since the old rules on investment relating to trade in goods that existed under GATT and were adopted by the WTO are very weak, the GATS is in fact the first multilateral agreement containing provisions that deal with investment to the extent that they relate to the supply of services. This is why it is often said that investment creeps into the WTO by way of the GATS's doorway.

Although the GATS does not impose the obligation to make market access or national treatment commitments in a particular sector, Article XIX stipulates a common obligation of WTO members to enter into successive rounds of trade negotiations with a view of achieving a progressively higher level of liberalization. When negotiating their commitments, WTO members use a classification system comprised of twelve core service sectors. Each of these sectors has a number of subsectors amounting to almost 160 in total:[7]

1. Business services (including professional services and computer services)
2. Communication services (including telecommunication and audiovisual services)
3. Construction and related engineering services
4. Distribution services
5. Educational services
6. Environmental services
7. Financial services (including insurance and banking)
8. Health-related and social services
9. Tourism and travel-related services
10. Recreational, cultural, and sporting services
11. Transport services
12. Other services not included elsewhere

The very first assessment of the GATS came soon after the Uruguay Round was over. The study was done before the completion of sectoral talks in the financial and telecommunication sectors a few years later. These initial results presented a largely disappointing picture, with developing countries partially liberalizing about 16 percent of their sectors and fully liberalizing less than 7 percent. In fact, four countries (Algeria, Bangladesh, Fiji, and Tanzania) only agreed to liberalize one sector out of a possible 155. Larger developing countries (defined as having a GDP above $40 billion) partially liberalized almost 40 percent and fully liberalized 14 percent. In comparison, the developed countries partially opened almost 50 percent of their sectors with about 23 percent fully liberalized.[8]

In September 2004, the WTO Economic Research and Statistics Division released a more recent study that contained data summarizing all the liberalizing commitments made by the then 146 members of the WTO. Table 5.1 and Figure 5.1 are taken from that study.[9] Table 5.1 shows that indeed the number of commitments progresses with the higher level of development of WTO members. Figure 5.1 demonstrates that those sectors that were subject to additional sectoral negotiations, namely financial and telecommunications, show the largest numbers of commitments undertaken. Tourism has been traditionally the most popular (and least politically con-

Table 5.1 Commitments by Country Group, January 2004

	Average Number of Subsectors Committed per Country	Range (lowest/highest number of scheduled subsectors)
Least-developed economies	20	1–110
Developing and transition economies	54	1–154
	(106)[a]	(58–154)[a]
Developed countries	108	87–117
Accessions since 1995	106	37–154

Source: World Trade Organization Secretariat, 2004.
Notes: Total number of subsectors, 160; total number of WTO members, 146.
a. Numbers in parentheses include transition economies only.

Figure 5.1 Number of WTO Members with Commitments in Each Sector, March 2004

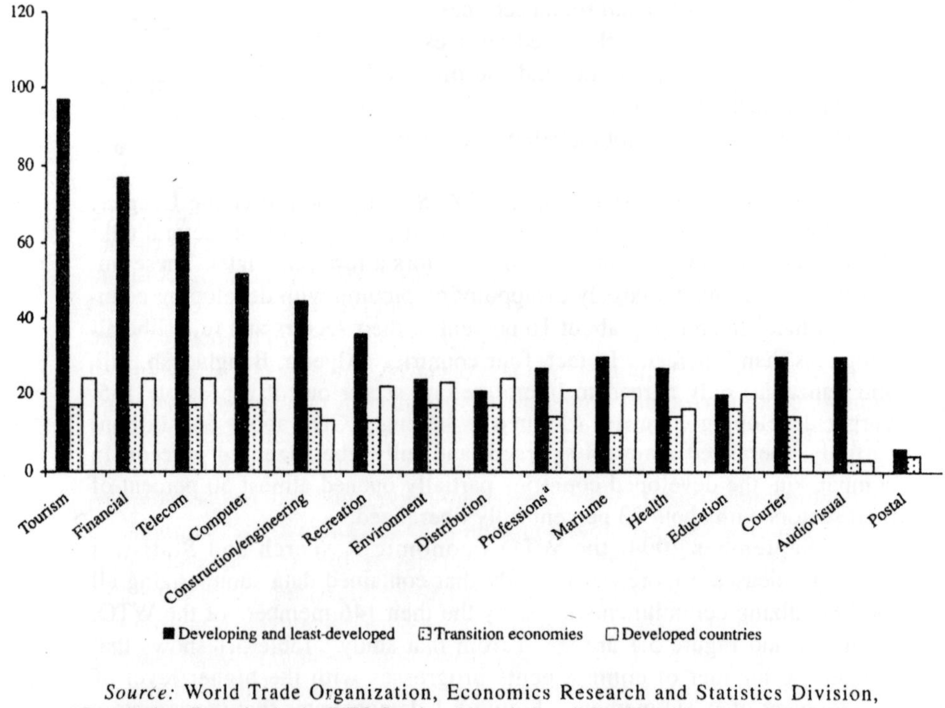

Source: World Trade Organization, Economics Research and Statistics Division, "Developing Countries in the WTO Services Negotiations," Staff Working Paper ERSD-2004-06, September 2004, chart 1.
Notes: Maximum number is 146.
a. Average for all professions.

troversial) sector and therefore it should be of little surprise that it leads the chart. It is often the case that those services that largely pertain to countries' social safety nets or traditionally have been a major focus for government involvement, such as health, education, postal, and audiovisual, are closed to foreign competition in most countries.

The conditions and limitations on market access and national treatment that appear in the schedules of the developed nations are quite extensive.[10] In contrast, the first twelve countries that acceded to the WTO after it was established have hardly listed any exemptions in their schedules of commitments. For example, the Kyrgyz Republic did not use any of the available limitations on liberalization of its service sectors.[11] It opened a large number of sectors to foreign competition without placing conditions on foreign firms. Nor did it delay liberalization of some sectors in order to enact relevant laws aimed at regulating these sectors in the future. By completely opening a given service sector with no limitations and no exemptions listed, the acceding countries prevent themselves from ever introducing any new regulatory measures that could affect such a sector. Once a commitment is made to open a sector to foreign competition, any new restrictive law would be considered a breach of the full liberalization commitment and a country could be taken to the WTO dispute settlement panel.

All the first twelve new members[12] have entered commitments in a large number of sectors, unlike some of the original members in the Uruguay Round. The broad picture is therefore one of wide sectoral coverage, although there are some relevant exclusions. In those sectors where commitments have been undertaken, the tendency is to have minor or no limitations, while more often a mode of supply is excluded. All twelve have undertaken commitments in professional services (mostly accounting, legal,[13] taxation, architecture, and engineering); business services (a very wide range of sectors); communication services, albeit with uneven coverage; financial services (in some cases with important modes 1 and 2 exclusions); construction services; and distribution services. Construction, distribution, and financial services are the sectors where the coverage is most complete. Eleven members have undertaken commitments in environmental, tourism, and transport services; ten members in health and social services and in education services; nine members in recreational services; and five in audiovisual services. Indeed, the first twelve countries that acceded to the WTO after 1995 have made remarkable liberalizing commitments in services. This can be directly attributed to the power-based nature of the accession process in which the existing WTO members are free to make any liberalizing demands as a price for membership in the WTO. The situation was, however, quite different in the case of China. Without jumping ahead to the chapter that discusses the results of the Chinese accession to the WTO, we should only note that China was able to resist those demands of its trading partners that it found to be excessive or not in line with China's own strategy for economic liberalization.

In almost all recently acceding and developing countries, the decision to liberalize a particular service sector often corresponds to the abolition of a monopoly in favor of competition. Since a majority of the underdeveloped countries—and this is certainly the situation in most of the acceding ones—have a very limited number of relevant laws and regulations pertaining to services, the task of liberalization necessitates an impossible task of simultaneously creating, opening, and regulating their service sectors. The success of regulatory reforms in acceding countries often depends on whether the authorities can deal with the overdeveloped industrial sectors that characterize the postinterventionist states.

Financial Services Sector

The financial sector has long been considered to belong exclusively in the hands of the governmental authority. From the time when the concept of money was first put into practice, only the monarch of a given territory would have a right to issue the legitimate coins. Given the fact that a healthy financial system is a necessary prerequisite of a well-functioning economy, one can understand the propensity of many governments to play a vital role in managing this sector. In recent years, however, rapid and significant changes have occurred in the structure of financial services industries around the world. Financial markets have become global and the tradition of territorial money is being seriously contested.[14] The need to make financial sectors more open globally can be attributed to a growing volume of international trade and a growing demand for commercial credit in foreign currency.

In spite of these global tendencies, it should come as no surprise that the Uruguay Round negotiators were facing serious difficulties when trying to liberalize this most heavily regulated sector. The resistance of many governments to opening their financial sectors to competition from private businesses, including foreign firms, was strong. Broad MFN exemptions based on reciprocity were taken by a number of countries.[15] When the round was heading toward its conclusion, very few meaningful commitments were made, as was the case with other sectors. Together with the financial sector, negotiations on basic telecommunications and maritime transport remained unfinished.

The Second Annex on Financial Services to the GATS and the Decision on Financial Services[16] adopted at the end of the round provided for extended negotiations in this sector. The talks concluded in July 1995,[17] but the results were still disappointing and the negotiating parties called for further negotiations in 1997. This time the negotiations were quite successful as an improved set of commitments in financial services under the GATS was agreed on December 12, 1997. A total of fifty-six schedules of commitments representing seventy WTO member governments and sixteen lists of MFN exemptions (or amendments thereof)[18] were annexed to the Fifth Protocol to the GATS. The total number of WTO members with commitments in financial services increased to 104 upon the entry into force of the Fifth Protocol.[19] As a result of the negotiations, several countries, including the United States, India, Thailand, Hungary, Mauritius, the Philippines, and Venezuela, reduced the scope of their MFN exemptions. The Fifth Protocol to the GATS set standards with respect to a level of liberalization of the financial sector around the world. The countries that have not yet made similar commitments and the countries that have been acceding to the WTO are now expected to follow this path of financial liberalization. The 1997 WTO deal on financial services ultimately set new higher standards for financial liberalization, which are often interpreted as minimum global standards, thus raising justified criticism about the ability of many less-developed countries to meet them.

It must be added that the timing of the deal on financial liberalization was not a coincidence. The financial crisis that engulfed the East Asian Tigers[20] in 1997 accelerated the reforms of the financial sector in these countries. These reforms included regulatory reforms and new liberalizing commitments made under the GATS. It was believed that increased financial liberalization would lead to badly needed revitalization of other service sectors, which are inevitably linked to financial services. Liberalization of financial services created new opportunities for banks, insurance companies, and ancillary services such as accounting, legal services, and computer-related services. In short, the events surrounding the financial instability in East Asia were actually accompanied by the growing pace of services liberalization, especially in this region.[21]

Liberalizing commitments in the financial sector are made in accordance with the Annex on Financial Services, which applies to all members. The annex complements the fundamental provisions of the GATS, and it contains an itemized list of financial services and a definition of excluded activities. Financial services include two broad categories of services: (1) insurance (and insurance-related) services and (2) banking and other services. These two categories are further broken down according to the list included in the Annex on Financial Services. Insurance and insurance-related services cover life and non-life insurance, reinsurance, insurance intermediation such as brokerage and agency services, and services auxiliary to insurance such as consultancy and actuarial services. Banking includes all the traditional services provided by banks such as acceptance of deposits, lending of all types, financial leasing, and payment and money transmission services. Other financial services include trading in foreign exchange, derivatives and all kinds of securities, securities underwriting, handling money, asset management, settlement and clearing services, provision and transfer of financial information, and advisory and other auxiliary financial services.

The GATS also contains rules on capital mobility. As we recall from the previous section, the scope of the GATS extends beyond border trade and into the area of domestic economic policies, which also can mean regulations concerning investment. Because the initial commitments on services made during the Uruguay Round were very modest, the consequences of some of the GATS provisions, especially the one on capital transfers (mobility of capital), gain particular significance in the context of future WTO negotiations and the ongoing accessions processes. By making new specific market access commitments under the GATS, candidates for accession and existing WTO members are expected to undertake commitments regarding the movement of capital. Article XVI of the GATS (Paragraph 1, footnote 8) states:

> If a Member undertakes a market-access commitment in relation to the supply of a service through the mode of supply referred to in subparagraph 2(a) of Article I and if the cross-border movement of capital is an essential part of the service itself, that Member is thereby committed to allow such movement of capital. If a Member undertakes a market-access commitment in relation to the supply of a service through the mode of supply referred to in subparagraph 2(c) of Article I, it is thereby committed to allow related transfers of capital into its territory.

The practical implications of this footnote are far reaching. Since the provision has not been subject to interpretation by a WTO dispute-settlement panel, there is no jurisprudence to act as a guide. From a legal point of view, there are no clearly defined limits with respect to interpretations of footnote 8. This can create a particularly difficult situation—bordering on unfair treatment—during accession negotiations. As a later chapter will show, the WTO accession process lacks procedural clarity. The accession negotiations are routinely conducted according to the rules dictated by the powerful WTO members. As a result, WTO members can use their unchecked bargaining power to interpret the above obligation in very broad terms. It is precisely because of such small-print provisions that the acceding countries and developing members of the WTO have been facing excessive demands for internal reforms to establish an environment congenial to foreign investment.[22]

Also, if we recall our earlier discussion in Chapter 3 regarding the distinction between internal and external democracy of the WTO, one question that arises in the context of the GATS concerns a situation when an authoritarian government (acting without consent of the people) makes far-reaching liberalizing commitments in services. Such commitments can drastically reduce the level of a government's autonomy over its economy. Furthermore, deep liberalization of the service sectors, especially the financial sectors, can lead to some permanent changes with respect to foreign ownership over the crucial aspects of the financial system of the state. In the future, democratically accountable governments can replace authoritarian governments, but under the GATS rules the minimum three-year period is required for notification about any changes and rolling back of the liberalization commitments made. In short, it means that governments deciding to liberalize services under the WTO framework have to be very careful and knowledgeable given the fact that such commitments become legally binding for years to come.

Discrepancies in interpretation of some provisions of the WTO create an unfortunate gap between a purely legalistic approach to the rules and how some WTO members chose to apply them. In principle, commitments under the GATS need not compromise the ability of governments to pursue autonomous regulatory and macroeconomic policies. What is problematic, however, is the more recent tendency by the major trading countries to demand a higher level of commitments from less-developed countries than they themselves undertook during the Uruguay Round. Yet, countries can, and should, use to their advantage certain provisions of the GATS. Experts point out the importance of Paragraph 2(a) of the Annex on Financial Services, which relates to prudential regulation (the so-called prudential carve-out): "Notwithstanding any other provisions of the Agreement, a Member shall not be prevented from taking measures for prudential reasons, including for the protection of investors, depositors, policy holders or persons to whom a fiduciary duty is owed by a financial service supplier, or to ensure the integrity and stability of the financial system."

Prudential measures are important regulatory measures that remain at the discretion of WTO members as long as they comply with other provisions of the GATS and are not used as a means of avoiding commitments: "Regulators would seem to have considerable discretion in their choice of prudential measures especially since no definition or indicative list of such measures is provided in the Annex."[23] Aaditya Mattoo provides examples of such measures: capital adequacy requirements, restrictions on credit concentration and portfolio allocation, disclosure and reporting requirements, and various licensing criteria imposed on financial institutions.

In addition to prudential regulations, WTO members are also free to conduct their own national macroeconomic policy. The financial sector could be affected when a national central bank raises interest rates, issues government bonds, or prints more money (increases money supply), but it should be stated that services supplied in the exercise of governmental authority, including activities conducted by a national central bank, are excluded from the scope of the GATS.[24] Also, to respond to the critics of the GATS who maintain that it forces countries to remove any restriction on capital flows between countries, the top expert in the field observes that this is not what the rules say: "If a Member undertakes a market access commitment in relation to the cross-border supply of a service and if the cross-border movement of capital is a[n] essential part of the service itself, that Member is committed to allow such movement of capital. Furthermore, if a Member undertakes a market access commitment in relation to the supply of a service through commercial presence, that Member is committed to allow related inflows of capital into its territory."[25] In conclusion, according to the rules, WTO members do not have any obligations with respect to capital outflows related to commercial presence.

No matter how much flexibility governments have under the GATS agreement, the demands placed on small developing and acceding countries to liberalize the financial sector remain substantial and difficult to withstand. In addition, the skillful maneuvering among legal provisions of the GATS requires an expert knowledge of the agreement—something with which many delegations from poorer countries have difficulties given the very limited size of their teams.[26] However, the bigger and economically confident economies—like India—can utilize the GATS to their advantage.[27] In addition, multiple linkages between government operations, the domestic private sector, and the international setting make it difficult to separate regulations impacting various service sectors, especially the financial sector. This causes regulatory problems for many governments and makes them resistant toward making liberalizing commitments without fully understanding how they are going to impact the domestic economy.

And yet, one of the opportunities presented by the GATS is the option to improve the overall regulatory framework of WTO members. Article VI:4 of the GATS specifies that members shall develop any necessary disciplines to ensure that "measures relating to qualification requirements and procedures, technical standards and licensing procedures do not constitute unnecessary barriers to trade in services."[28] Therefore, it was proposed that WTO members should agree on the *necessity test* to ensure that no regulatory measures are more trade-restrictive than necessary. According to a note prepared by the WTO Secretariat, the necessity test is the means by which an effort is made to balance between two potentially conflicting priorities: the promotion of trade expansion and the protection of the regulatory rights of governments.[29] The necessity test thus would help assess whether regulatory measures affecting trade in certain service sectors are adequate or are more restrictive than is necessary to achieve the objective they seek. That is, if two or more measures exist that can achieve the same objective, the one with the least restrictive impact on trade should be chosen.

Some critics of the necessity test observe, however, that as a consequence of applying the necessity test governments have to compromise the very objective they are pursuing.[30] A major worry would be a compulsory application of the necessity test in the form of universal regulatory standards without any consideration given to each country's specific economic situation. Furthermore, the initiative behind the necessity test assumes that countries are overregulated, or, in other words, that they have too many unnecessary regulations in place. This misses the point that many poorer members of the WTO have very few regulations in place (even if they are burdensome) and their primary focus should be on working toward designing effective country-specific regulatory systems and not just getting rid of the existing impediments to trade.

In the final analysis, it appears that financial liberalization under the GATS has a different meaning for the prosperous and administratively stable industrialized economies that are characterized by highly mature regulatory frameworks and experienced bureaucracies. Developed countries are interested in gaining market access in a number of service sectors in the developing world, and they want to ensure an investment-friendly environment for their services and goods—and thus they expect financial sectors they can rely on. For developing countries that are lacking sometimes even the most basic regulations, liberalization of financial services could mean opening their borders to unregulated foreign investment. Such countries need to improve their regulatory systems first. This must be done on a country-by-country basis, with countries in question retaining full ownership of the reforms process. It has been documented that foreign investors prefer dealing with a stable and predictable set of demanding rules than dealing with a lax and uncertain system.[31] In truth, the most economically successful countries are characterized not by low taxes, unchecked foreign capital flows, and weak standards (including labor and environmental), but rather by a transparent and predictable administrative and legal regime. It is essential for the future development of reforming countries to ensure that effective regulatory frameworks are established in those countries. Such a move would best prepare underdeveloped members of the WTO to face the fast-changing pace of global economic transactions.

The Professional Services—Legal

In the WTO Services Sectoral Classification List, "Legal services"[32] are listed as a subsector of "Professional services."[33] The analysis of this sector should begin with pointing to the legalistic nature of the WTO itself. It used to be that only a few law schools offered courses leading to a specialization in international trade law. Today it would be difficult to find a school that does not have such a program.

The need for legal services and, by extension, for lawyers versed in different aspects of commercial, criminal, trade, labor, intellectual property, and economic law that can work not only on cases that touch upon both domestic and international law is growing steadily. The practice of law has been experiencing extraordinary changes as a result of global market integration and the increasing salience of international law in world politics after the Cold War. Increasingly, lawyers are required to provide services and advice in more than one jurisdiction. The legal turn in the world trade system and progressive codification of international economic law have also created demand for lawyers as trade and economic policy consultants. The point previously made about the importance of developing a sound regulatory framework—with its laws, legal acts, and rules—in many less developed countries further illustrates this need. Currently, there are more lawyers than economists assisting the developing members of the WTO with legislative and regulatory reforms, preparations for negotiations, and finally WTO implementation processes.

While all modes of supply are used in the context of trade in financial services, most of the trade in legal services is done via modes 1 (cross-border) and 4 (the temporary stay of employees of foreign law or consulting firms). The cross-border supply using the Internet has already changed the practice of law because of new communications technologies that enable anyone to market and sell legal services anytime, anywhere, and on any subject. This raises the question about how to maintain high standards and accountability of such virtual services providers. These questions are particularly important given the fact that lawyers who take advantage of this new global market to promote their legal services mostly reside in the developed economies.

As we are witnessing increasing legalization of many aspects of world politics, it is difficult not to notice that this tendency has a strong Western element. Writers such as Hugo Grotius and Samuel Pufendorf first conceived the doctrine of international law in seventeenth-century Europe. This tradition was further enriched by the principle of state sovereignty first articulated by Thomas Hobbes.[34] The present international legal rules are very much rooted in this long-established tradition. The two main overarching influences are the continental practice of civil law and the British and US tradition of common law. The increased demand for trade lawyers who are trained in one of these traditions comes from a need for legal advice about the proper interpretation of WTO agreements. The same, however, is true for bilateral treaties. When the United Stated signed a free-trade agreement with Jordan, it was negotiated and written in English. The agreement also drew its format from US jurisprudence.

Western lawyers have definitely become the custodians of international legal rules. This means that when developing countries around the world open their legal services to foreign competition, there is no basis for reciprocity arrangements. Local lawyers simply cannot compete with their counterparts from the industrial nations. In reality, then, liberalization of this service sector under the GATS mostly corresponds to a one-way movement of lawyers from industrial countries to the developing world.

In truth, the need for such services is particularly immense in the developing world. The invitation of foreign lawyers is not only a matter of learning to interpret the rules of the WTO, it is also a matter of developing countries needing the expertise of Western lawyers to draft relevant laws and regulations necessary to establish the essential regulatory framework of the state. Many WTO members decided to fully liberalize their legal services sectors as a result.

The potentially problematic issues regarding liberalization of legal services are more nuanced in nature. When they open their borders to foreign lawyers, many developing countries assume the political neutrality of these foreign experts, and they tend to rely on them to provide advice on aspects of their economies that are deemed to be of vital importance. Such experts sometimes create the most fundamental domestic laws without fully knowing the specific characteristics of the local economy and domestic politics. Foreign lawyers may draft essential regulations in developing countries, although their legitimacy rests solely upon their proficiency in understanding and interpreting the legal texts of the WTO agreements. The industrialized countries have complex administrative schemes to ensure that their own standards are maintained. Many of these relate to qualification requirements and accreditation recognition procedures. Such regulations, however, are virtually absent in developing countries. The only regulations in place are those that supervise the performance of local professionals, as it is often assumed that foreign lawyers represent the highest international standards. Nonetheless, with the emergence of international consultancy and e-commerce, this situation can create many problems. There is nothing to stop unqualified and sometimes dubious experts from developed countries from misleading the policymakers in developing countries.

Naturally, it is in the interest of all countries to develop high international standards for legal services. The two major international associations of lawyers, the International Bar Association (Anglo-Saxon/common law) and the International Advocates Union (Latin/civil law) are champions of the harmonization of such standards. Both associations are distinctively Western but are represented worldwide. Only those individuals who are already members of a national bar association can join them, and their membership predominantly consists of lawyers from the developed countries.

As of June 2007 the International Bar Association (IBA), which has its headquarters in London, England, has a membership of 30,000 individual lawyers and more than 195 bar associations and law societies. Article 1 of the 2005 IBA constitution lists the following objectives that are of particular relevance to trade in legal services: (1) to establish and maintain relations and exchanges between bar associations and law societies and their members throughout the world; (2) to assist such associations and societies and members of the legal profession throughout the world to develop and improve the profession's organization and status; and (3) to assist members of the legal profession throughout the world, whether in the field of legal education or otherwise, to develop and improve their legal services to the public.[35] Furthermore, in September 2006 the IBA produced general principles for the legal profession, which "aim at establishing a generally accepted framework to serve as a basis on which codes of conduct may be established by the appropriate authorities for lawyers in any part of the world." Among the ten listed principles, the ones insisting on independence to provide an unbiased opinion; the high standards of honesty, integrity, and fairness; the competence of the lawyers; and the principle to expect only reasonable payments are especially worth mentioning.[36]

The International Advocates Union (UIA) was founded in Charleroi, Belgium, in 1927 by the bars of Charleroi, Luxembourg, and Paris. According to its website in 2007, the UIA consists of over 200 bar associations, organizations, or federations (representing nearly two million lawyers) as well as several thousand individual members from more than 110 countries. The UIA does not have a constitution and its goals are broad. The first three declared goals make a noble claim, which is still nonbinding: (1) to promote the basic principles of the legal profession; (2) to participate in the development of legal knowledge at an international level; and (3) to contribute to the establishment of an international legal order based on the principles of human rights and justice among nations, through law and for the cause of peace.[37] Gaining a membership in one of these two organizations is a necessary prerequisite to work as a lawyer across borders. Their inherently Western nature poses an interesting question about the growing reach of Western law principles around the world.

In conclusion, we must remember that international institutions were first created by Western powers. Despite the fact that they are becoming more global in scope and their influence is widening, the WTO, the IMF, and the World Bank continue to reflect fundamentally Western values. The GATT/WTO is grounded in the Anglo-Saxon legal tradition that favors the precedent rule. Those countries that have different legal traditions, most notably the Arabic countries, some Asian states, and China, find it particularly challenging to be on an equal footing with countries whose views of a legal contract and domestic regulations may be quite different.

There is also the corresponding issue of dominant languages. The WTO, with its 152 members as of May 2008, recognizes only three official languages: English, French, and Spanish. The argument could be made that this is done for the sake of legal clarity. The negotiators often spend hours arguing over the proper use of individual words. The issue of translation is then very carefully approached by the WTO Secretariat to ensure that there is neither confusion nor misunderstanding of a particular legal provision or commitment made. Because of the WTO's legal character, those who want to take advantage of its rules have to become fluent in its legal texts and its legal language, even if the WTO legal framework inherently clashes with their distinct cultural and legal understanding of trade relations. The legal professionals who are skilled in the WTO jurisprudence and are helping developing countries with the implementation of WTO agreements have then special responsibility to conduct themselves according to the highest standards.

Telecommunications and the Audiovisual Services Sector

So often in this book, new inventions in telecommunications are credited with furthering trade expansion. The ability of individual states to develop the newest and most cost-efficient networks is a prerequisite for moving the society up the ladder of socioeconomic development. Arriving at a substantial telecommunication agreement under the GATS was a priority for many countries, and yet when the Uruguay Round was completed, the liberalizing commitments in basic communications were found to be unsatisfactory. Similar to the case with the financial sector, the new talks were scheduled for a later date, to be finally officially concluded in February 1997. The agreement was added to the GATS as the Annex on Telecommunications and was regarded as quite successful with sixty-nine WTO members participating. Because the initial talks under the Uruguay Round saw many developed countries making commitments in this sector, the 1997 deal led many developing countries to open this particular sector to foreign and domestic competition.[38]

As defined in the Services Sectoral Classification List, telecommunication services (together with postal, courier, and audiovisual services) are a subsector of "Communication Services." The telecommunication sector then includes fifteen subsectors, among them voice telephone, fax, e-mail, electronic data interchange, packet-switched data transmission services, circuit-switched data transmission services, etc.[39] The audiovisual sector has six subcategories: (1) motion picture and videotape production and distribution services, (2) motion picture projection services, (3) radio and television services, (4) radio and television transmission services, (5) sound recording services, and (6) other. Now, if this appears to be confusing, consider, for example, television shows or motion pictures sent over the Internet. David Luff notes that if "they are not supplied through an uninterrupted chain of transmission, as they require switching nodes, they are not, in the EC at least, considered as broadcasting services. They could qualify as packet- or circuit-switched data transmission services."[40] Indeed, the Services Sectoral Classification List often creates many scheduling problems. In the case above, it is unclear how to classify the transmission of a TV show via the Internet. Instinctively, we consider a television show to belong to the audiovisual sector, a very controversial sector, as will soon be discussed. However, from a technical point of view, an expert engineer would insist on classifying it as a telecommunication service. This can potentially create a dead-end debate. If a particular WTO member's cultural policy prohibits such a transmission without paying a proper licensing fee but that same member made full liberalizing commitments under the GATS telecommunication services, even the WTO dispute settlement panel would have some considerable difficulty deciding whether such a transmission should be freely allowed.

The above example is important for two reasons. First, it illuminates the problem of scheduling commitments, and second, it brings us to the controversy surrounding the audiovisual sector. Before we examine the enigma of the audiovisual sector, it will be helpful to summarize one of the most recent trade disputes that also involved the issue of interpretation of the scope of commitments made under the recreational, cultural, and sporting services sector (other than audiovisual services).[41] Antigua and Barbuda initiated a dispute in 2003 against the United States because the laws of the United States effectively prohibited delivery via the Internet of any gambling and betting services from these islands.

The US schedule of commitments made does not include the actual words "gambling and betting."[42] However, this very sector (recreational, cultural, and sporting services) only contains the following subsectors according to the Sectoral Classification List: (1) entertainment services (including theater, live bands, and circus services); (2) news agency services; (3) libraries, archives, museums, and other cultural services; (4) sporting and other recreational services; and (5) other. The United States made a full liberalizing commitment with no restrictions for cross-border supply in the last (other) subsector. Antigua and Barbuda claimed that this widely open category implicitly contains services like gambling and betting. As a result Antigua and Barbuda challenged a series of US regulations: three federal laws (the Wire Act, the Illegal Gambling Business Act, and the Travel Act) and a number of laws in four US states (Louisiana, Massachusetts, South Dakota, and Utah) that prohibited cross-border delivery of gambling and betting services.

In short, then, this dispute, brought to the WTO by the two tiny islands against the biggest trading state, centered around the interpretation of the scheduling commitment under the GATS, but it also targeted the regulatory regime of the United States. Antigua and Barbuda alleged that certain US regulations were inconsistent with the US obligations under the WTO and hence should be changed if not abolished altogether. The United States defended its laws based on Article XIV of the GATS, which allows WTO members to make exemptions to their obligations in order to protect "public morals and public order." The DSU disagreed with the position taken by the United States in its panel report issued in November 2004.[43] It concluded that indeed the United States made the liberalizing commitment in its schedule under other recreational services, which should be understood as including gambling and betting. The DSU panel also rejected the US defense, which claimed the exemptions from its WTO obligations for protecting public morals.

The story does not end here. The United States appealed the decision of the DSU panel. The Appellate Body of the WTO then issued its report in April 2005.[44] It upheld most of the findings of the DSU panel's report. However, the Appellate Body reversed the DSU panel's finding that the United States had not shown that the three federal statutes are "necessary to protect public morals or to maintain public order" within the meaning of Article XIV (a). Furthermore, the Appellate Body concluded that the United States used these laws in a discriminatory manner. For example, the suppliers of gambling and betting services from within the United States were allowed to do so. The Appellate Body then concluded that the United States discriminated against Antigua and Barbuda by selectively applying the laws. Because of this decision, there was an expectation that the United States would either modify its laws to allow Antigua and Barbuda to conduct its gambling business across the border with the United States or it would apply them fairly to include US suppliers.

Immediately after the report was issued, the United States asked for additional time to modify its laws to comply with the findings of the Appellate Body panel. In June 2006, Antigua and Barbuda informed the WTO Dispute Settlement Body that, given their frustration and disagreement as to the existence of measures taken by the United States to comply with the rulings of the report, they requested consultations under Article 21.5 of the DSU. This meant that Antigua and Barbuda were considering a new dispute with the United States. In August 2006, the new WTO trade dispute (DSU) panel was put together. On March 30, 2007, the DSU panel report was circulated to WTO members.[45] The report concluded that the United States failed to comply with the recommendations and rulings of the WTO Dispute Settlement Body. Under the circumstances, there is very little that Antigua and Barbuda can do. Once again a major weakness of the WTO Dispute Settlement Body was confirmed. Even if a small developing country wins a dispute at the WTO, it can only hope that the losing party will comply with the decision that may be perceived as unfavorable. Consequently, this dispute outcome also demonstrates the limits of the WTO as an organization capable of influencing the domestic preferences of its members. The organization is only as fair, as lawful, and as reasonable as its members allow it to be.

The paradox of the WTO was discussed in previous chapters. The multilateral organization with democratic decisionmaking bodies succumbs nevertheless to the mercantilist logic that self-interested countries pursue their own interests and try to put demands on others. The relationship between culture and trade in the WTO has evolved with conflicting claims over the need for protecting and promoting domestic culture. The cynics, however, maintain that the call for exempting culture from any commercial consideration is false and smells of old-fashioned protectionism. Still, the debate over culture and trade should not be underestimated.

Global trade liberalization combined with new means of distributing information and artistic creations have caused many concerned individuals to lobby their governments for more protective cultural policies. Some of the countries, most notably France and Canada, that are concerned about the sociocultural impact of global market integration want to limit the liberalization of certain service sectors related to the issue of cultural identity. Because there is no specific sector under the GATS identified as cultural or artistic services, the audiovisual sector has been used to negotiate the liberalization of services that are associated with various aspects of cultural policy. Governments have traditionally subsidized domestic cultural and heritage-oriented sectors; they have also routinely restricted the distribution of foreign entertainment and cultural productions, especially motion pictures and television programs.

The evidence of international tension in the audiovisual sector can be traced back to the interwar years, that is, to the era of early film production. US movies began dominating European movie theaters after 1918. The British were particularly concerned about this, to the point of producing a special study in 1926 entitled "Exhibition Within the Empire of Empire Films." This paper was in fact a major effort by the British industry to pressure the government to introduce special measures, namely quotas, that would support domestic productions and limit the distribution of US shows.[46] After the imposition of such measures, conflict and disagreement over the protective European screen quotas only grew stronger. An eventual solution to this dilemma was the inclusion of Article IV of GATT 1947, which specifically authorized screen quotas.[47] Hence, despite GATT's overall prohibition of using quotas as an instrument of commercial policy, the exemption was made for screen quotas. In addition, Article XX of GATT permits countries to introduce measures "for the protection of national treasures of artistic, historic, and archeological values."

Subsequent international conflicts over trade and culture developed with the growth and spread of television broadcasting in the 1960s. The disagreements between the United States and Europe concerned the question of whether trade in TV programs concerned trade in goods or trade in services. GATT only applied to goods, thus leaving trade in services to fall under the sole jurisdiction of national governments. The outcomes of three European court cases established that transmission of television signals was a service, but trade in sound recordings and films was about goods. During the Tokyo Round of Multilateral Negotiations (1973–1979), the United States officially complained about the subsidization of the movie industry and television in a number of countries.[48] In 1981 the European Parliament issued the Schall Report, which suggested the creation of a special TV channel to promote the European Community.

In 1991 the United States challenged the European Community restrictions on the televised showing of non-European films by invoking Article IV of GATT 1947, which discusses quota restrictions. This is when the Europeans contested the challenge by arguing that television broadcasting was a service and thus it was not covered under the goods regime of GATT. At issue was the question of national identity and to what extent "the term 'culture' became synonymous with the word 'audiovisual.'"[49] The European Communities and its allies[50] pushed for maintaining the subsidies in the audiovisual sector in the name of preserving cultural identity and heritage. The United States opposed this position on the grounds that it was a protectionist measure in disguise. The conflict over culture persisted during the Uruguay Round, with Canada suggesting an exemption in the draft negotiating text on services liberalization. Canada already negotiated a cultural *carve-out* in the 1988 Canada-US Free Trade Agreement.

Despite continuing disagreements, the audiovisual sector was included in the GATS schedules, although most WTO members refrained from making commitments in this sector. As many European countries, and Canada, remain active advocates of strong domestic cultural policies, we will see very limited liberalization of this sector in years to come. There are those who contest the very idea of cultural policies on the grounds that such policies are politically motivated, and emotionally charged, while mainly protecting existing interests and thereby retarding creative responses to new opportunities.[51] It is true that any policy that is formulated away from any economic consideration risks being politically motivated. However, it is also true that an economic approach too often assumes away political context, of which every government has to be aware. Cultural policies may not be the most efficient economically and they may not be always fair in terms of the benefits they confer and distribute, but they may also be a necessary response to those that fear the consequences of current global economic transformations.

The conflict over the right to protect culture and the benefits of free trade will continue, especially given the criticism regarding the homogenizing effect of economic globalization. It may well be that this issue necessitates deeper sensitivity from the trade practitioners when it comes to understanding the peculiar nature of cultural policies. Patricia Goff puts it well:

> Cultural policies are not motivated by the same considerations that typically inspire conventional interventionist policies. Cultural products clearly have economic value. Nevertheless, an understanding of their regulation based strictly on economics overlooks the importance that Canadian and European governments attribute to them as vectors of culture and identity. Emphasizing the ways in which cultural policies sometimes resemble discriminatory trade practices ignores the fact that the same policies provide national governments with important tools for offsetting the cultural costs of economic liberalization.[52]

Other Sectors: Health and Social Services

Health and social services are considered to be at the core of the public sector in many countries. The high quality and effectiveness of these services often testifies to the quality of life and the level of developmental progress in societies. The decision to open the health and social services sector to foreign investment is thus particularly politically sensitive. Although the idea behind the GATS agreement was a voluntary liberalization of selective service sectors, by 2004 only fifty-seven of the WTO's then 146 member states had made commitments in this sector.[53] Since the agreement also allowed member countries to decide how much of each sector should be liberalized, WTO members that decided to liberalize put severe limitations on how it could be done.[54] Still, the late 1990s witnessed an increased move toward market-based reforms in the area of health and social services. Governments burdened with serious budgetary constraints decided in the name of improved efficiency to privatize some of the services traditionally run by various governmental agencies. These initiatives are sometimes met with serious criticism from the employees working in the affected sectors and members of the civil society at large. The main worry concerns the for-profit objectives that, by default, guide the performance of the private sector. The issues, however, can be resolved given the flexibility of the GATS and the restrictions it allows to be placed on liberalizing commitments under its Article VI. There is nothing in the agreement that prevents the relevant authorities from designing and implementing a consistent set of policy goals and, consequently, creating a regulatory framework that would encourage high standards and quality control in pursuit of these goals. Nevertheless, a wise liberalization scheme requires an active role to be played by competent government officials capable of balancing well the societal needs with the efficient allocation of governmental resources.

While governments have a role to play and many WTO members have well-developed regulatory regimes, the challenge is to keep up with the fast pace of changes presented by the competition in service industries. One can only imagine how difficult it is to ensure the proper level of regulation in a country with limited experience in the field of regulatory efficiency and quality control.

Another concern with respect to domestic policy making is the dilemma over which services fall under the government's responsibility as socially necessary services, and hence are exempted from the rules of the GATS, and which can be open to competition from private and foreign service suppliers. The GATS does not present good definitions in this respect, and the confusion over what services can be subject of negotiations under the GATS often leads to conflicts among the parties. Countries often struggle over the way in which public interest objectives can be reconciled with objectives that advance international trade. A top expert on the GATS presents this dilemma particularly well:

> Government measures, whose focus is on consumers (patients, students, train or bus passengers) rather than suppliers (hospitals, universities, transport operators), tend to be compatible *per se* with all relevant provisions of the Agreement. This presupposes, of course, that there is no built-in bias favoring the use of domestic over foreign supplies (e.g. via restrictions on insurance portability or the use of scholarships). However, many policy schemes are structured differently. Subsidies are often extended to producers rather than to users, domestic producers have easier access than foreign competitors, or whole sectors are reserved exclusively for government providers. While there may be doubts whether the underlying policy objectives, normally related to quality and equity, necessarily call for such arrangements, the GATS is nevertheless able to accommodate them. National concepts of public services—in particular in consumer-related areas such as health and education—have evolved over decades, if not centuries, and are deeply rooted in countries' institutional fabrics. While a trade agreement may help to improve access conditions to individual markets, it can hardly be expected to redefine the scope of genuine government responsibilities.[55]

Still, the very inclusion of the health and social services sector on the GATS Sectoral Classification list provoked much hostility from NGOs and civil society groups. Such groups see the WTO as a champion of globalization, which erodes the state's ability to provide important public services and play an active role in promoting development. Indeed, economic globalization does carry a warning about the changing role of the state. In one extreme form, one doomsday scenario conceives of a world dominated by multinational corporations and global institutions like the WTO, which elbow the state into an irrelevant position. The state is definitely under a new set of external and internal pressures, but it still has a major role to play. In reality, there is mounting evidence that a domestic environment conducive to social stability and characterized by transparent regulatory regimes facilitates the increased inflow of foreign direct investment and often constitutes the prime determinant of economic prosperity and social stability. The countries with the most successful economies have large public sectors, sophisticated regulatory regimes, and complex tax systems. In this context, Paul Hirst and Grahame Thompson offer a few words of caution: "One key effect of the concept of globalization has been to paralyze radical reforming national strategies, to see them as unviable in the face of the judgment and sanction of international markets."[56]

The authors further observe that the danger of the rhetoric of globalization is that it tends to ignore the questions of uneven distribution, since the world's wealth and output remain local and are extremely unevenly distributed. Moreover, globalization treats the world as a single open competitive market and the location of economic activity as dictated by purely commercial considerations. Thus, as Jagdish Bhagwati wisely tells us, "pro-globalization and pro-privatization economic reforms must be treated as complementary and indeed friendly to both the reduction of poverty and social agendas."[57]

Conclusion

The negotiation of the GATS agreement during the Uruguay Round created considerable controversy. At issue were the negotiations on services liberalization and the effect of this liberalization on regulatory regimes of countries, which are difficult to modify. In contrast to visible tariffs, which can be changed smoothly, administrative laws and regulations are engrained in domestic politics and thus are difficult to reform. The domestic political scene is routinely subject to conflicting pressures, with progress hampered by resistance by vested interests "often serving protectionist purposes."[58] The GATS does not help in this respect. In fact, its flexibility unfortunately means that the agreement lacks precise definitions and clear scheduling guidelines. In short, the responsibilities placed on individual governments in the context of services liberalization should not be underestimated. This is why developing countries are very reluctant to respond to calls in the Doha Round for deeper liberalization.

The GATS-driven services liberalization can support domestic financial liberalization by consolidating policy reform in a binding multilateral framework. However, under the pressure of negotiations, it is possible to downplay some socioeconomic aspects of financial-sector reform. The hasty and excessive opening of underdeveloped banking sectors to foreign competition could lead to costly systemic failures or hamper macroeconomic management and lead to financial instability. Some developing countries worry that this instability can be exacerbated by quick movements of speculative capital in and out of the local economy via a liberalized capital account under the GATS. Such concerns make many less-developed countries resist undertaking substantial liberalizing commitments. This is one of the reasons why the talks on progressive services liberalization that commenced in 2000 have faltered.

It depends, however, how the performance of the GATS is assessed. The novelty of the agreement and the slow learning process that parallels the attempts to use the GATS as a negotiating framework have not stopped WTO members from making many important commitments that, for example, unquestionably improved the spread of new telecommunication inventions. This development demonstrates its relevance, but it does not make the GATS into an engine of services liberalization. The final results are mixed. This is how one of the top counselors in the WTO Services Division evaluates the role of the GATS:

> On average, the schedules of commitments submitted at the end of the Uruguay Round in 1993/94 cover no more than one-third of the approximately 160 service sectors contained in a classification list developed by the WTO Secretariat. Yet there are wide variations between and within individual groups of Members. The number of sectors scheduled by developed countries exceeds 100 on average, which is 2.5 times the average for developing countries and more than 4 times the average for least developed countries. Virtually all initial offers submitted in the current negotiations between March 2003 and August 2005 have remained modest, both in terms of sector coverage and proposed access conditions, and do not significantly change the picture. More than one-third of the WTO's current 148 Members had not even submitted an offer by mid-2005, including the vast majority of African countries and virtually all least-developed countries. This contrasts with an increasing number of—relatively ambitious—regional or bilateral arrangements in services that have been or are being negotiated among WTO Members. (By end-June 2005, 29 preferential agreements had been notified under the relevant provisions of Article V:7(a) of the GATS.)[59]

Even following the apparent intensification in the Doha Round talks after the 2005 Hong Kong Ministerial Conference, the situation has not improved, and it becomes difficult to predict whether liberalization of services will proceed according to a reciprocal logic or whether the multilateral GATS will remain relevant.

Notes

1. WTO, *The Results of the Uruguay Round of Multilateral Trade Negotiations.* (Geneva: GATT/WTO, 1995). The General Agreement on Trade in Services (GATS) is Annex 1B.

2. WTO/GATT, "Basic Instruments and Selected Documents (BISD), Thirty-Third Supplement," in *Ministerial Declaration on the Uruguay Round—Punta del Este* (Geneva: WTO, 1986).

3. John Croome, *Reshaping the World Trading System—A History of the Uruguay Round* (Geneva: World Trade Organization, 1995), p. 31.

4. See Article XIV of the GATS, *The Results of the Uruguay Round of Multilateral Trade Negotiations*..

5. Aaditya Mattoo, "National Treatment in the GATS: Corner Stone or Pandora's Box?" *Journal of World Trade* 31, no.1 (1997): 107–135.

6. Geza Feketekuty, "Improving the Architecture of GATS," in Pierre Sauve and Robert M. Stern (eds.), *GATS 2000—New Directions in Services Trade Liberalization* (Washington, DC: Brookings Institutions Press, 2000), pp. 90–91.

7. WTO/GATT, *The Services Sector Classification List* (MTN.GNS/W/120) (July 10, 1991).

8. Bernard Hoekman, "Assessing the General Agreement on Trade in Services," in Will Martin and L. Alan Winters (eds.), *The Uruguay Round and the Developing Countries* (Cambridge, UK, and New York: Cambridge University Press, 1996), pp. 98–105.

9. Juan A. Marchetti, "Developing Countries in the WTO Services Negotiations," Table 1, Chart 1, in WTO Working Paper ERSD-2004-06 (2004).

10. See, for example, WTO, *Schedule of Specific Commitments—Canada* (GATS/SC/16) (April 15, 1994).

11. WTO, *Schedule of Specific Commitments on Services—the Kyrgyz Republic* (WT/ACC/KGZ/26) (July 31, 1998).

12. Ecuador, Mongolia, Bulgaria, Panama, Kyrgyz Republic, Latvia, Estonia, Jordan, Georgia, Albania, Oman, and Croatia.

13. Mongolia did not make any commitments in the legal services sector.

14. Benjamin J. Cohen, *The Geography of Money* (Ithaca, NY: Cornell University Press, 1998), pp. 147–149.

15. *Reciprocal* arrangements are the basis of bilateral trade agreements where countries make reciprocal liberalizing commitments in such a way as to balance benefits on both sides; the gains arising out of foreign trade are distributed fairly only between the two signatories. *Reciprocity* implies a preferential agreement. Thus it contradicts the very principle of nondiscrimination (MFN) the WTO system is based on.

16. GATS, *The Results of the Uruguay Round of Multilateral Trade Negotiations*.

17. Those improved commitments were annexed to the Second Protocol to the GATS. WTO, *Second Protocol to the General Agreement on Trade in Services (Financial Services)—Done at Geneva on 6 October 1995* (WT/Let/93) (June 21, 1996).

18. Submitted by Australia, Canada, Honduras, Hungary, India, Mauritius, Nicaragua, Pakistan, Peru, the Philippines, Senegal, Switzerland, Thailand, Turkey, the United States, and Venezuela.

19. WTO, *Fifth Protocol to the General Agreement on Trade in Services (Financial Services)—Done at Geneva on 27 February 1998* (WT/Let/221) (May 21, 1998) and (WT/Let/223) (May 27, 1998).

20. South Korea, Taiwan, Indonesia, Malaysia, the Philippines, Singapore, and Thailand.

21. Takatoshi Ito and Anne O. Krueger (eds.), *Trade in Services in the Asia Pacific Region* (Chicago: University of Chicago Press, 2003).

22. Roman Grynberg and Roy Mickey Joy, "The Accession of Vanuatu to the WTO—Lessons for the Multilateral Trading System," *Journal of World Trade* 34, no. 6 (2000): 164–165.

23. Aaditya Mattoo, "Financial Services and the WTO: Liberalization Commitments of the Developing and Transition Economies," *World Economy* 23, no. 3 (2000): 354.

24. Under Article I:3 of the GATS and the Annex on Financial Services.

> Article I:3: For the purposes of this Agreement:
> (a) "measures by Members" means measures taken by:
> (i) central, regional or local governments and authorities; and
> (ii) non-governmental bodies in the exercise of powers delegated by central, regional or local governments or authorities;
>
> In fulfilling its obligations and commitments under the Agreement, each Member shall take such reasonable measures as may be available to it to ensure their observance by regional and local governments and authorities and non-governmental bodies within its territory;
>
> (b) "services" includes any service in any sector except services supplied in the exercise of governmental authority;
>
> (c) "a service supplied in the exercise of governmental authority" means any service which is supplied neither on a commercial basis, nor in competition with one or more service suppliers.

25. Mattoo, "Financial Services and the WTO," p. 355.

26. This problem will be discussed in greater detail in the chapter about developing countries in the WTO. However, it can be noted here that some delegations consist of three to four people responsible to a multiplicity of issues, agreements, and international treaties that often extend beyond the WTO.

27. Asoke Mukerji, "Developing Countries and the WTO—Issues of Implementation," *Journal of World Trade* 34, no. 6 (2000): 59–61.

28. Subparagraph (b) of Article VI:4 (GATS) further specifies that such disciplines shall aim to ensure that regulatory measures are "not more burdensome than necessary to ensure the quality of the service."

29. WTO, *Application of the Necessity Test: Issues for Consideration* (Informal Note by the Secretariat, Job No. 5929) (October 8, 1999).

30. Gregory Palast, "The WTO Agreement on Services," *The Observer*, April 15, 2001.

31. Ha-joon Chang, "Globalization, Transnational Corporations, and Economic Development: Can the Developing Countries Pursue Strategic Industrial Policy in a Globalizing World Economy?" in Dean Baker, Gerald Epstein, and Robert Pollin (eds.), *Globalization and Progressive Economic Policy* (Cambridge, UK, and New York: Cambridge University Press, 1998), pp. 97–113.

32. The category "legal services" is further subdivided into the following subcategories: "legal advisory and representation services concerning criminal law"; "legal advisory and representation services in judicial procedures concerning other fields of law"; "legal advisory and representation services in statutory procedures of quasi-judicial tribunals, boards, etc."; "legal documentation and certification services"; and "other legal and advisory information."

33. "Professional services" as a GATS category includes legal services, accounting, auditing and bookkeeping services, taxation services, architectural services, engineering and integrated engineering services, urban planning and landscape

architectural services, medical and dental services, veterinary services, and services provided by midwives, nurses, physiotherapists, and paramedical personnel.

34. Ernst-Ulrich Petersmann, "From the Hobbesian International Law of Coexistence to Modern Integration Law: The WTO Dispute Settlement System," *Journal of International Economic Law* 1, no. 2 (1998): 175–198.

35. Constitution of the International Bar Association (IBA) Article 1 (2005).

36. See IBA General Principles for the Legal Profession, www.ibanet.org.

37. See www.uianet.org/index.jsp.

38. For an in-depth analysis of this agreement see Mary Marko, "An Evaluation of the Basic Telecommunications Services Agreement," CIES Policy Discussion Paper 98/09 (1998).

39. WTO/GATT, *The Services Sectoral Classification List* (MTN.GNS/W/120) (July 10, 1991).

40. David Luff, "Current International Trade Rules Relevant to Telecommunication Services," in Damien Geradin and David Luff (eds.), *WTO and Global Convergence in Telecommunications and Audio-Visual Services* (Cambridge, UK: Cambridge University Press, 2004), p. 38.

41. WTO, *United States—Measures Affecting the Cross-Border Supply of Gambling and Betting Services* (WT/DS285/R) (November 10, 2004).

42. WTO, *Schedule of Specific Commitments—United States* (GATS/SC/90) (April 15, 1994).

43. WTO, *United States—Measures Affecting the Cross-Border Supply of Gambling and Betting Services* (WT/DS285/R) (November 10, 2004).

44. WTO, *United States—Measures Affecting the Cross-Border Supply of Gambling and Betting Services* (WT/DS285/AB/R) (April 7, 2005).

45. WTO, *United States—Measures Affecting the Cross-Border Supply of Gambling and Betting Services* (WT/DS285/RW) (March 30, 2007).

46. Keith Acheson and Christopher Maule, *Much Ado About Culture—North American Trade Disputes* (Ann Arbor: University of Michigan Press, 2001), pp. 56–57.

47. Mary E. Footer and Christoph Beat Graber, "Trade Liberalization and Cultural Policy," *Journal of International Economic Law* 3, no. 1 (2000): 117.

48. WTO/GATT Document MTN/3B1, cited in ibid., p. 118.

49. Ibid., p. 119.

50. Mainly, Canada, Australia, India, Egypt, and Brazil.

51. Acheson and Maule, *Much Ado About Culture,* p. 5.

52. Patricia M. Goff, *Limits to Liberalization—Local Culture in a Global Marketplace* (Ithaca, NY: Cornell University Press, 2007), p. 169.

53. See Figure 5.1.

54. WTO, *Health and Social Services—Background Note by the Secretariat* (S/C/W/50) (September 18, 1998).

55. Rolf Adlung, *Public Services and the GATS,* WTO Working Paper ERSD-2005-03 (2005), p. 5.

56. Paul Hirst and Grahame Thompson, *Globalization in Question; The International Economy and the Possibilities of Governance* (Cambridge, UK: Polity Press, 1999), pp. 1–3.

57. Jagdish Bhagwati, "Poverty and Reforms: Friends and Foes?" *Journal of International Affairs* 52, no. 1 (Fall 1998): 34.

58. Akira Kawamoto, "Regulatory Reform on the International Trade Policy Agenda," *Journal of World Trade* 31, no. 4 (1997): 86.

59. Adlung, *Public Services and the GATS,* p. 7.

CHAPTER 6

Intellectual Property

In a striking opening to their book, Christopher May and Susan K. Sell provide a compelling example of the disquieting connection between the somehow obscure concept of intellectual property rights and the tragic lives of many people:

> It is not an exaggeration to state that intellectual property rights are a matter of life and death. This is most obvious in the case of the patent protection of acquired immunodeficiency syndrome (AIDS)–related medicines. Since the late 1990s, pharmaceutical patents have been a lightning rod for criticism of the manner in which intellectual property rights function within the global system. The yearly cost of keeping human immunodeficiency virus (HIV)–positive patients alive on the cocktail of drugs currently available in the developed countries has in the past cost up to a thousand times the typical annual health expenditure per capita for developing countries.[1]

The rational solution to the apparent crisis described above would be the promotion of international free trade in pharmaceutical products. The idea would be to stimulate production of required medications by inciting global competition among different firms. Such a move would produce a steady supply of such medications to the developing world at a cheaper price. Yet, this is not going to happen because patented formulas are not free. The proposed solution would necessitate free reproduction of the patented formula on which the life-saving drug is based by a variety of large and small pharmaceutical firms. These firms would then freely compete with each other in their attempt to sell the drugs at a reasonable price to the people in need.

The problem arises because the patents protecting pharmaceutical formulas are exclusive rights. The owner of the patent is free to set a price for a license to use the patent at a level that could be prohibitively high or refuse it altogether and only decide to sell the final product. In other words, intellectual property rights allow patent owners to restrict the use of their inventions. Intuitively speaking, intellectual property rights contradict the idea of free trade because they guard and restrict the use of patented inventions. In truth the whole concept has more in common with monopoly rights than with the principles of free competition and nondiscrimination that are supposed to frame the world trade system. Despite this contradiction, however, an agreement aimed at ensuring protection of intellectual property rights worldwide is now part of the WTO system.

This chapter explains TRIPs, the rationality behind its creation, and the most prevalent problems associated with its implementation. Although TRIPs includes under its purview many different kinds of intellectual property, the main focus of the chapter is on patents and, to a lesser degree, on copyrights and trademarks. This is because most of the criticism about the agreement stems from its requirements concerning patent protection. My task here is to convey to the reader the multiplicity of issues brought about by making an agreement on intellectual property into a third pillar of the WTO. The consequences are far reaching in terms of the impact that TRIPs now has on the regulatory autonomy of WTO members with respect to its costly implementation requirements.

The inclusion of TRIPs in the multilateral trading system was a curious development in the history of the world trading system. Many countries responded to the geopolitical transformations of the post–Cold War period with ideas favoring strong multilateral cooperation to deal with global market integration. The increased significance of intellectual property rights and the call for a multilateral agreement to protect such rights was a sign of the changing priorities in international economic relations. Following a surge in a number of revolutionary inventions in the 1980s, businesses began to acknowledge the importance of being on the cutting edge of creative technology. Many firms felt compelled to obtain an absolute (intellectual property) right to new innovations and discoveries. Given the fact that new technological solutions had entered such diverse fields as data processing, computerized manufacturers' production lines, biotechnology, sound and digital image productions, forensic science, medicine, satellite transmission, nuclear physics, and transportation, the protection of new inventions became an inseparable part of the new competitive logic underlying the global economy. However, this race to be ahead of the competitive global game can have its dark side if new barriers to fair competition and technological progress are enacted in the name of protecting intellectual property rights.

Developing countries especially have strong and growing interests in obtaining access to new technologies. There are many different ways of calculating poverty and underdevelopment. The invisible border between countries with economies encouraged by technological inventions and those with very limited access to new technologies is often called the "digital divide." Quite often intellectual property rights play a role in reinforcing this divide. As the Uruguay Round was ending, most developing countries continued to view the argument behind TRIPs with suspicion that it was an instrument to combat global networks of counterfeiting and piracy. One of its most vocal critics in fact concluded that it was predominantly "a component of a policy of *'technological protectionism'* aimed at consolidating an international division of labor where Northern countries generate innovations and Southern countries constitute the market for the resulting products and services."[2] More than a decade later, TRIPs remains as controversial as ever.

The Contradictions of TRIPs

TRIPs opens with a revealing preamble. Here are arguably its most relevant paragraphs, followed by the first part of Article 1:

> *Desiring* to reduce distortions and impediments to international trade, and taking into account the need to promote effective and adequate protection of intellectual property rights, and to ensure that measures and procedures to enforce intellectual property rights do not themselves become barriers to trade; . . . .
>
> *Recognizing* the need for a multilateral framework of principles, rules and disciplines dealing with international trade in counterfeit goods;
>
> *Recognizing* that intellectual property rights are private rights;
>
> *Recognizing* the underlying public policy objectives of national systems for the protection of intellectual property, including developmental and technological objectives; . . . .
>
> Article 1: Nature and Scope of Obligations
>
> 1. Members shall give effect to the provisions of this Agreement. Members may, but shall not be obliged to, implement in their law more extensive protection than is required by this Agreement, provided that such protection does not contravene the provisions of this Agreement. Members shall be free to determine the appropriate method of implementing the provisions of this Agreement within their own legal system and practice.

The preamble highlights the obvious contradiction of the agreement. First, it claims that the priority of TRIPs is to facilitate international trade, but at the same time it expresses protectionist concerns by asserting that intellectual property rights are private rights. In this way TRIPs sets to reconcile two conflicting aims: the goal of open free trade and the right to restrict access to one's private property.

Article 1 then obliges WTO members to provide protection of intellectual property that is not more extensive than what is required by TRIPs. Consequently, it is said that TRIPs is only limited to the minimum standards of protection of intellectual property. Critics, however, question the level of these standards, especially from the perspective of a developing country that has never before established an intellectual property rights regime. The legal standards under TRIPs are modeled on the Western legal tradition and are set at a level comparable to those in the developed countries.

Most problematic, however, is the assumption that intellectual property is private property. The elusive concept of intellectual property continues to divide economists when it comes to assessing its long-term effect. Somehow, this was not a problem here, as the interpretation of intellectual property as private property is unequivocally assumed. In firmly linking the notion of intellectual property with private rights, TRIPs borrows from the Western tradition of property as elaborated by John Locke. According to Locke, a person could rightfully claim the land if he improved it by transforming it with his own productive labor. It is important to stress that it is the productive labor that goes into improvement of the land and not a simple takeover of the land that is crucial in understanding Locke, as Richard Ashcraft has demonstrated.[3]

In his book contemplating the influence of ideas on economic development, Francis Fukuyama recalls the assertion made by economic historians that the creation of a stable system of property rights in the West was the crucial development that permitted the process of industrialization to begin. In countries like the United States, a system of property rights was established early on such that even family businesses were usually also incorporated as legal entities. This, however, was not the case elsewhere. In China, for example, there has never been a tradition of property rights; instead, businesses remain contained within large families where transactions are based on trust and do not require legal protection.[4] The Chinese culture traditionally placed a higher value on the community than the individual. Accordingly, copying and imitating the work of past scholars and authors has been a traditional way of learning for the Chinese.[5]

The extension of the *private rights* approach to intellectual property rights under the TRIPs agreement is additionally troubling because it obscures the distinction between intellectual property and tangible property rights. The two most-cited definitions of intellectual property stress its intangibility. According to the World Intellectual Property Organization (WIPO), "Intellectual property refers to creations of the mind: inventions, literary and artistic works, and symbols, names, images, and designs used in commerce." Black's Law Dictionary defines *intellectual property* as a "category of intangible rights protecting commercially valuable products of the human intellect. The category comprises primarily trademark, copyright, and patent rights, but also includes trade-secret rights, publicity rights, moral rights, and rights against unfair competition." It is then particularly misleading to confuse tangible goods with intellectual property and apply the same economic laws to both concepts. This mistake is well exposed by May and Sell. In fact, the authors use the fundamental economic concept of scarcity to explain why it makes no sense to treat intellectual property as a tangible competitive resource.

> Intellectual property constructs a scarce resource from knowledge or information that is not formally scarce. Unlike material things, knowledge and information are not necessarily rivalrous, and therefore coincident usage seldom detracts from social utility. Whereas two prospective users must compete to use a material resource (and this competition may be mediated through markets and the setting of a price), two or more users of any particular item of knowledge or information can use it simultaneously without competing.[6]

Overall, the idea that intellectual inventions, which by default rely on knowledge and experience of past generations, are now treated and restricted as if they were commodities does not play well with those who see the broader societal context of such inventions. Consider a comment by Lord Sydney Templeman:

> The term "intellectual property" infers that there is some perpetual asset which belongs to an inventor or author. This theory is employed to obtain extensions of the protection afforded by statute and provokes cries of "theft" and "piracy" when the rights granted by parliament are infringed. From the point of view of the consumer and the general public, however, a patent right is a grant of a monopoly and copyright is a grant of a restriction on trade. The monopoly and restriction can only by justified to the extent that they are necessary for the public benefit. It is assumed that patent and copyright protections are necessary to ensure that an inventor continues to invent and that an author continues to publish. The validity of this assumption cannot now be tested. . . . The first thing to be done is for governments and courts to recognize that patents and copyright create monopolies, which are injurious to free trade and impose exorbitant prices. Recent disclosures of the enormous sums paid to directors (not to inventors) by pharmaceutical companies and recent increases in profits and share values of companies exploiting monopoly rights sufficiently demonstrate the need for monopoly rights to be resisted wherever possible.[7]

If there are so many arguments against strong intellectual property rights, why then have an agreement on intellectual property that is now an inseparable part of the WTO? The simple answer would acknowledge that the perception of globalization as it emerged following the end of the Cold War elevated the value of new inventions as an engine of progress. Businesses started looking for investment and trade opportunities beyond the borders of the states in which they were located. Governments around the world wanted to attract them. The growing pressures of this new competitive global logic made it possible to talk about intellectual property during the multilateral trade talks.

Indeed, for decades, the GATT system would not even consider the issue of intellectual property as part of its trade agenda. First, discussions about this subject in GATT took place during the Tokyo Round of multilateral trade negotiations conducted between 1973 and 1979. Still, they were narrowly focused on trade in counterfeit goods.[8] In the final stage of the Tokyo Round, the Levi Strauss Corporation organized the International Counterfeiting Coalition that lobbied for the creation of an anticounterfeiting code. A group of industrial countries started to work on a draft proposal, although it was too late to finalize it before the Tokyo Round was concluded. However, only three years later, Canada, the EC, and the United States agreed on the draft, which would later become a basis for pushing the issue of intellectual property on the negotiating agenda of the Uruguay Round.[9] At the end of the round, the TRIPs agreement was incorporated firmly in the WTO. Even though, the 1986 Punta del Este Declaration launching the Uruguay Round only mentions trade in counterfeit goods, TRIPs is the most comprehensive multilateral agreement on intellectual property ever negotiated.

TRIPs covers the following categories of intellectual property: (1) copyright and related rights, (2) trademarks, (3) geographical indications, (4) industrial designs, (5) patents, (6) layout designs (topographies) of integrated circuits, and (7) protection of undisclosed information.[10] Copyrights protect original creative works of authorship like films, books, songs, and computer programs. Trademarks are words, signs, or symbols that identify a certain product or company. Similar to trademarks, geographical indications identify a product (such as Champagne) with a certain geographical region. Wine and spirits are given special protection here. Industrial designs protect the ornamental features of consumer goods, such as shoes or cars. Patents are legal titles granting the inventor the exclusive right of ownership to make commercial use of inventions. Layout designs for integrated circuits protect producers of semiconductors. Protection of undisclosed information (trade secrets) does not grant a legal title to the creator of an original work. Instead, it protects business from the unauthorized disclosure or use of confidential information.

The broad scope of TRIPs is widely attributed to the sustained efforts of private business groups who pursued an active lobbying campaign to publicize the damages they faced from weak international intellectual property standards. Especially, three powerful industries—pharmaceuticals, entertainment industries, and high-tech firms—recognized the opportunity afforded by the Uruguay Round to create a major multilateral agreement on intellectual property.[11] By the time the Uruguay Round negotiators met in

Montreal in 1990, intellectual property became a core issue for the United States trade representative (USTR). This attitude also had a coercive side. In 1984, the US Congress amended the 1974 Trade Act to include in it a "Special Section 301," which stated that a failure by a foreign country to protect intellectual property rights should be considered as an unfair trade barrier subject to US retaliation. In 1988 an additional amendment was included that made intellectual property an annual issue for surveillance and possible action by the USTR. To complement these initiatives, the USTR conducted a series of bilateral talks with a number of developing countries demanding, under the treaty of "Special 301," that they would establish strong intellectual property regimes.[12]

One of the world's best-known economists, Jagdish Bhagwati, uses the word "crusade" when commenting on the campaign that resulted in creating the agreement. He sees no place for TRIPs in the WTO except for the sinister purpose of redistributing income from the developing to the developed countries. He also notes that during the Uruguay Round the arguments against such an agreement expressed by economists from developing countries, as well as the negotiating objections of some of their governments, were simply ignored.[13]

Most developing countries were against bringing an agreement on intellectual property to the WTO, and this is why it was important for its supporters to break down this quasi anti-TRIPs coalition and have an ally in Mexico. Perhaps one of the reasons for including a chapter on intellectual property in a trilateral free-trade agreement negotiated among Canada, Mexico, and the United States at the beginning of the 1990s was to set a precedent. The message was clear: an agreement on intellectual property had to be included in the final package of any trade agreement. When Canada and the United States signed their bilateral free-trade agreement in 1988, intellectual property was not mentioned in it. However, when in 1991 the United States started negotiations with Mexico, soon joined by Canada, a chapter on intellectual property was proposed as a necessary part of the deal.

NAFTA Chapter 17 closely resembles TRIPs, which in turn was first proposed as part of the Uruguay Round single undertaking in the previously discussed December 1991 Dunkel Text. While both Canada and the United States already had strong intellectual property rights regimes (although the Canadian system was much weaker in allowing, among other things, shorter patents), Mexico had only rudimentary laws and essentially had to construct a whole new regulatory system for the protection of intellectual property.[14] Considerable costs were involved in establishing such a system.

During the Uruguay Round, the US and European negotiating teams continued to be influenced by business coalitions asking for TRIPs to provide the necessary protection against theft of their technologies and other creative inventions. To bring a sense of urgency to the table, the argument was made that the firms would stop exporting and investing in the developing world if an agreement on intellectual property was not signed.[15] The agreement was to establish certain global standards applicable within national legal systems, and since foreign investors would be protected by these rules, the agreement was said to be inherently investment-related.[16] It would be claimed that foreign investors were more willing to invest and transfer technology when enforceable laws protected their patents, copyrights, trademarks, and other secrets.

However, there is no clear evidence that strong intellectual property rights protection is a significant determinant of foreign direct investment flows. Keith E. Maskus, who is one of the top experts in the field, has consistently demonstrated the complexity of the relationship between intellectual property, economic development, and foreign direct investment. Multinational corporations face a multiplicity of options when designing their investment strategies. Concerns over intellectual property definitely play a role in reaching a decision, but hardly any generalization can be made about how important those concerns are for any particular firm as "their importance varies by industry and market structure."[17] In fact, some of the more radical economists have suggested the possibility that strong universal protection of intellectual property around the world may in fact deter some multinationals from directly investing in foreign countries.[18]

In fact, China offers an interesting example supporting the hypothesis of a weak connection between the level of foreign direct investment and intellectual property rights protection. Since it started to trade with the world in the late 1970s, China hardly possessed a rudimentary intellectual property rights regime, and it has actually been one of the most consistent violators of foreign patents and copyrights. Still, the flows of foreign investment into China have grown significantly over the last twenty years. The requirements of TRIPs, however, did play a major role in China's WTO accession negotiations. WTO members demanded that China introduce relevant new laws.[19] The government of China has made enormous progress since the 1980s to develop its legal and administrative system, although many complaints have been heard in the WTO regarding the enforcement of intellectual property rights.

More recently, two top experts specializing in intellectual property rights have expressed their uneasiness about the move to strengthen them globally via TRIPs. The authors issued a warning about the consequences of the agreement on developing countries in the era of globalization. With respect to TRIPs and its potentially detrimental impact on small firms in the developing world, they raise some fundamental concerns

> about the implications of the new regime for the ability of firms in developing countries to break into global—or even domestic—markets and compete effectively. It seems increasingly likely that stronger global IPRs could reduce the scope for such firms to acquire new, and even mature, technologies at manageable costs. The natural competitive disadvantages of follower countries may become reinforced by a proliferation of legal monopolies and related entry barriers that result from global minimum intellectual property (IP) standards. Such external restraints on competition could consign the poorest countries to a quasi-permanent status at the bottom of the technology and growth ladder.[20]

If there is a genuine economic rationale for the protection of intellectual property rights, it indicates a compromise "between the incentives they create for innovation and the inefficiencies that arise from granting a monopoly over the use of the patented good/technique."[21] The best-known economic theoretical perspective for establishing a formal regime for the protection of intellectual property has to do with the "appropriability of knowledge problem"[22] caused by the "public-good" nature of knowledge. To the extent that intellectual property rights enhance the *appropriability* of knowledge, they are expected to foster investment into activities that stimulate creation of new knowledge (inventions and innovations). However, economic theory also recognizes that intellectual property rights cause a market distortion because they limit the consumption and spread of knowledge by enhancing the market power of titleholders.[23] In other words, since knowledge itself is noncompetitive in nature, and it has been an engine of progress for generations, all knowledge-based inventions and creations should be freely available. If this were the case, however, inventors would not invest in new discoveries, because they would not be able to recover their costs. In conclusion, by granting inventors the exclusive rights to commercialize their intellectual creations, the intellectual property rights laws offer a necessary incentive for enhancing the existing body of knowledge.

Global Standards of Intellectual Property Rights Under TRIPs

The problem that developing countries have with TRIPs is twofold: the implementation process of TRIPs routinely exceeds their administrative and financial capabilities, but countries that do not fully implement the agreement can find themselves in violation of their WTO obligations and become a target of a trade dispute. To be clear, TRIPs does not create a universal regime for the protection of intellectual property rights; it nevertheless establishes minimum standards describing the level of protection that each WTO member must provide via its domestic laws. TRIPs also imposes an obligation of MFN, under which advantages accorded by a WTO member to the nationals of any other country must also be granted to the nationals of all WTO members. Full implementation of the agreement by a country means that the relevant laws are drawn, administered, and enforced in a way that they protect all patents, copyrights, and other intellectual property registered on its territory. Furthermore, equal protection is given to domestic and foreign intellectual property rights originating in any other WTO member country.

Instead of listing the details of how each of the intellectual property rights categories should be protected, TRIPs requires each WTO member to become a signatory to the past intellectual property rights conventions that already contain detailed rules regarding different categories of intellectual property. However, the agreement does contain descriptions on how to enforce the rules of these conventions in the domestically established regimes. Most developing countries did not belong to such conventions prior to the establishment of the WTO. This requirement is specified in Article 1, which goes on to say that TRIPs incorporates the following conventions: the Paris Convention for the Protection of Industrial Property (1967); the Berne Convention for the Protection of Literary and Artistic Works (1971); the Rome Convention—the International Convention for the Protection of Performers, Producers of Phonograms and Broadcasting Organizations (1961); and the Washington Treaty—the Treaty on Intellectual Property in Respect of Integrated Circuits, or the ICIP Treaty (1989). The Paris and Berne conventions were first established at the height of the Industrial Revolution at the end of the nineteenth century and have been revised several times. Since 1967 both have been administered by the WIPO. TRIPs also obligates members to provide for the protection of plant varieties, either by patent or by an effective sui generis system. This system has been routinely associated with the plant breeder's rights established in the International Union for the Protection of New Varieties of Plants (UPOV) convention. This intergovernmental organization is based on the International Convention for the Protection of New Varieties of Plants first signed in Paris in 1961.[24]

The oldest is the Paris Convention, for it was initially drafted in 1883 by a small group of countries and it was last revised in 1967.[25] It covers industrial intellectual property such as patents, industrial designs, trademarks, geographical indications, and trade secrets. To qualify for patent protection, inventions must be new, nonobvious, and commercially applicable. The main principle of the Paris Convention is "national treatment" to indicate that authors and inventors should be treated the same in all member states. Other principles include nondiscrimination and priority of application. The latter means that any application filed in foreign countries will be treated as if it had been filed on the same date as the first application. TRIPs incorporates the Paris Convention, but it also specifies that the length of patent protection must be granted for a minimum of twenty years from the filing date. In addition, it requires that WTO members fully enforce such protection.[26] It is in this context that Susan Sell notes the difference between the past conventions, which reflected the existing consensus among their signatories, and TRIPs, which often necessitates creation or transformation of laws in many countries. The Paris Convention did not provide a list of what should be protected and how, and it did not indicate the length of protection to be offered.[27]

Therefore, some critics argue that "these [are] not 'minimum' standards of intellectual property protection in the classical sense of the term; rather, they collectively expressed most of the standards of protection on which the developed counties could agree among themselves. Moreover, these relatively high substantive standards were reinforced by new and heretofore untried procedural standards mandating minimum level of enforcement in all member countries and by the reformed dispute-settlement."[28] The demands posed by the implementation of TRIPs are indeed enormous, even if only "the minimum" standards are required. However, let's briefly address the issue of enforcement first, which is one of the most difficult aspects of meeting the obligations under TRIPs. The newly acceding countries and most developing WTO members in particular experience great difficulties in this respect.

There are four main principles relating to the enforcement provisions as stipulated in Article 41. First, each WTO member must ensure that the specific and effective enforcement measures and procedures are available and capable of deterring further infringing activity. Second, the relevant procedures must be expeditious, fair, and not too costly. Third, it requires that the evidence be presented to all parties in courts, which are expected to be efficient and competent. Fourth, each WTO member should also provide a form of appeal. Within this context, Articles 42 through 49 particularize the "civil and administrative procedures and remedies" that must be available in respect to any activity infringing on intellectual property rights covered by TRIPs. Special requirements that relate to border measures are listed in Articles 51 through 60. In fact, a distinction is made between infringing activity in general and counterfeiting (trademarks) and piracy (copyright) in respect to which additional border measures and criminal procedures must be provided to prevent the release of infringing imports into free circulation.[29] Finally, Articles 61 and 62 of the agreement deal with criminal procedures, which must be available in cases of willful trademark counterfeiting or copyright piracy on a commercial scale. TRIPs allows WTO members to decide whether to provide for criminal procedures and penalties to be applied in other cases of infringement of intellectual property rights. Penalties should be sufficient enough to provide a deterrent against future infringement.

Overall, the minimum procedures and legislative measures required under the enforcement provisions of TRIPs place an enormous burden on WTO members. They also inevitably limit the regulatory autonomy of WTO members by creating obligations that must be reflected in domestic laws and administrative bodies.

TRIPs contains provisions linking it with the WTO dispute settlement system to ensure that all WTO members fully implement it or risk engaging in a trade dispute, which can end up in retaliatory measures. The enforcement provisions under the agreement are particularly demanding on developing countries. This can be a particularly challenging process for developing countries, which often not only have to create a completely new administrative and regulatory framework for protection of intellectual property, but also have to satisfy all remaining WTO members that the new laws and regulations will be enforced. Otherwise, they risk engaging in a trade dispute.

A peculiar feature of the WTO dispute settlement is the so-called nonviolation clause, which permits one WTO member to complain (and start a formal trade dispute under the DSU) against another WTO member based on "an allegation a benefit that should accrue is being nullified or impaired as a result of a measure taken by another Member, which does not itself conflict with that Member's obligations."[30] The TRIPs agreement specifically recognizes the nonviolation clause (Article XXIII of GATT 1994 incorporated into Article 64 of TRIPs). This could have a potentially detrimental effect on developing countries, which could have disputes initiated against them on the basis of an incomplete, or deemed unsatisfactory, implementation of the agreement. The vocal opposition of developing countries to such a possibility led to a compromise. In the final stage of the Uruguay Round, a moratorium on the application of such nonviolation complaints under TRIPs was agreed for the period of five years until January 1, 2000. During this time, the WTO was expected to examine how such nonviolation complaints could be initiated.

The issue was revisited in 2000. However, since a decision taken by consensus was necessary to extend the moratorium, the unequivocal position of the US delegation effectively paralyzed the debate on the subject.[31] This happened despite how developing countries were expressing concerns that such nonviolation complaints in the field of intellectual property rights can lead to questionable complains (e.g., citing inadequate enforcement procedures being put in place, imprecise laws, unqualified judges, etc.) within the WTO system. Several countries, like Canada, the EU, and Malaysia, maintain that the whole concept is dubious with respect to TRIPs, especially given the fact that now under TRIPs the burden of proof rests on the defendant.

TRIPs does talk about the need to maintain a proper balance between the rights of the owners and the obligations they have toward higher social values. References to "technological innovation" as well as to the "transfer and dissemination of technology" should serve as the basic recognition of the matters that are of major concern to developing countries. As stated in Article 7:

> The protection and enforcement of intellectual property rights should contribute to the promotion of technological innovation and to the transfer and dissemination of technology, to the mutual advantage of producers and users of technological knowledge and in a manner conducive to social and economic welfare, and to a balance of rights and obligations.

However, according to scholars from the developing world, the first six years of implementing TRIPs were characterized by industrialized nations focusing attention mainly on securing the intellectual property rights for their corporations and paying almost no attention to their obligations to transfer and disseminate technological knowledge to address the issue of developmental objectives.[32]

The Doha Round was expected to address the long-standing complaints of developing countries in this area. The adoption of the Doha Declaration by the WTO members at the Fourth Ministerial Conference in Qatar in 2001 was perhaps the most important event in the history of multilateral trade relations from the point of view of developing countries. For the first time, the WTO recognized and acknowledged the firm link between trade and development. It was hoped that by changing the focus on developmental concerns of WTO members many problems associated with the implementation of TRIPs could be resolved. For example, the protection of products bearing geographical indications other than wines and spirits was also included in the Doha program.

Under the standards required under TRIPs, WTO members must provide special protection for wines and spirits. It was France that succeeded in its lobbying efforts, although not all issues relevant to the protection of geographical indications were resolved during the Uruguay Round. Many countries consequently argued that protection was also needed for geographical indications for products other than wines and spirits. Special rice that is sold under the Indian geographical indication "Basmati" and beers clearly identified under the Czech geographical indication "Pilsner" are the most widely cited examples. If these products are marked as Basmati rice and Pilsner beer but are actually produced in another region or country, this would, by implication, constitute unfair usage of the commercially valuable geographical indication. Furthermore, it would mislead consumers as to the place of origin of that product.

This issue of affording special recognition to Champagne, Burgundy, and Bordeaux points out yet another contradiction of TRIPs. From the legal point of view, there is an explanation for the distinction in Section 3 of Part II of TRIPs that places wines and spirits on a higher ground while ignoring the fact that geographical indications for other categories of goods are equally important for trade. The requests from many countries that the extra degree of protection of geographical indications that are granted exclusively to wines and spirits under TRIPs be extended to cover other products often traditionally produced in developing countries have been well justified.[33]

Patents, TRIPs, and the Resulting Controversies

TRIPs extends the scope of the Paris Convention in many significant ways. Keith E. Maskus points out how broad is the definition of what qualifies as patentable as specified by Article 27 of TRIPs: "Patents shall be available for any inventions, whether products or processes, in all fields of technology, provided that they are new, involve an inventive step and are capable of industrial application." This means the extension of patent protection to industries previously not covered by many domestic intellectual property laws, for example, chemical, pharmaceutical, and food.[34] The same Article 27 goes on to list exemptions from patentability.

> [Para 2.] Members may exclude from patentability inventions, the prevention within their territory of the commercial exploitation of which is necessary to protect *ordre public* or morality, including to protect human, animal or plant life or health or to avoid serious prejudice to the environment, provided that such exclusion is not made merely because the exploitation is prohibited by their law.
>
> [Para 3.] Members may also exclude from patentability:
>
> (a) diagnostic, therapeutic and surgical methods for the treatment of humans or animals;
>
> (b) plants and animals other than micro-organisms, and essentially biological processes for the production of plants or animals other than non-biological and microbiological processes. However, Members shall provide for the protection of plant varieties either by patents or by an effective *sui generis* system or by any combination thereof. The provisions of this subparagraph shall be reviewed four years after the date of entry into force of the WTO Agreement.

The exemption for biotechnological inventions was controversial since it "permits exclusion from patentability for traditional breeding ('essentially biological') methods and higher life organisms (plants and animals)," despite obliging countries to provide protection for plant breeders' rights.[35] The industrialized countries have hoped to expand patent rights to all biotechnological inventions and methods during the post–Uruguay Round review of the agreement. This move, however, was met with opposition, often ethically motivated, against designing and then patenting life forms.

Inside the WTO, developing countries expressed their strong resistance by pointing out how the agreement is already imbalanced to favor the interests of the developed countries. Developing countries, in turn, have been demanding that traditional knowledge and biodiversity should become eligible for protection under TRIPs.[36]

Article 27.3 of TRIPs does not call for establishing standards for the protection of indigenous plant varieties or traditional knowledge, thereby allowing for the exploitation of biological resources and traditional recipes in developing countries by commercially driven corporations. With regard to traditional knowledge, developing countries maintain such knowledge often has been the foundation of modern agriculture and medicine, but now their societies have to pay for patented products that are derived from their traditional knowledge or bioresources. For example, Vanuatu, a small least-developed country, so far has been unsuccessful with its WTO accession process and unable to meet many demands as a condition of membership. Consider the establishment of a regulatory regime for protection of intellectual property to comply with TRIPs. While the costs are obvious and difficult to meet, the benefits are hard to envision. Vanuatu is the biological home of the root crop kava. Kava is a traditional beverage in Vanuatu and has been consumed by the people of Vanuatu since long before the arrival of Europeans. However, large pharmaceutical companies in the United States and the EU now produce, and have patented, kava pills.[37] Apart from exporting the unprocessed kava root for pennies, Vanuatu gains nothing from the international sales of the increasingly popular natural sedative. The implementation of TRIPs will not protect the indigenous traditional rights that Vanuatu claims to have to kava.

In addition, by requiring patenting of plant varieties (micro-organisms) via the sui generis system, TRIPs clashes with the provisions of the 1993 Convention on Biological Diversity (CBD), which stipulates in Article 3 that countries exercise sovereign rights over their biological resources subject to their national legislation.[38] Article 8 of the convention established the obligation to "respect, preserve and maintain knowledge, innovations and practices of indigenous and local communities." Under the terms of the convention, access to genetic resources is granted by "the country of origin" defined in Article 2 as "the country which possesses those genetic resources in *in-situ* conditions," which, in turn, mean those "conditions where genetic resources exist within ecosystems and natural habitats, and, in the case of domesticated or cultivated species, in the surroundings where they have developed their distinctive properties." The convention then in principle allows an individual state where the genetic resources exist to have an unchallenged right over them. The convention also stresses the need for conservation of such resources and urges transfer of technology on preferential terms to the developing world with the aim of ensuring sustainable development. Much to the dismay of developing countries, the framers of TRIPs did not take into account the principles of the convention.

In fact, there is also an additional problem with the agreement on this issue. It has to do with automatically associating sui generis protection with the International Union for the Protection of New Varieties of Plants. TRIPs does not mention the UPOV by name, but many industry lobbyists pushed for this association because the UPOV places very few limitations on the monopoly rights of plant breeders. It only allows that plant breeders can use UPOV-protected varieties for research purposes.[39] Most important, in its 1991 revision the UPOV has eliminated the so-called farmers' privilege that allowed farmers to reuse their seeds in the future. This has particular implications for genetically modified seeds, which are now patented. Farmers therefore have to annually renew a license if they want to use the seeds again, although those in the developing world are particularly interested in retaining their farmers' rights over the seeds that they are using. They need free access to often more-efficient genetically modified seeds to ensure that agriculture remains sustainable in many poor countries.[40]

India has been the champion of a campaign to rebalance TRIPs. Its attempts to bring the attention of activists and other governments to the issues of biopiracy and traditional knowledge became stronger after two famous cases involving turmeric and neem trees. Both of these natural resources were traditionally used in India for generations, for turmeric is used as a component of various home remedies and neem tree as a source of natural pesticide for farmers. However, in the 1990s the US Patent and Trademark Office granted a patent to US researchers on the use of turmeric as a healing agent and another patent was granted to an agrochemical company on using an extract from the neem tree in the production of a pesticide. The Indian government contested both patents and was supported in its efforts by a growing coalition of farmers and activists worldwide. The turmeric patent was eventually overturned but the case "raised a larger question of the status of traditional methods and practices passed down orally, what is sometimes referred as 'folklore.' Many so-called 'scientific discoveries' are nothing more (or less) than folklore that researchers may stumble upon or seek out among indigenous peoples, farmers, shamans, and healers."[41] TRIPs, in line with the previous intellectual property rights conventions, does not grant protection to traditional knowledge.

India has consistently argued for the recognition of the CBD, which in Article 8 recognizes the right of indigenous cultures to protect their communal knowledge. However, in pointing out the principle of the sharing of knowledge, which is one of the crucial themes of the convention, India also proposed an alternative solution. This proposal is a response to the attitude expressed by the industrialized nations. They resist the inclusion of traditional or indigenous knowledge under TRIPs by claiming that it is not an intellectual property but rather involves subject matter that is widely known. It thus should remain widely accessible in the public domain. Consistent with this view, India suggested that unrestricted and unpaid access to all plant genetic resources for food and agriculture should be maintained to the advantage of all countries. This would include free access to genetically modified seeds, for which patents would no longer be applicable. The Indian proposal advocated open exchange of genetic material to improve knowledge and produce more productive and sustainable agriculture around the world. Rather than seeking a solution in intellectual property rights, some developing countries, most notably India, have suggested that voluntary agreements involving firms, governments, and indigenous people could provide for benefit-sharing and technological cooperation.[42]

Developing countries are increasingly more influential in setting the international agenda for future trade negotiations, but their position is particularly prominent when it comes to traditional knowledge, farmers' rights, genetic resources, and access to pharmaceutical inventions. On the eve of the Fourth Ministerial Conference in Doha, a number of developing countries forwarded their proposals to address these issues. For example, *Declaration of the Group of 77 and China* includes very strong language in this context:

> [Para 12.] We consider that negotiations should make operational the provisions under the TRIPS Agreement relating to the transfer of technology, to the mutual advantage of producers and users of technological knowledge, and seek mechanisms that allow for the disclosure of the sources of traditional knowledge and genetic resources used in inventions, in order to achieve a fair and equitable sharing of benefits. In this regard, the TRIPS Agreement should be supportive of and not run counter to the objectives and principles of the CBD with view to ensuring the protection of biological resources and to promote disciplines to protect traditional knowledge and genetic resources. The TRIPS review shall fully take into account the developmental dimension and during the course of this review Members should agree not to invoke dispute settlement procedures against the developing countries.
>
> [Para 13.] We affirm that nothing in the TRIPS Agreement should prevent governments from taking measures for protecting public health and nutrition as well as from ensuring affordable access to essential medicines and life saving drugs in keeping with public health concerns of developing countries.[43]

As a result, the 2001 declaration launching the Doha Round of multilateral negotiations explicitly acknowledges the above issues as part of the work program.[44]

The most controversial area, however, with respect to patent protection under TRIPs concerns pharmaceutical products. Patents, by design, increase the price of medicines to consumers, because they enable pharmaceutical firms to keep prices much higher than their marginal costs of production by discouraging the emergence of competitors.[45] It is virtually impossible to compete with such dominant monopolies because of the unprecedented financial resources at their disposal and their supreme research capabilities. In taking advantage of their dominant market position, the pharmaceutical companies have tried to maintain similar drug prices around the world despite the wide gap in the per capita income level between the developed and developing countries. Add to that the "novelty" impact of TRIPs on developing countries. Among the ninety-eight developing countries that were members of the WTO at the time of its establishment, twenty-five did not have patent laws covering pharmaceutical products. And among those that had it, the length of patent protection was much shorter in fifty-six developing countries than the twenty years required by TRIPs.[46] Most important, however, the governments widely employed certain legal mechanisms like compulsory licensing[47] to limit the scope of the pharmaceutical patents in order to facilitate production of cheaper generic medications and, more generally, to advance new inventions and technologies.

TRIPs does allow for the granting of compulsory licenses, but it implicitly discourages countries from using this option by restricting their use. The leading developed countries are not in favor of compulsory licenses and they have used a threatening tone toward those countries that have proposed granting compulsory licenses.[48] Moreover, the conditions under which compulsory licensing is allowed are sufficiently ambiguous to deter the governments from doing it. Article 31 of TRIPs sets out a long checklist of complicated procedures a government must follow before it can legally override a patent and issue a compulsory license. For example, before a government can issue a compulsory license, it must negotiate with and essentially obtain permission from the owner of the patent. The owner of the patent must be given a satisfactory compensation fee for overriding the patent. The compulsory license can only be temporary and only for the domestic market.[49]

The provision regarding compulsory licensing created uproar among developing countries, and it became a top issue in the argument for changing the process with respect to patented pharmaceutical products. Paragraph 6 of the *Doha Declaration of the TRIPS Agreement and Public Health* singled out this issue and committed WTO to negotiate a mutually agreeable solution.[50] After a marathon of contentious negotiations, a deal allowed a special waiver of Article 31(f) of TRIPs to be granted to any WTO member lacking facilities to produce the necessary medications. The waiver allowed for importing of such medications from any other WTO member. And although it was not restrictive to a number of specific diseases (as the United States wanted), it included a number of procedural requirements to prevent a wide-reaching spread of sales of low-cost pharmaceutical products.[51] During the Hong

Kong Ministerial Conference in December 2005, WTO members made a decision to permanently amend TRIPs in this context as recognized by Paragraph 40 of the Ministerial Declaration.[52] However, one has to keep in mind that the legal authority of this decision is untested given the uncertainty of whether the Doha Round will ever be completed.

In addition, TRIPs mandates that when it comes to the adjudicating process in patent infringement cases, the burden of proof be reversed. In other words, a defendant country would now have to persuade the WTO panel that it was innocent. The reversal of the burden of proof has only recently become a norm in many industrialized countries, because it is normally difficult to prove an infringement case.[53] It may be considered worrisome that there is nothing in the agreement to prevent large companies from engaging in strategically motivated preemptive litigations to eliminate potential competition.

The connection between TRIPs, access to affordable medicines, and litigation-prone corporate behavior was firmly made at the end of the 1990s. However, it would take over a decade before a unique coalition of developing countries, supported by international activists and enjoying global media coverage, led to the recognition during the 2005 Hong Kong conference that TRIPs needed to be permanently amended.[54] What energized a coalition of developing countries and attracted widespread public attention was the dispute between the South African government and a number of leading pharmaceutical companies. Although there were almost 3.5 million HIV-infected people in South Africa in 2000, the existing treatments were too expensive for most patients there. In South Africa the average annual income was around $3,000 in 1995, while the HIV/AIDS regimens could cost between $6,000 and $10,000 a year. In 1997, the South African government took steps to address this problem by introducing the Medicines Amendment Act.[55]

The 1997 act authorized two practices that are implicitly discouraged under TRIPs. One is referred to as parallel imports, which allow a country to import from abroad cheaper pharmaceutical products even if the owner of the patent did not approve it. The other was compulsory licensing, which would allow the government to license South African companies to produce generic substitutions of the drug and hence significantly reduce the prices. The ratification of the Medicines Amendment Act of 1997, however, was stalled by a lawsuit filed in February 1998 by a group of forty-two pharmaceutical companies from Europe and the United States that challenged the act. They claimed that it was unconstitutional because it allowed the minister of health to act in an "arbitrary way" to determine the conditions for compulsory licensing. At the time of the lawsuit, the US lobby group working in support of the pharmaceutical industry, the Pharmaceutical Research and Manufacturers of America (PhRMA), asked the Office of the USTR to put South Africa on its watch list, which it did in April 1999. It cited South Africa for the 1997 act, which the United States said could potentially "abrogate patent rights" and hence presented this already socially and politically charged issue as a simple case of intellectual property rights violation. Such a move could lead to trade sanctions or to the withdrawal of aid to South Africa.[56]

In fact, soon after TRIPs and other WTO agreements came into force, the Office of the USTR established in 1996 an Office of Monitoring and Enforcement to ensure that all countries fulfill their WTO obligations. Throughout the 1996–2000 period, the USTR repeatedly put on its "Special 301 watch list" countries that supposedly did not provide the kind of adequate intellectual property rights protection they were required to have. It was done upon the requests submitted to the USTR by private businesses. During the post-TRIPs period, two groups in particular became active in the process; one was the already-mentioned PhRMA and the other was International Intellectual Property Alliance, which includes a number of trade associations. It should be noted that the strengthening of Special 301 in the US Trade Act in the 1980s was a culmination of a campaign organized by the business lobby group called the Intellectual Property Rights Committee, which initially included twelve corporate executives from US corporations as well as business groups from the EU and Japan. This group in fact first presented a proposal for a multilateral agreement on intellectual property to be included under GATT.[57]

The lawsuit in South Africa happened at a moment when the unavailability of the life-saving drugs needed to address the growing HIV/AIDS epidemic was attracting growing criticism. Consequently, the South African case ignited a massive global campaign supported by critical editorial coverage in the media around the world. A growing number of activists, scholars, and organizations such as Oxfam and the Nobel Prize–winning Doctors Without Borders publicized the consequences of excessively priced life-saving medicines due to internationally enforced pharmaceutical patents. In response to resounding global pressure, on April 19, 2001, the pharmaceutical companies dropped the case they had been pursuing for three years. The end of the lawsuit cleared the path for the 1997 Medicines Amendment Act to go into force, thus allowing the importation of affordable medicines and increased use of generic drugs in South Africa.

The proponents of strong patent protection in the WTO, especially the United States and European Communities, point to Article 27.1 (Patentable Subject Matter) of the agreement, which stipulates that "patents shall be available and patent rights enjoyable without discrimination as to the place of invention, the field of technology and whether products are imported or locally produced." They maintain that this provision should be interpreted as prohibiting the use of any domestic policy measures that would threaten the absolute right of the patent's owners. As a result, any national policy initiative that overrides an existing patent can be interpreted as discriminatory, trade restricting, and violating TRIPs.

This interpretation of TRIPs has been contested by many developing countries, most notably by India and Brazil. For example, Brazil's law stipulated that a patent could be subject to compulsory licensing if the patent was not worked in the territory of Brazil. The United States and European Communities threatened Brazil with DSU panel proceedings under the WTO. In July 2001 Brazil reached an out-of-court understanding with the United States, when the Brazilian government agreed that in the event it would deem necessary to grant compulsory licenses on patents held by the US companies it would hold prior talks on the matter with the USTR office.[58] The US government subsequently withdrew its complaint in the WTO. However, the outcome of this disagreement questions Brazil's autonomy, since it obliges the government of Brazil to consult with a foreign country prior to making a decision on what is really a matter of domestic policy making.

The pressure to make some amendments to TRIPs has been intense in the WTO, but with the AIDS crisis on the horizon the traditional advocates of strong patents began to change their attitudes. Finally, the anthrax scare has forced many policymakers in Europe and North America to take a close look at the TRIPs agreement and its implications. In October 2001, the Canadian government asked Apotex, a Canadian-based company, to make copies of Cipro, which was a drug under a patent owned by Bayer of Germany. Cipro is considered to be the preferred treatment for anthrax. Immediately, some US business leaders criticized Canada's decision, while many politicians called upon the US government to do the same, arguing that a decision not to produce cheaper generic medicines would prevent many US citizens from obtaining Cipro, which sold between US$4 to $5 per pill commercially. Apotex offered to supply Canada with generic Cipro at 99 cents a tablet. Even, the US Department of Health and Human Services demanded that Bayer reduce the price to allow them to replenish the emergency supplies. The US Health and Human Services secretary Tommy G. Thompson announced that he would approach generic manufacturers if Bayer did not significantly lower the price of Cipro. The threat worked and Bayer delivered the medicine more cheaply. The Canadian government also withdrew its decision to override Bayer's patent.[59] Still, the anthrax scare demonstrated how the inflexible approach to patents, as currently encouraged by TRIPs, could dangerously exacerbate conflicts between private interests and public needs by limiting governments' options to act.

The growing concerns over global patent rules and the unyielding plea by developing countries to modify TRIPs have finally produced some tangible results. First, during its Fourth Ministerial Conference in Doha, Qatar, in November 2001, WTO members adopted the *Declaration on the TRIPS Agreement and Public Health,* addressing for the first time on a multilateral level, the problem of inaccessibility of medicines by the poor nations. Second, as previously discussed, the ensuing talks actually resulted in an amendment to TRIPs solidified by the Hong Kong Declaration.[60] Still, the uncertain legal status of the Hong Kong Declaration prevents us from considering it as a permanent addition to the WTO agreements.

Copyrights, Trademarks, and the Commercial Aspects of TRIPs

Although the controversy surrounding TRIPs is perhaps most closely linked with the protection it affords to patents, the incorporation into the agreement of the Berne Convention has its problems too. The Berne Convention concerns copyrights; it was first signed in 1886 by a handful of countries. It is said that it took over twenty-five years to negotiate the treaty under the leadership of publishers, academics, and writers such as Victor Hugo.[61] The convention was last amended in 1979. Copyright protection under TRIPs must be afforded for the life of the author plus fifty years. The two fundamental principles of the Berne Convention are national treatment and automatic protection.[62] The principle of automatic protection indicates that copyright protection must not be conditional upon compliance with any formality. In contrast to TRIPs, no procedures for enforcing the rules are mentioned in the convention.

As we know, TRIPs became reality because of the concerted efforts by the European Community and the United States. There was, however, one area where these two allies did not agree, and it had to do with two different views on copyrights. During the Uruguay Round of negotiations, the United States insisted on removing the concept of *moral rights* from the provisions covered by TRIPs. The Europeans, who first invented and solidified the concept in the 1928 revision of the Berne Convention, wanted to uphold it. The United States maintained that moral rights unnecessarily restricted the ability of copyright owners to freely market the product commercially. In the end, the US argument prevailed.

In accordance with Article 9 of TRIPs, WTO members are not obliged to enforce moral rights, which were guaranteed under Article 6bis of the Berne Convention. Article 6bis says that an author has a moral right to her creative work in order to protect the integrity of the work. This right allows an author to object to any modification to the author's work that would be prejudicial to her reputation. To be in compliance with the Berne Convention, publishers who normally acquire copyrights to the literary, musical, or software creations before they can distribute them are not able to make any changes to these works without first obtaining a permission from the author. By removing this obligation from TRIPs, the creators of the agreement gave priority to the commercial interests of copyright owners (publishers), who prefer to have unlimited authority over the copyrighted material they purchase for publication. Of course, countries can still introduce moral rights in their domestic laws, but under TRIPs they do not have to.

The US legislative tradition has never recognized the principle of moral rights.[63] In fact, for a long time the United States was unwilling to establish a strong copyright regime, fearing its impact on dissemination of knowledge. The free reprinting of books brought from Europe was a norm for decades during the time when the United States was developing its economy. The first US copyright explicitly permitted "importation of vending, reprinting or publishing within the United States, of any map, chart, book or books, written, printed, or published by any person not a citizen of the United States."[64] It was not until US-based businesses made demands during the Uruguay Round to establish a multilateral agreement on intellectual property that the United States finally signed the Berne Treaty in 1989.[65]

TRIPs removes the Berne requirement to respect the moral rights of authors. It is in this way that it once again reinforces the industry-driven attitude to copyrights. This attitude places the owner of the title at the center, while the author is given a secondary role in the name of commercial considerations. In short, TRIPs promotes a strictly commercial view of intellectual property rights, which goes against a historical understanding of the concept. There is a growing need to take a different approach to intellectual property rights—one that strikes a delicate balance between granting the inventors recognition and the right to protect their work without compromising the ability of governments to take advantage of such inventions for the benefit of society.

This view of intellectual property rights prevailed for generations until TRIPs strengthened the private rights approach. The first intellectual property laws were designed to ensure a diffusion of knowledge, award prestige to inventors, and encourage importation and creation of new inventions. Patents originated in Europe during the Renaissance, where European sovereigns commonly awarded patent letters to favored artisans and inventors to induce the transfer of new technologies. The first formalized patent system is traced back to 1474 when Venice passed its first patent statute. Its purpose was to stimulate invention and innovation, and for this reason the award of the grant contained the requirement for working the patent locally. In fact, the patent grant could be forfeited if it was not used within a specified time. The government also retained a complete right to grant a compulsory license for production of the patented invention.[66]

In England, patents in the legal sense originated in section 6 of the 1624 Statute on Monopolies, which, while generally condemning monopolies, provided "the first and true inventor" with a patent lasting up to fourteen years of exclusive rights to his invention with the following conditions: "it must not be contrary to the law nor mischievous to the State by raising of prices of commodities at home, or must not hurt trade, or be generally inconvenient."[67]

The developments that led to the signing of the Paris Treaty in 1883 reflected the need of a handful of countries that were leading the Industrial Revolution to have their new inventions monopolized and protected. Under the leadership of Great Britain and Germany, these countries wanted to maintain their competitive edge by restricting access to their inventions, thereby allowing them to be dominant economic players in Europe. Consequently, countries like Switzerland and the Netherlands were pressed to establish new patents laws. Many Swiss industrialists of the era were against this move. This was because Swiss industries were able to develop since, in the absence of intellectual property rights, they were free to copy foreign inventions without restrictions. A similar situation occurred in the United States and Canada in the early stages of their nation building. This leads to the conclusion that countries at the early stages of their economic development not only do not have intellectual property rights, but they actually develop by sharing and copying the inventions.

The first copyright law originated in England in 1710 when the British Parliament enacted the Statute of Anne. The law contained legal protection for consumers of copyrighted works by curtailing the term of a copyright, thus preventing a monopoly on the part of the booksellers. It also created a "public domain" for literature by limiting the length of term of a copyright and by restricting the rights granted to the copyright owner (print, publish, sell) so that the publishers were not able to maintain a perpetual monopoly over the publishing of books. The statute dramatically changed the allocation of entitlements among authors, publishers, and readers. It also removed literary works from the censorship of the booksellers and in effect unleashed a free market for literary creations.[68] Again the interest of the state and the broad socioeconomic benefits of the patents were the crucial criteria for enacting the first intellectual property laws.

Compliance with TRIPs is nonoptional and since the agreement is part of the single undertaking, the domestic intellectual property rights regimes of WTO members are now under the jurisdiction of the WTO dispute settlement system. This extension of GATT provoked fears about the diminished capacity of WTO members to conduct their domestic policy making. In the words of Deborah Z. Cass: "The Uruguay Round agreements have ushered in a new era of positive integration in which states became obliged to incorporate particular standards into their legal systems in areas such as intellectual property (rather than just an interdiction against discrimination), and it has therefore impeded national regulatory choice."[69]

Indeed, it is TRIPs that has raised the most vocal concerns that the legal interpretation of the agreement may entail diminutions of state prerogatives in creating its own regulations. The case of tobacco and the use of trademarks in that industry offer an interesting example. Cigarette manufacturers often distinguish their products as being "light" and "mild" to ostensibly show that such cigarettes pose less of a risk to the smoker's health than normal cigarettes and are also not as addictive. This is done by registering trademarks as such "Marlboro Lights™" and "Marlboro Ultra Lights™." Notwithstanding the internal documents of these manufacturers that explicitly reveal the deceptiveness of these labels by acknowledging how the perception of "healthier" cigarettes may win more buyers, medical studies have proven that smokers that partake in cigarettes branded as "light" and "mild" tend to smoke more to ensure certain nicotine levels in their bodies. In the interest of public health by curbing tobacco use, members might cancel the registration of such trademarks and/or prohibit their usage.[70]

Although Article XX(b) of GATT allows trade restrictions to be used when "necessary to protect human, animal or plant life or health,"[71] the use of trademarks as addressed in Article 20 of TRIPs is stipulated to "not be unjustifiably encumbered by special requirements, such as use with another trademark, use in a special form or use in a manner to distinguish the goods or services of one undertaking from those of other undertakings." However, as Benn McGrady pointed out, the language in this provision is vague. On the one hand, it can be interpreted narrowly to mean that prohibitions on the use of trademarks may be restricted because there is no explicit interdiction over the use of such measures, although the word "encumbered" is itself ambiguous. On the other hand, favored by the tobacco industry, a broader approach to understanding this provision can be taken that would permit no restrictions on the use of trademarks. Already, the majority of WTO members utilize advertising restrictions that limit the use of trademarks. In many states, these are further complemented by health warnings that alert potential consumers, and remind users, of the harms caused by cigarette smoking. How one regards these measures to be lawful and consistent with TRIPs is contingent on whether the narrow or broad interpretation is undertaken. One can only guess where the industry stands on this issue. The Philip Morris company launched a campaign by releasing documents in which it argued in favor of broad interpretation, claiming that prohibiting the use of the light in "Marlboro Lights™" would violate Article 20 of TRIPs.[72]

From the point of view of governments, they must apply a strict definition of the necessity of protecting "public health" when restricting tobacco trademarks. Fortunately, the uncertain meaning of Article 20 provides certain leeway for policymakers in applying the provision to justify their own restrictions. Because of the general understanding about the hazards of smoking tobacco, countries that support the position expressed by Philip

Morris may be reluctant to start a WTO dispute panel on this issue. If such a dispute is nevertheless initiated, given the public health costs associated with tobacco consumption incurred by states, the standard of public interest may be appropriate to justify domestic regulations that limit trademark use.[73] Still, the way the tobacco industry has been utilizing and interpreting TRIPs in their attempt to limit the regulatory autonomy of WTO member states is troublesome.

Conclusion

Since its inclusion within the multilateral framework of the WTO, TRIPs has generated much criticism from scholars, diplomats, activists, and politicians around the world. Representatives of developing countries have been particularly vocal in contesting an agreement that essentially favors monopoly rights within the system based on the idea of open and free trade. With the entry into force of the TRIPs agreement, many countries found themselves in a difficult situation since only some WTO members, mostly industrialized countries, were signatories to the conventions that became mandatory under TRIPs. Under the WTO, all the present and future WTO members not only have to comply with the obligations established by the past intellectual property conventions, but will additionally have to apply new provisions and enforcement requirements provided in TRIPs.

There are many contradictions surrounding the agreement. We know, for example, that economies of WTO members vary not only because of differences when it comes to their size and economic performance, but also because of differences in regulatory regimes. In a similar vein, distinct interpretations of what constitutes intellectual property and how, if at all, it should be protected by law divide countries around the world. Many countries never developed legal protection for inventions or for written texts since it would be contrary to their cultural understanding, which might favor unlimited sharing of knowledge for the benefit of future societies. As a result developing member countries are very concerned about the impact that TRIPs can have on their socioeconomic development, especially since the governments in Europe and North America have prioritized the issue of intellectual property rights. The high standards of protection afforded to intellectual property follow the developments in the globalizing economy driven by huge investments made in new technological inventions. Developing countries worry that the growing emphasis on strong intellectual property rights would deny them access to new technologies and pharmaceutical formulas that could lead to further marginalization of the South.

Developing WTO members and countries that are applying for WTO membership must implement TRIPs under the scrutiny of the industrialized nations. Among the difficulties faced by countries in the implementation of TRIPs, the following merit particular consideration. First, developing countries lack technical and financial support to develop rules and necessary institutional infrastructure for establishing an effective intellectual property rights regime. Second, developing countries are unsure of benefits from the costly implementation of TRIPs. They, however, recognize a tangible threat of misappropriation of their natural resources. They also contest prohibitively high prices for new technological, pharmaceutical, agricultural, and chemical creations, which can exacerbate many social and economic problems in the developing world.

The demands placed on developing countries with respect to TRIPs demonstrate that the agreement is a problematic attempt to globalize intellectual property rights. This is why the WTO membership must adopt a broader developmental focus when interpreting TRIPs. Yet, paying attention to the development needs of all WTO members would likely require a considerable departure from the approach that has been institutionalized in TRIPs.

Notes

1. Christopher May and Susan K. Sell, *Intellectual Property Rights—A Critical History* (Boulder, CO, and London: Lynne Rienner Publishers, 2006), p. 1.

2. Carlos M. Correa, *Intellectual Property Rights, the WTO and Developing Countries—The TRIPS Agreement and Policy Options* (Penang, Malaysia: Third World Network, 2000), p. 5.

3. For an insightful discussion on the subject, please see Richard Ashcraft, "Lockean Ideas, Poverty, and the Development of Liberal Political Theory," in John Brewer and Susan Staves (eds.), *Early Modern Conceptions of Property* (London and New York: Routledge, 1996), pp. 43–61.

4. Francis Fukuyama, *Trust—The Social Virtues and the Creation of Prosperity* (New York: Penguin Books, 1996), pp. 63–64.

5. William P. Alford, *To Steal a Book Is an Elegant Offence—Intellectual Property Law in Chinese Civilization* (Stanford, CA: Stanford University Press, 1995).

6. May and Sell, *Intellectual Property Rights*, p. 5.

7. Lord Sydney Templeman, "Intellectual Property," *Journal of International Economic Law* 1, no. 4 (1998): 604–605.

8. "Counterfeit" refers to goods to which a trademark has been applied without authorization. See GATT, *Agreement on Measures to Discourage the Importation of Counterfeit Goods* (L/4817) (July 31, 1979).

9. Susan K. Sell, *Private Power, Public Law—The Globalization of Intellectual Property Rights* (Cambridge, UK, and New York: Cambridge University Press, 2003), pp. 40–41.

10. WTO, "Annex 1C: The Agreement of Trade-Related Aspects of Intellectual Property Rights. TRIPS," in *The Results of the Uruguay Round of Multilateral Trade Negotiations,* Sections 1–7 of Part II (Geneva: WTO). Article 1, Paragraph 2

reads: "For the purposes of this Agreement, the term 'intellectual property' refers to all categories of intellectual property that are the subject of Sections 1 through 7 of Part II."

11. Sell, *Private Power, Public Law*, pp. 43–55.

12. Michael P. Ryan, *Knowledge Diplomacy: Global Competition and the Politics of Intellectual Property* (Washington, DC: Brookings Institution Press, 1998), pp. 10–11.

13. Jagdish Bhagwati, *The Wind of the Hundred Days—How Washington Mismanaged Globalization* (Cambridge, MA: MIT Press, 2000), p. 279.

14. Maxwell A. Cameron and Brian W. Tomlin, *The Making of NAFTA—How the Deal Was Done* (Ithaca, NY, and London: Cornell University Press, 2000), pp. 140–142.

15. Frederick M. Abbott, "The Enduring Enigma of TRIPS: A Challenge for the World Economic System," *Journal of International Economic Law* 1, no. 4 (1998): 489.

16. Ibid., p. 518.

17. Keith E. Maskus, *Intellectual Property Rights in the Global Economy* (Washington, DC: Institute for International Economics, 2000), p. 119.

18. Edson K. Kondo, "The Effect of Patent Protection on Foreign Direct Investment" *Journal of World Trade* 29 (1995): 97–122.

19. WTO, *Communication from China—The Chinese Laws* (WT/ACC/CHN/40) (November 9, 2000).

20. Keith E. Maskus and Jerome H. Reichman, "The Globalization of Private Knowledge Goods and the Privatization of Global Public Goods," in *Journal of International Economic Law* 7, no. 2 (2004): 282.

21. Will Martin and Alan Winters, "The Uruguay Round: A Milestone for Developing Countries," in Will Martin and Alan Winters (eds.), *The Uruguay Round and the Developing Countries* (Cambridge: Cambridge University Press, 1996), p. 25.

22. "Appropriability of knowledge" relates to the fact that certain tangible goods gain public utility because of the knowledge that has been invested in their creation. In other words, as certain products become publicly desirable, or even essential, the inventors may want to improve them to further enhance the quality of life. The argument is made that the inventors will only do this if intellectual property laws protect their inventions.

23. Carlos A. Primo Braga, "Trade-Related Intellectual Property Issues: The Uruguay Round Agreement and Its Economic Implications," in Will Martin and Allan Winters (eds.), *The Uruguay Round and the Developing Countries* (Cambridge: Cambridge University Press, 1996), p. 370.

24. The first 1961 International Convention for the Protection of New Varieties of Plants was signed exclusively by a group of top industrialized countries. The convention has been revised several times (1972, 1978, and 1991) and following the inclusion of TRIPs within the WTO framework, many developing countries have signed it. As of June 2007, the UPOV membership includes sixty-four countries.

25. The ten founding members were Belgium, Brazil, France, Italy, the Netherlands, Portugal, Spain, Switzerland, Tunesia, and the UK. As of June 2007, the Paris Convention has 171 members.

26. WTO, "Annex 1C," Article 33.

27. Sell, *Private Power, Public Law*, pp. 40–41.

28. Jerome H. Reichman, "Securing Compliance with the TRIPS Agreement After US v India," *Journal of International Economic Law* 1, no. 4 (1998): 586.

29. Jerome H. Reichman, "Universal Minimum Standards of Intellectual Rights Protection Under the TRIPS Component of the WTO Agreement," in Carlos M. Correa and Abdulqawi A. Yusuf (eds.), *Intellectual Property and International Trade: The TRIPS Agreement* (Boston and London: Kluwer Law International, 1998), pp. 72–75.

30. Adrian Otten, "Implementation of TRIPS Agreement," *Journal of International Economic Law* 1, no. 4 (1998): 533.

31. WTO, *Scope and Modalities of Non-Violation Complaints Under the TRIPS Agreement—Communication from the US* (IP/C/W/194) (July 17, 2000); WTO, *Non-Violation Nullification or Impairment Under the TRIPS Agreement—Communication from Canada, the Czech Republic, the EC, Hungary and Turkey* (IP/C/W/191) (June 22, 1999); WTO, *Non-Violation Nullification or Impairment Under the TRIPS Agreemen—Communication from Cuba, the Dominican Republic, Egypt, Indonesia, Malaysia and Pakistan* (IP/C/W/141) (April 29, 1999); WTO, *Non-Violation Nullification or Impairment Under the TRIPS Agreement—Communication from Canada* (IP/C/W/127) (February 10, 1999).

32. Asoke Mukerji, "Developing Countries and the WTO—Issues of Implementation," *Journal of World Trade* 34, no. 1 (2000): 55.

33. WTO, *Annual Report of the Council for TRIPS* (IP/C/22) (December 6, 2000); WTO *General Council: Implementation-Related Issues and Concerns* (WT/L/384) (December 19, 2000); and WTO, *Annual Report of the Council for TRIPS* (IP/C/23) (October 5, 2001).

34. Maskus, *Intellectual Property Rights,* p. 20.

35. Ibid., p. 21.

36. Thomas Cottier, "The Protection of Genetic Resources and Traditional Knowledge: Towards More Specific Rights and Obligations in World Trade Law," *Journal of International Economic Law* 1, no. 4 (1998): 555–584.

37. Roman Grynberg and Roy Mickey Joy, "The Accession of Vanuatu to the WTO—Lessons for the Multilateral Trading System," *Journal of World Trade* 34, no. 6 (2000): 166.

38. The full text of the convention is located at: www.cbd.int.

39. Sell, *Private Power, Public Law,* p. 143.

40. Correa, *Intellectual Property Rights,* pp. 167–171.

41. Sell, *Private Power, Public Law,* p. 141.

42. WTO, *Report of the Council for TRIPS* (IP/C/8) (November 6, 1996).

43. WTO, *Declaration of the Group of 77 and China on the Fourth WTO Ministerial Conference at Doha, Qatar* (WT/L/424) (October 24, 2001).

44. WTO, *Ministerial Declaration* (WT/MIN(01)/DEC/W/1) (November 14, 2001).

45. Frederick M. Abbott, "The TRIPS Agreement, Access to Medicines, and the WTO Doha Ministerial Conference," *Journal of World Intellectual Property* 5, no. 1 (2002): 18.

46. Primo Braga, "Trade-Related Intellectual Property Issues," p. 356.

47. A compulsory license is a license typically granted by a government, with or without the consent of the title owner, which permits a party other than the original titleholder to use a patent.

48. Abbott, "The TRIPS Agreement," p. 24.

49. Maskus, *Intellectual Property Rights,* pp. 21, 178.

50. WTO, *Declaration on the TRIPS Agreement and Public Health* (WT/Min/[01]/Dec/W/2) (November 14, 2001).

51. John S. Odell and Susan K. Sell, "Reframing the Issue: The WTO

Coalition on Intellectual Property and Public Health, 2001," in John S. Odell (ed.), *Negotiating Trade—Developing Countries in the WTO and NAFTA* (Cambridge, UK, and New York: Cambridge University Press, 2006), p. 106.

52. WTO, *Hong Kong Ministerial Declaration—Doha Work Programme* (WT/Min/[05]/W/3/Rev.2) (December 18, 2005).

53. Ryan, *Knowledge Diplomacy,* pp. 42–45.

54. Odell and Sell, "Reframing the Issue," pp. 85–114.

55. Tshimanga Kongolo, "Public Interest Versus the Pharmaceutical Industry's Monopoly in South Africa," *Journal of World Intellectual Property* 4, no. 5 (2001): 609.

56. Ibid., pp. 609–621.

57. Sell, *Private Power, Public Law,* pp. 124–129.

58. WTO, *Brazil—Measures Affecting Patent Protection—Complaint by the US* (WT/DS199/1) (June 8, 2000); WTO, *Request to Join Consultation by the EC* (WT/DS199/2) (June 20, 2000); WTO, *Request for Establishment of the Panel* (WT/DS199/3) (January 8, 2001); WTO, *Mutually Agreed Solution* (WT/DS199/4) (July 19, 2001); WTO, *India—Patent Protection for Pharmaceutical and Agricultural Chemical Products—Complaint by the US* (WT/DS50/1) (July 9, 1996).

59. See the following articles: "US in Talks on Anthrax Patent," *Financial Times,* October 21, 2001; "Editorial Comment: Patent Abuse," *Financial Times,* October 22, 2001; "Ottawa Pays Twice for Cipro," *Globe and Mail,* October 23, 2001.

60. WTO, *Hong Kong Ministerial Declaration.*

61. The eight founding members were Belgium, France, Germany, Italy, Spain, Switzerland, Tunisia, and the UK. It has 163 members as of June 2007.

62. See all the relevant documents at www.wipo.org.

63. The framers of the US Constitution ensured that copyright law was under federal jurisdiction (Article I, Section 8[43]). Congress subsequently enacted the Copyright Act of 1790 and major revisions to it in 1831, 1870, 1909, and 1976.

64. As cited in Paul Goldstein, *Copyright's Highway—From Gutenberg to the Celestial Jukebox* (New York: Hill and Wang Publishers, 1994), p. 184.

65. The United States did sign the Paris Convention in 1887, but for decades its patent system remained quite weak.

66. May and Sell, *Intellectual Property Rights*, pp. 58–87.

67. Ibid., p. 83.

68. Goldstein, *Copyright's Highway,* pp. 42–43.

69. Deborah Z. Cass, *The Constitutionalization of the World Trade Organization—Legitimacy, Democracy, and Community in the International Trading System* (Oxford, UK: Oxford University Press, 2005), p. 212.

70. Benn McGrady, "TRIPS and Trademarks: The Case of Tobacco," *World Trade Review* 3, no. 1 (2004): 55–56.

71. This was in fact affirmed by the GATT panel *Thailand—Restrictions on Importation and Internal Taxes on Cigarettes* (BISD/37S/200) (November 7, 1990), as explained in McGrady, "TRIPS and Trademarks," pp. 53–82.

72. Ibid., pp. 60–61.

73. Ibid., p. 78.

PART 3

Emerging Concerns

CHAPTER 7

New Trade Issues on the World Trade Organization Agenda

Following the completion of the Uruguay Round, questions have been raised about how many more trade-related issues should be included under the WTO legal umbrella. If intellectual property rights had been brought into the WTO on the premise that they are strongly connected with international trade policy to the point of establishing TRIPs, the same argument could be made in favor of designing and including within the WTO framework new agreements on the environment, investment, and labor standards. Any extension of WTO rules to additional areas could be supported by the contention that as a global organization the WTO should be responsible for covering a broad range of activities related to trade. This line of reasoning, however, does not sit well with the economically weaker members of the WTO. If one takes into account the ongoing WTO implementation problems experienced by many developing countries, it is hard not to feel apprehensive about creating even more obligations by adding new agreements.

Nonetheless, soon after the WTO was established, the idea of further expanding the scope of the organization has been continuously advanced. At the First Ministerial Conference in Singapore in December 1996, WTO members under the leadership of the EC and the United States started contemplating agreements on investment, trade facilitation, competition policy, and government procurement. These so-called Singapore issues were viewed as a necessary progression of the Uruguay Round, although their supporters varied when prioritizing among them. The EC together with Switzerland called for the establishment of a multilateral framework on trade and investment within the WTO. The United States supported enhancing all present investment-related provisions, but together with the UK and

Japan they particularly stressed the importance of creating a multilateral government procurement agreement. Furthermore, at the same ministerial meeting, the WTO Committee on Trade and Environment released its strongest report to date. As a result, WTO members spent a considerable amount of time talking about the environmental aspects of trade. The United States in concert with a number of European countries made headlines when their representatives suggested the WTO should aspire toward promoting core labor standards on a multilateral level.

From the start, developing countries as a group were very reluctant to negotiate additional agreements and became particularly frustrated with calls for establishing a formalized arrangement connecting investment, labor, and environment with the existing WTO agreements. They felt that any new obligations concerning such issues would be used for protectionist purposes to target and isolate developing countries with weaker regulations in these areas. During the Third Ministerial Conference in Seattle in 1999, a talk given by President Bill Clinton in support of including labor standards in the WTO received massive condemnation by developing countries. Heavily contested by the majority of WTO membership, the Singapore issues eventually lost their sense of urgency in the WTO, but they have never quite disappeared. This is because many European states, the United States, Canada, and Australia are facing growing demands from their domestic constituencies to link, if not directly include, the issues of environment, labor, and investment within the WTO. While civil society groups insist on placing the environment and labor on the WTO agenda, business groups note that a multilateral investment agreement is long overdue.

However, as has been shown in the previous chapters, the changing power relations within the world trading system and the altered dynamics inside the WTO make it impossible for the developed countries to press forward their demands on the WTO agenda in a unilateral fashion. Difficulties in advancing new trade issues in the WTO compelled the developed countries to look for an alternative approach to enlarging the scope of the existing multilateral obligations. This approach starts with bringing new trade-related issues onto the stage of international economic relations by negotiating them first outside the formal decisionmaking structures in the WTO. This approach relies on setting new precedents during bilateral trade deals and the WTO accession negotiations. By having new issues accepted by their trading partners in bilateral negotiations and WTO accession negotiations, the developed countries, most notably the EC and the United States, hope to have them eventually acknowledged by the majority of WTO members and then included in the formal multilateral talks.

This chapter first examines some of the most prevalent new trade-related issues and tries to determine how suitable they are for inclusion in the WTO. The second part of the chapter explains the WTO accession as a power-driven process, which is progressively being used to enlarge the scope of the WTO obligations. It also briefly describes the US-Jordan free-trade agreement as an example of a bilateral deal used as a precedent to formally include new issues in a free-trade agreement. Jordan was a new member of the WTO in 2000 when it was invited to negotiate a unique trade deal with the United States that for the first time ever included formal provisions on the environment and labor standards.

Investment and Competition Policy

Among the four Singapore issues identified during the First WTO Ministerial Conference as subjects of future multilateral talks, investment has remained perhaps the most vital focus of discussions. Since the 1980s the international investment flows have been persistently rising. New improvements in telecommunication and transportation technologies provided corporations with incentives to create new patterns of production by investing and establishing offshore manufacturing facilities. In time the unprecedented growth in foreign direct investment worldwide became a major globalizing force in the world economy. Nonetheless, no consistent set of global rules ever existed to help regulate, manage, and monitor international investment. By the 1990s many countries had negotiated bilateral investment treaties with their major trading partners, thus creating many inconsistencies, ambiguities, and uncertainties for investors caused by a multiplicity of treaties.[1]

The investment-related issues became part of the Uruguay Round from the beginning. Together with services and intellectual property, investment provisions were supposed to transform GATT into an organization that is sensitive to the needs of investors operating in a global trade system. Yet the investment negotiations fell short of the initial expectations. Developing countries, fearing being overburdened with new obligations, kept resisting most of the new issues listed in the Punta del Este Declaration. However, they also feared being left behind in the momentum generated during the Uruguay Round. In the end, the major trading countries had to seek a compromise and save the agreements on services and intellectual property. Hence, they lowered their ambitions when negotiating investment-related provisions.

The result is the Agreement on Trade-Related Investment Measures (TRIMs) that singles out and brings together two of the GATT articles that form the basic GATT obligations about national treatment and the requirement to avoid quantitative restrictions on trade.[2] These provisions are relevant in the context of foreign investment because they state that certain performance requirements, which host countries can be imposing on foreign investors, are inconsistent with WTO obligations. At the insistence of developing countries, TRIMs only concerns the most-recognized trade-distorting restrictions. These include local content requirements and export performance requirements.[3] TRIMs requires all WTO members to eliminate the prohibited measures, but only those affecting trade in goods since the agreement does not cover services. However, there are separate provisions in the GATS that relate to the commercial presence of service providers that were discussed in Chapter 5. TRIMs does not provide any investment security guarantees against expropriation, nor does it give any right to compensation. Overall, these scattered provisions resemble a loosely connected patchwork of rules rather than a comprehensive legal framework on investment.

One of the reasons why the major developed countries gave up on negotiating a stronger investment agreement during the Uruguay Round had to do with moving the negotiations on such an agreement to the Organization for Economic Cooperation and Development. Established in 1961 in France as the institutional facilitator of sustainable growth among the twenty major developed countries, the OECD has continued to be viewed as an organization with limited membership.[4] When the OECD started to negotiate a Multilateral Agreement on Investment (MAI) in 1995, the negotiators hoped that the final deal would serve as a blueprint for the future WTO agreement on investment. Controversial from the start, the MAI negotiations provoked a wave of protests on the streets, with many civil society groups openly campaigning against the agreement and criticizing its proposed safeguards for social, labor, and environmental policies that they deemed to be weak. Furthermore, there was also a sense that the OECD was not the right forum to negotiate such an agreement. After all, the OECD is still a restricted club of the major industrialized countries. As the world economy was undergoing major transformation in favor of new emerging economies, the scheme of keeping developing countries as a group outside the talks on global investment turned out to be unworkable. The MAI talks eventually collapsed in 1997.

Agreeing to a set of global investment rules is very difficult since foreign private investment remains controversial and heavily restricted in many parts of the world. In an attempt to revitalize the talks, investment issues came back to the WTO. There are several factors that support the idea of establishing a multilateral agreement on investment within the WTO. The first one takes an argument that precipitated the creation of GATT, namely the goal to abolish discriminatory investment practices worldwide. Bringing the investment into the WTO would mean the application of the MFN principle of nondiscrimination. The second factor has to do with predictability and transparency of investment provisions. Currently, it is almost impossible to properly assess various investment provisions given the hundreds of bilateral investment treaties (BITs) that exist around the world. By the end of 2003, there were more than 2,332 such BITs concluded, with 85 percent of them finalized after 1990.[5]

It is argued that to harmonize numerous international investment provisions under a single multilateral treaty would greatly improve transparency of investment worldwide. It would allow better understanding into how investment flows are regulated and managed around the world. The next factor in favor of bringing rules on investment into the WTO has to do with regulating market access to ensure elimination of unfair restrictions. A unified set of global standards would be identified to prevent unfair practices. Another factor relates to the most chronic apprehension experienced by foreign investors: fear of expropriation and security of investment. It is believed that under the formal WTO the investment-related practices could be properly monitored. Any violations would be brought to the attention of the WTO dispute settlement mechanism with hope of settling the dispute in a formal and transparent manner. Finally, it is often argued that bringing investment into the WTO would greatly facilitate foreign investment activities, including flows to developing countries. In 1992 the World Bank elaborated official "Guidelines on the Legal Treatment of Foreign Investment" that would take into account the above factors. These guidelines represent a nonbinding legal framework consisting of broadly accepted and already existing legal instruments intended to promote foreign investment by the global harmonization of standards.[6] The guidelines have been used as a starting point during the multilateral investment talks.

Following the decision undertaken in Singapore, the Working Group on the Relationship Between Trade and Investment was established. Its report, released just before the Doha Ministerial Conference in 2001, contributed to placing the investment on the ministerial declaration, although the findings of the working group were deemed inconclusive.[7] Some WTO members in fact defended their preference for biiateral investment agreements, and they expressed the view "that bilateral investment treaties provided adequate transparency, stability and predictability of host countries' investment regimes. They permitted host countries to liberalize their investment regimes autonomously, and while doing so to maintain flexibility in the policies they adopted towards FDI."[8] Other WTO members continued to cautiously advocate a multilateral investment agreement in the WTO, such that

> the value-added of multilateral investment rules in the WTO should be seen primarily in light of the role they could play in increasing the attractiveness of the investment climate in host countries by providing legal certainty for foreign investors. In this regard it was felt that they could contribute to increasing flows of FDI, but it was acknowledged there could be no guarantee of this given that FDI flows were dependent on such a wide range of economic and other factors.[9]

A representative of India expressed the first view. It reflected a position taken by most developing countries. It was clear that any additional agreement that necessitates changes in regulatory or administrative policies would be strongly resisted by developing members of the WTO, even if such an agreement would claim as its goal enhancing world economic welfare. There is a growing skepticism among WTO membership regarding the argumentation used to promote new agreements. In the words of Brian Hindlay: "One problem is that 'world economic welfare' includes the welfare of countries that would have to change their policies as a consequence of the new agreement. The right of a Member of the WTO to pursue policies that, in the view of other Members, amount to shooting itself in the foot, becomes an issue."[10]

The lofty rhetoric about enhancing economic welfare is no match for the high costs of implementing new agreements as estimated by developing countries. This is why the Singapore issues have slowly faded from the WTO talks. The 2005 Hong Kong Ministerial Declaration hardly even mentions them. For example, it only says that on government procurement WTO members should engage in more focused discussions. The Agreement on Government Procurement was first negotiated during the Tokyo Round as a separate code with optional membership. Almost thirty years later it still has the same status. It is one of the two agreements that remain plurilateral, the other being an agreement on civil aircraft. The talks during the Uruguay Round significantly extended its coverage, but mainly developed countries participated in the negotiations.[11] Because of the resistance of developing countries, it was agreed to keep the agreement on government procurement outside the WTO single undertaking until the next round of talks. Furthermore, the Hong Kong Declaration does not list any new initiative on investment. In fact, it has been difficult enough to implement the existing WTO provisions. For example, least-developed countries receive a break with respect to their TRIMs implementation problems. They are allowed to maintain, on a temporary basis, their old policies and trade measures that deviate from their obligations under the TRIMs agreement.[12]

The Hong Kong Declaration, however, does contain a special annex on trade facilitation. This makes sense as the enhancement of trade facilitation capacity in developing countries is supported by technical assistance and means the improvement of essential auxiliary services and procedures that tend to be overly cumbersome in the developing world. The annex prioritizes some areas like publication procedures, border and customs measures, measures to enhance impartiality and nondiscrimination, and formalities and fees connected with cross-border trade. Despite being considered a new trade issue, trade facilitation was never intended to grow into a formal agreement. Perhaps the least controversial, trade facilitation is an important aspect of modernizing the way goods are traded by eliminating the proverbial "red tape" that hinders many trade-related procedures.

Competition policy has also vanished from the WTO list of priorities, although after the meeting in Singapore it was closely linked with the investment talks. To complicate things further, arguably it is difficult to define competition policy as "any policy that promotes the contestability of markets—for instance, trade liberalization, more open government procurement arrangements, control of the protectionist abuse of technical standards, and the reduction of subsidies."[13] Competition policies are most often governmental policies and laws that are designed for regulating the activities of firms, both domestic and foreign, operating under particular jurisdiction. The push for an international framework that would establish standards to guide the domestic application of competition policies is meant to reduce distortive effects of such policies. A commonly cited example is Japan, known for its vertical monopolies *(keiretsu)* that engage in both production and distribution. The United States has long been contesting these vertical corporate monopolies, claiming that they effectively restrict access to foreign suppliers.[14] A proposed WTO agreement on competition policy would attempt to limit the influence of such anticompetitive behavior. Still, even the United States is reluctant to fully support an international treaty that would potentially have a say about the way its domestic regulations are designed. In the end, most WTO members think that these matters should, at least for now, be kept under the jurisdiction of individual states.

Labor Standards and Trade

One of the more controversial linkages to enter multilateral trade negotiations has been that between trade and labor. Historically speaking, labor standards have been primarily monitored and regulated domestically by individual states. If they become linked with trade and monitored under the legal system of the WTO, many countries would perceive such a move as a direct loss of their autonomy. Bringing labor standards into the WTO would mean that countries that violate them could be the subject of trade disputes and possible retaliation. Very few countries want their domestic laws to be shaped and adjudicated by the WTO dispute settlement mechanism. Nonetheless, domestic labor laws are informed by international law as shaped by the conventions articulated by the International Labour Organization (ILO). In terms of enforcement, however, it remains the domain of the individual state. More recently, however, the steady growth of international trade, new flexible modes of production, cross-continental spread of foreign investment, and the emergence of new powerful economies in Asia and Latin America challenged the ability of states to promote and enforce fair and equitable labor standards.[15]

According to those who consider globalization to largely be an unrestrained force of economic liberalization, we are living in a world where multinational corporations are reaping benefits by moving their production activities to countries with low labor and environmental standards. This new international division of labor allows companies to make huge profits by using low-paid workers in the developing world, most notably in China. Indeed, China is a major recipient of foreign direct investment, the largest among developing countries. During the 1990s, over US$320 billion flowed into its economy.[16] Whether or not this investment is connected with a lower-paid and abundant labor force in China is hardly debatable. From an economic point of view, China does possess comparative advantage with respect to lower-cost labor.

Due to the asymmetrical distribution of global wealth and the lack of economic development in a number of exporting countries, concerns have been raised that goods manufactured in many developing countries may have been made under impoverished labor conditions. A lack of implementation and enforcement may mean that in some societies certain labor laws understood as core or basic in the developed world are denied to workers. Such labor laws would concern, for example, minimum wage and/or maximum hours, the minimum age for children to work, gender discrimination at the workplace, compulsory and forced labor, as well as health and safety. As a result, there are calls for bringing a labor agreement into the WTO.

From the point of view of developing countries, the problematic aspect of linking labor with trade is the fact that the calls demanding global enforcement of appropriate labor standards via trade agreements mostly come from governments and lobbying groups located in the developed world. Their demands may be rooted in an altruistic desire to see that a bar of morality and ethics are upheld in order that the goods purchased in department stores would be untainted with the fact that they were produced under unjust labor conditions. After all, at the very crux of the issue is not simply the relationship between the employer and the employee, but human rights. Developing countries, nevertheless, charge that these supposed moral concerns disguise protectionism for fear that domestic industries in the West would lose their edge to companies that invest in the developing world.[17]

Furthermore, companies may direct their investment to those areas where labor standards are relatively lower to reduce their expenditures. Indeed, this issue is not at all dissimilar to those concerns raised with respect to the environment: If there are no rules governing the production processes of exported goods in the multilateral trading system, then states may be tempted to reduce their standards in a “race to the bottom” to attract new investment and maintain the competitiveness of their industries. Given how the WTO manages world trade within the global economy, it therefore makes sense, according to those who demand greater appreciation and sensitivity toward labor issues, for the organization to incorporate a set of labor laws in its legal framework and provide allowances for trade action, not unlike antidumping measures and countervailing duties, to use against offending states. The official position of the WTO is that labor standards are outside its jurisdiction and that the only organization competent to deal with the labor issues is the ILO. The 1948 Havana Charter of the proposed ITO explicitly incorporated provisions aimed at eliminating unfair labor conditions, although the critics may speculate about whether this was not yet another reason for its collapse.[18] It is a point that is all too pervasive that the Havana Charter was too ambitious in trying to address a variety of trade-related issues.

The argument of the WTO's institutional competence is worth exploring. One must wonder if the WTO would be the appropriate organization to fulfill these admittedly normative demands and apply a set of rules that govern trade-labor linkages, especially since there is already an international organization that is tasked with the duty of advancing and monitoring workers' rights.

The ILO was created pursuant to the 1919 Treaty of Versailles to establish international labor standards and thereby ensure the protection of workers around the world. Its humanitarianism is complemented by real political concerns that worker injustices could lead to domestic unrest that may spill over regionally. Economic considerations are also a factor. As the website of the ILO itself states, "because of its inevitable effect on the cost of production, any industry or country adopting social reform would find itself at a disadvantage vis-à-vis its competitors."[19] Over the years, subsequent conventions were signed at ILO conferences, which are held yearly. They become part of international labor law once they are adopted by a required number of countries, and some are legally binding; however, there is no mechanism to enforce compliance. Governments are nevertheless required to submit reports to describe the fulfillment of their treaty obligations. Since its establishment, the ILO has adopted more than 400 binding conventions and nonbinding recommendations. The ILO Declaration on Fundamental Principles and Rights at Work lists a number of core standards, but their precise definition and the scope of how they should be applied remains under debate.[20] This seems to indicate that the ILO is more competent to deal with labor-related subjects than the WTO. The WTO already suffers from a poorly developed institutional structure that does not adequately support its decisionmaking processes. Add to that a limited number of experts on hand. The WTO Secretariat in Geneva employs just over 600 people, the lowest number for any such organization.

The WTO may not even be the appropriate organization to deal with labor-related issues simply because of the potential use of measures that may bear inadvertent consequences that would exacerbate the problems that are sought to be resolved. For instance, should there be greater appreciation of labor rights within the WTO's legal framework, it may open the door for countries to apply trade measures against those states in which local industries are able to benefit from lower labor standards. But those trade sanctions may have unintended consequences. Suppose then that the United States levies a set of restrictions on imports from Bangladesh to compel the South Asian country to adopt higher labor standards. The prices of those imports would rise and fewer of them would be bought, thus leading to a contraction of the targeted industry. That industry in Bangladesh would then have to release its workers from employment, leaving them to find employment in other sectors or even in an underground economy. Unemployment would subsequently rise and poverty would be made worse. This perverse outcome would be true should Bangladesh fail to accede to US demands for higher labor standards, and this has been shown to happen in cases where economic restrictions enacted to reduce child labor have forced children into more egregious forms of employment (e.g., prostitution).[21] If Bangladesh were to respond favorably to the sanctions, then the higher labor standards that would become implemented would not reflect the preferences of Bangladeshi society.[22] However, the enforcement of basic labor rights could entail an increase in domestic welfare if markets had hitherto failed because of worker intimidation and slave labor.

What should be noted is that, as a number of empirical studies have demonstrated, differences in labor standards do not have as much of an impact on comparative advantage as some critics have long pointed out.[23] The claims that foreign producers benefit from lower labor standards such that the competitiveness of a country in which firms and workers are subject to lower standards is higher have little basis in the theory of comparative advantage and are prone to be manipulated by protectionist interests. Furthermore, abstract economic theory has shown that wages are, part and parcel, a function of a country's level of economic development and wealth. For example, workers in our Bangladeshi example may earn a third of the real wages earned by their US counterparts, but they could also be less productive. If the former were only a third as productive as the latter, owing to differences in equipment and expertise, the firm would be indifferent about basing its operations there. Alternatively, a company that prefers to make shoes in Bangladesh rather than the United States may realize that US productivity levels are higher but recognizes that the lower costs of Bangladeshi workers offset the losses in productivity, as well as transportation and other administrative costs that are associated with outsourcing production overseas. In other words, differences in wages can be balanced by differences in productivity. Trade restrictions would have perverse effects on the problems they attempt to fix.

Although Article XX(e) of GATT states that trade measures may be pursued against those goods that were produced using prison labor, there is no provision in GATT, which is now part of the WTO, that explicitly permits trade action to be taken against goods produced in circumstances where labor standards are not upheld.[24] The reference to "public morals" in Article XX(a) may conceivably be "invoked to justify trade sanctions against producers that involve the use of child labor or the denial of basic workers' rights."[25] As of 2008 no complaints have ever been brought forth in either GATT or the WTO that bore witness to this possibility.

The United States, along with other Western states such as France, insisted on the inclusion of a "social clause" that would be added on the multilateral trade agenda. The social clause would have entailed the availability of trade sanctions as a means to legally discriminate against foreign products in order to observe a core set of labor rights enshrined through the legal framework provided by the ILO. Developing countries, unsurprisingly, rejected these proposals and articulated a statement that reaffirmed the promotion of labor rights but recognized that it is through trade liberalization and economic development, rather than measures that may be protectionist in actual intent, that higher labor standards can be obtained.[26] Notwithstanding the implicit paternalism underpinning the social clause, the position of the developing countries here stems from the recognition that such sanctions would have perverse consequences that may potentially worsen the very work environments that they are targeted to improve.

In the event that a country does place trade sanctions on another country out of concern over the circumstances under which the targeted imports were produced, one can infer from several key WTO rulings that the restrictions would face a host of legal problems. As Patrick Macklem points out, the 1998 *Shrimps/Turtle* case demonstrated well the difficulties of placing trade restrictions for noneconomic purposes. The Appellate Body had found that the US ban on shrimp imports from countries deemed to practice unacceptable catching methods that endanger the lives of sea turtles was unfair and discriminatory. After all, the United States did not pursue meaningful negotiations with banned countries nor did it provide all countries with appropriate technologies and transition periods to adjust their practices. The certifying process itself was peremptory as it left little opportunity for affected countries to repeal the ban.[27]

The reasons provided by the Appellate Body in justifying its decision do give some insight on how a trade restriction imposed for noneconomic purposes should be pursued. To quote Macklem at length:

> First, a state seeking to restrict market access to goods produced under conditions that violate international labor rights must adopt the least trade restrictive means of accomplishing this purpose. Secondly, a state must treat all states in a similar manner and take into account different but comparable policies in countries that might be adversely affected by such an initiative. Thirdly, trade restrictions cannot be imposed in the absence of an adjudicative process in which alleged rights violations are tested in a procedurally fair manner. Fourthly, a state is under a duty to negotiate with all those affected before implementing trade restrictions. Fifthly, it must provide a transition period to enable compliance before imposing a trade restriction. Finally, a state should offer technical assistance to assist in the rectification of conditions that might otherwise trigger trade restrictions.[28]

There is, needless to say, little space to maneuver for a state wishing to enact a trade restriction that would satisfy the rules of the WTO-managed trading system.

The Environment and Trade

In the last several decades, the one issue that has gathered greater attention and focus has been that of the environment. As climate change appears increasingly apparent, with its attendant natural disasters, droughts, and floods, the environment has gained much coverage in becoming a more salient "low politics" issue in international relations. The 1972 United Nations Conference on the Human Environment helped initiate international environmental law and paved the way for the World Commission on Environment and Development (the Brundtland Commission), which in 1987 released a report calling for development that meets the needs of the present without compromising the ability of future generations to meet their own needs. Five years later a series of multilateral documents dealing with the issue of sustainable development were adopted by more than 178 governments at the United Nations Conference on Environment and Development held in Rio de Janeiro, Brazil, in June 1992. The Rio de Janeiro Earth Summit led to the adoption of legally binding treaties that enunciated the imperatives to reduce greenhouse gas emissions and strive for biological conservation.

Contemporaneous with these developments was of course the greater economic liberalization that the global economy has seen under the WTO. Some might view the parallel salience of environmental awareness and neoliberal economics as contradictory. After all, a principal concern is that economic liberalization, and the concomitant need for global harmonization, would put pressures on governments to relax environmental standards and regulations to maintain their economies' competitiveness. Moreover, certain treaties place restrictions on what goods may not be traded. The

Basel Convention, which banned the trade of hazardous waste materials from developed to developing countries, comes to mind.[29] One must then wonder whether an organization like the WTO should be more appreciative of environmental concerns and therefore less aloof about how free trade and economic liberalization may affect the environment.

A number of scholars and decisionmakers within the WTO itself argue that the organization should remain a technical organization that maintains a primary focus on monitoring international trade. According to this view, environmental issues are beyond its purview and, furthermore, outside its competence. Yet, as Chantal Thomas points out, the inclusion of intellectual property rights within the disciplines of the WTO show that certain subjects that are prima facie unrelated to exchange and transactions can be included under the WTO's legal framework. The precedent set by including TRIPs in the WTO also means that other trade-related matters (such as the environment) may be disciplined.[30]

By placing TRIPs under the multilateral framework of rules, the negotiators indicated there need not be cross-border activity involved in creating new agreements since TRIPs may be violated when there are no foreign parties to a transaction involved. Under the agreement, domestic transgressions of intellectual property rights protections are deemed to have adverse effects on the international economy. Environmental agreements are similar such that domestic noncompliance may have ramifications for the global environment.[31] This is all to say nothing of how TRIPs has been negotiated and implemented under the ambit of the WTO.

Given the very pervasiveness of trade in many facets of daily life, it now seems too naïve to presuppose that an organization concerning trade should simply restrict itself, crudely speaking, to the mere reduction of tariffs and abolition of quota systems. In fact, one of the arguments for inclusion of services and intellectual property in the WTO suggested that the changing patterns of production and greater global market integration necessitated the creation of new agreements.

While environmental issues can at times be very normative, for the values espoused by sympathetic activists are at odds with the seeming indifference that permeates the usually environmentally neutral language of GATT/WTO trade agreements, the wide effects economic activity can have on the environment, locally and even globally, may warrant a certain degree of attention to be paid to the environment on the WTO's agenda. The general agreement had already certain provisions that remarked on the need for trade to be sensitive to animal and plant life. Article XX of GATT allows certain measures to be exempt from the usual prohibitions of the WTO when they are used, both nonarbitrarily and not to disguise actual protectionism, to "protect human, animal or plant life or health" and to conserve "exhaustible natural resources if such measures are made effective in conjunction with restrictions on domestic production or consumption."[32] While the word "environment" itself is conspicuously absent in the language of Article XX, the drafters thought that these clauses were sufficient. Furthermore, given the predilections of national governments for self-interest, much concern was dedicated to the prospects that environmental concerns would be pursued to further ulterior state motives that in actuality place greater priority on protectionism than the conservation of wildlife habitats.

It may also be difficult to enforce domestic environmental standards and regulations with respect to exports of like products. The infamous *Tuna/Dolphin* case was illustrative of these challenges. The dispute began when Mexico filed a grievance against the United States in 1991 for its embargo on Mexican tuna. US authorities contended that the netting practices of catching tuna used by Mexican fishermen were destructive toward the dolphin population. After all, US tuna producers are subject to the law because the Dolphin Protection Consumer Information Act requires producers to catch tuna in such a way that the lives of dolphins are not placed at risk. Because Mexican practices of catching tuna were insufficient in reducing the endangerment of dolphins, they faced an import ban in the United States. Mexico had therefore argued that this amounted to a violation of Article XI of GATT, which stipulated the prohibition of quantitative restrictions on imports with certain exemptions. The panel agreed with Mexico's contention, further adding that Article XX could not justify the ban because the United States could not provide animal protection beyond its borders. As the panel elucidated in its closing remarks, "a Contracting Party may not restrict imports of a product merely because it originates in a country with environmental policies different from its own."[33]

Even though Mexico and the United States would eventually resolve the dispute bilaterally, the never-adopted ruling on the *Tuna/Dolphin* case was a public relations blow to the WTO. The fears of activists that an institutional body supervising the liberalization of the global economy would be aloof and indifferent, if not hostile, to environmental issues seemed vindicated—especially when the penalized domestic policies seemed attuned to the imperatives of safeguarding biodiversity. Moreover, the ruling also galvanized concerns that the decisions made by the WTO would impinge on national sovereignty by compelling states to adjust their regulations, be they pertaining to the environment or not, in a teleological pursuit of economic liberalization.

The desire to make the WTO more sensitive to environmental issues nevertheless lacks an appreciation of the many difficulties of making the environment a subject matter for the WTO's agenda. One significant part of the problem is that, in the words of Gary P. Sampson, "while the rationale for environmental regulation is to make discrimination between goods and services mandatory, the rationale for WTO rules is to avoid it, at least for those goods that enter into international trade."[34] Moreover, some WTO rules are ambiguous, for they allow a certain flexibility of interpretation in order to seek greater consensus in a multilateral environment. To impose a greater emphasis on the environment would probably mean that the language of agreements and regulations concerning trade and the environment would have to lose its ambiguity in order to provide more effective solutions and unbending rules geared toward the protection of the environment.[35] Obtaining such an agreement would be difficult, notwithstanding the very challenge of even commencing a new round of multilateral trade negotiations that would center on the environment.

Another challenge would be how the Technical Barriers to Trade (TBT) Agreement already allows WTO members to adopt different domestic standards and regulations. The implications of this provision have led critics to believe that the WTO permits a race to the bottom. According to this argument, which admittedly views the law of comparative advantage as an apparent nonfactor, a country with stringent environmental standards may appear less appealing to businesses as a base for operations should there be another country with more relaxed regulations. The aforementioned agreement delimits the ability of an importing country to impose its standards on production processes on a sovereign territory. Just as the WTO panel ruled that the United States cannot oblige Mexican fishermen to follow its own rules for the fishing of tuna, a country's domestic laws cannot be used to penalize imports. Interestingly enough, as Sampson notes, the discordance of standards between the countries may mean that the industries in the country with the lower standards are hence provided some form of subsidization. How this argument would be addressed and resolved under existing WTO rules is unclear, however.

It would still be erroneous to believe that the WTO has not provided any institutional response to the increasing salience of environmental issues and the possible impacts of environmental policies on international trade. The Committee on Trade and the Environment (CTE) was created following the Marrakesh Decision on Trade and Environment in order to examine "trade measures for environmental purposes including those taken pursuant to multilateral agreements, the relationship between multilateral trading norms and environmental taxes and charges, ecolabelling, and exports of domestically prohibited goods."[36] Though it was partly convened to assuage the demands of US environmental lobbies, a significant impetus for the formation of the CTE was the growing awareness that environmental regulatory policies may influence international trade. After all, as the above discussion has already related, the *Tuna/Dolphin* case had brought negative light over the WTO, and it was clear that there would be similar disputes in the future. The widening use of labels and packaging requirements also necessitated the formation of a committee tasked to explore the linkages of the environment and trade, for European countries feared that such practices would threaten their exports. Rather than the pressure of environmental lobbyists, it was the overall threat to the freedom of international trade, perceived and aggrieved by domestic producers, that helped spur the establishment of the CTE.[37]

A key issue on the CTE's agenda has been that of market access. A number of agricultural exporting countries have in fact invoked environmental rationales to remonstrate with the EU and Japan because of their protectionist policies in agriculture. The trade-distorting subsidies and minimum price guarantees provided by the EU's Common Agricultural Policy (CAP) create incentives for overproduction, which in turn is wasteful. While this is certainly an issue for developing countries, they also wish to restrict the exports of goods from developed countries that are forbidden to be sold domestically in those countries. Nigeria invoked this argument to ban the trade of waste materials out of the enunciated concern that they would damage African ecosystems and wildlife. While this sounds not too unreasonable, it nevertheless ran afoul of the WTO's rules of extraterritoriality that expressly forbid a developing country to be subjected to the domestic standards of developed countries.[38] Not much of the agenda, it seems, is shaped by the lobbying efforts of nongovernmental organizations.

In fact, as a study conducted by Gregory C. Shaffer has shown, the CTE is essentially a microcosm of the WTO itself, as its agenda, and whatever negotiating stalemates may ensue, are determined and shaped by the interests and positions of member states. The WTO does not pass decisions against the wishes of members. Indeed, the seeming lack of accomplishment that has frustrated the CTE's mandates is the result of conflicting interests that are determined at the national level.[39] The conclusions reached here by Shaffer fly in the face of the oft-repeated critiques of the WTO that it is undemocratic and seeks to obtain the powers and status of a world government. The WTO, according to these criticisms, is bent on gradually stripping away the powers of sovereign states to legislate laws that articulate domestic standards and regulations. It is a neoliberal outfit exerting states to abide by its preferences for trade liberalization and reduced government intervention. This is not the case, as Shaffer points out, as states still prioritize the interests of domestic constituencies over the mutual gains made by freer trade in wishing to preserve protectionist policies, which is a reality in direct odds with the liberalizing spirit advocated by neoliberalism. Environmental groups and their sympathetic advocates thereby misplace their criticisms on the organization by inadvertently downplaying the agency and influence of their own governments.

Whatever the fate of the ongoing Doha Round, the Doha Declaration was critical in demonstrating a greater appreciation of the importance of the trade-environmental linkages within the WTO by affirming the necessity to examine the relationship of multilateral environmental agreements and the rules and obligations that underpin the WTO's legal framework, and by furthering trade liberalization with respect to environmental goods and services.[40]

Setting Higher Standards During WTO Accessions

As a universal organization, the WTO invited all countries still outside the system to join it. However, WTO accession is an incredibly challenging process that can take years of negotiations to complete. Countries that have been joining the organization must implement all WTO agreements and they have to meet additional accession-related demands by the existing WTO members. Some of these demands are being called WTO-plus obligations because candidate countries are asked to make commitments that exceed the obligations made by the existing members. In this way, the WTO accession process is being used to establish new standards and to introduce new issues in the WTO.

In order to explain the peculiar nature of the WTO accession process, we must first note that there is a big difference between accession to GATT and accession to the WTO. Under GATT, the protocols of accessions specifically allowed for a limited application of Part II of GATT because of its provisional character. Part II included many of the principal obligations, like those relating to national treatment, quotas, customs procedures, subsidies, and antidumping, and it was given an exception from full implementation because of the provisional nature of GATT. This exemption meant that contracting parties could deviate from those GATT Part II obligations that did not comply with their preexisting laws and legislation.

GATT did not stipulate any membership criteria and the terms of accession were agreed between the contracting parties and the candidate state. Furthermore, because GATT related only to trade in goods, accession negotiations centered on tariff levels and import quotas. Such concerns could be accommodated without placing demands on candidate countries to reform their domestic economies. GATT's contracting parties employed different legal techniques and safeguard clauses in negotiating accession protocols. Nonmarket economies were allowed to join GATT under Article XVII, as previously explained, but they were treated differently within the system. These differences were reflected in respectively different protocols of accession.

In contrast to GATT practice, the WTO protocols of accession bind the acceding governments to observe all rules contained in the WTO agreements, and in addition each protocol binds the new member to observe the specific commitments.[41] These commitments can vary in their depth and their numbers among the acceding countries. The accession of Ecuador, the first country to accede to the WTO, was a novelty for the world trading system. With Ecuador, WTO members began to request commitments concerning compliance with WTO rules, the introduction of new measures and regulations, and the implementation of WTO obligations by the acceding country.[42] The commitments listed in the protocol of accession are legally binding and enforceable via the WTO Dispute Settlement Understanding.

The commitments can be classified according to the following three categories: (1) commitments to abide by the existing WTO rules; (2) commitments about the recourse to particular WTO provisions, such as transitional periods and developing country status under certain agreements; and (3) commitments to abide by rules created by the commitment paragraphs and not contained in the Uruguay Round agreements, which relate to privatization, state-trading, competition policy, regulatory standards, investment-related measures, trade facilitation, and membership in other international organizations. We are particularly interested in the third category because it means that a candidate country can be asked to make excessive commitments on a wide range of issues.

The Accession Protocol of Ecuador incorporates twenty-one specific commitments.[43] Comparable commitment figures for some other governments that have acceded are (in chronological order): Bulgaria, twenty-six;[44] Kyrgyz Republic, twenty-nine;[45] Estonia, twenty-four;[46] Jordan, twenty-nine;[47] Georgia, twenty-nine;[48] Croatia, twenty-seven;[49] Albania, twenty-nine;[50] and Lithuania, twenty-eight.[51] China was required to make eighty-two commitments.[52] The entire package of the Working Party Report, the Protocol of Accession, and the Schedules of Concessions and Commitments in Goods and Services constitute the conditions under which the acceding government is permitted to join the WTO.[53]

It is especially important to recognize that the current commitment approach to WTO accession is possible because of the changes introduced to the dispute settlement mechanism. Under GATT, the weak dispute settlement process provided little assurance as an enforcement mechanism. The legalization of the WTO dispute settlement procedures has created a powerful mechanism to enforce WTO rules and obligations and the commitments made by the acceding countries.

Taken together, the GATT Protocol for the Accession of Poland[54] and the GATT Report of the Working Party are only ten pages long. In contrast, the shortest WTO report of the working party (including protocol) to date under the WTO concerned the accession of Mongolia, which has 30 pages, while the one on the accession of Albania has 60 pages. The Report of the Working Party on the Chinese Accession has 176 pages. The current length of the WTO working party reports reflects the complexity of the negotiations and the depth of the commitments made.

Most important, a large portion of the commitments made by the newly acceding countries concerns the Singapore issues. Most acceding countries were asked to make commitments facilitating the creation of an investment-friendly trade environment, and their laws and regulations, including competition policies, were under scrutiny of the WTO members. Almost all of them—most notable exemptions were Ecuador (the first country to join the WTO) and Nepal (because of least-developed country status)—were asked to join the Agreement on Government Procurement.[55]

In summary, the developed countries have been using the WTO accession process to include the Singapore issues as part of the formal obligations placed upon the newest WTO members. This is possible because of the peculiar character of the WTO accession process, which allows the existing WTO members to set criteria for WTO membership. This, of course, means that despite the legalistic nature of the organization and the democratic nature of the decisionmaking inside the WTO, the organization's accession process seems to be outside these rules, as it is still dominated by the historically powerful trading nations. Let me explain how the process actually works.

Interested countries can apply for membership under WTO Article XII of the Marrakesh Agreement Establishing the World Trade Organization.[56] In order to initiate the accession process, the government of an aspiring country must send an official request for accession under Article XII to the office of the director-general of the WTO. This request is then forwarded to a meeting of the General Council, where a decision is made to establish a working party and designate its chairman.[57] Every interested WTO member can join the working party and become actively involved in the resulting accession negotiations. This is intended to ensure the transparency of the multilateral phase of the accession negotiations. The size of the working party can vary considerably: at the final stages of the Chinese accession, its working party consisted of more than eighty WTO members, while the working party for Vanuatu has less than thirty members. The length of any particular accession is also difficult to predict. The accession of the Kyrgyz Republic was the shortest so far (two years, ten months), while the Chinese accession was the longest (fifteen years, five months).[58]

Article XII of the agreement establishing the WTO concerns the accessions. It is a vague article that does not stipulate any membership criteria, and no procedures are in place to facilitate the process. The "terms to be agreed" are left to the accession negotiations between the existing WTO members and the candidate. The political considerations often influence the demands placed on the acceding countries, causing some accessions to become very lengthy. In this context a very special case of accession is

China, which turned out to be the longest and the most complex to date. In the next chapter, I will discuss some of the implications of the Chinese accession. Russia is another peculiar case exemplifying the intrusiveness of politics. Following the political breakdown of the Soviet Union in 1991, Russia sent an application to join the WTO in June 1993. The negotiations started soon afterward and appeared to be close to their conclusion in 2006. During that year, however, a cavalier position of Russian president Vladimir Putin on the issue of East-West economic and security relations created open hostilities among Russia, several European countries, and even the United States. These hostilities spilled over into the WTO. As of January 2009, the Russian accession to the WTO still looks uncertain.

The WTO accession negotiations in principle should relate only to three main areas: concessions and rules for trade in goods, for trade in services, and in trade-related aspects of intellectual property rights. However, during multilateral meetings, the implementation of the accepted offers and the ability of a state to comply with the WTO obligations are also at issue. Hence, the overall regulatory framework of the country, its administrative institutions, and its capacity to consolidate the promised reforms, are carefully evaluated. We also note here another striking change that took place with the establishment of the WTO. Presently, the acceding countries are routinely asked to submit a legislative plan of action indicating how the implementation of the requested legislative changes and the introduction of the new commercial laws and regulations would proceed. In addition, candidate countries are pressed to present a plan outlining implementation of their commitments with respect to privatization, an investment regime, and other administrative reforms processes. These demands for the so-called WTO-plus commitments have been regarded as an abuse of economic power exercised by a number of countries.[59]

The standards of the WTO accession have evolved in such a way as to provide the existing WTO membership with assurances that a newly acceding country not only complies with the current WTO agreements, but, most important, that it is investment-friendly and willing to harmonize its regulatory framework with the model advanced by the major industrialized countries. To meet these much higher WTO entry requirements, acceding countries routinely go through a thorny and unpredictable structural adjustment process under the supervision of incumbent WTO members.

From an institutional point of view, accession negotiations in each working party follow procedures stipulated in a note by the Secretariat and were partially developed during the GATT era.[60] In the first stage of the accession negotiations, the applicant government is required to provide all members of the working party with a trade policy memorandum describing all aspects of its trade and economic policies that are relevant in the context of the accession negotiations. This particular phase in the accessions process is one of fact finding and is designed to give WTO members an in-depth understanding of the candidate country's economy, with special attention focused on its trade regime. This stage of the process is inevitably intrusive, but the memorandum forms the basis for negotiating the terms of accession.

The memorandum describes in detail the applicant's foreign trade regime and provides relevant statistical data for circulation to all WTO members. It also contains information about the regulatory framework, socioeconomic development, and even political environment of the candidate country.[61] As a rule, no meeting of the working party would take place until a detailed memorandum is prepared by a candidate country and submitted to all interested members. Members of the working party must be satisfied with the quality of the memorandum in terms of the details it provides in order to accept it as a basis for launching the actual negotiations between them and the acceding country. Apart from the many intrusive questions that must be answered in the memorandum, its preparation is costly and it poses serious technical difficulties to the acceding governments, which often have trouble understanding the economic and legal concepts involved.

The established procedures also require that relevant laws and regulations be made available to members of the working party at the same time as the memorandum to ensure that they comply with WTO rules. As is made clear in the technical note,[62] only laws and regulations that are relevant to the particular accession in question should be submitted. In practice, all kinds of laws and regulations are submitted in response to the demands of some members of the working party. After scrutinizing them, any member of the working party can demand that laws and regulations of the acceding country be modified if they do not meet the expected standards. Discussions over the legislative developments and the evaluation of the existing laws of the acceding country by the working party can be very frustrating. This aspect of the accession process is particularly controversial because an economically vulnerable country often feels pressured to design its regulatory framework under the guidance and scrutiny of some members of the WTO. The biggest trading nations are quite involved in every step of the accession processes. This makes the WTO accession negotiations deeply asymmetrical, since the candidate country has no choice but to meet these demands should it desire membership in the WTO.

Since the WTO reflects the free-market perspective and approach toward economic development, many aspects of the acceding countries' agricultural policies require immediate reforms as part of their accession process. One such area is the issue of domestic subsidies that are difficult to maintain by the acceding countries, despite the fact that the major industrialized nations are having tremendous problems with reducing their own level of agricultural domestic support. One of the primary achievements of the Uruguay Round concerning market access for agricultural trade was to replace all existing nontariff quantitative restrictions with bound tariffs. The amount of work that has to be done by the candidate country to fulfill minimum requirements under the WTO Agreement on Agriculture is enormous, to say nothing of the challenges of negotiating new tariff levels.

As a necessary condition to join the organization, WTO members expect candidate countries to offer significant economically liberalizing commitments in a number of important service sectors. The WTO Secretariat, in consultation with its members, has put together a document designed to assist acceding governments in submitting data and information about their policies affecting trade in services.[63] Given the complexities of the trade in services and the flexibilities of the GATS, which are discussed in Chapter 5, it is understandable that acceding countries have experienced difficulties in collecting and presenting the information called for in the note.

Once all the information is collected and the memorandum is completed, the first official meeting of the working party takes place and the negotiations begin. After the meeting, members of the working party submit the comments, questions, and demands posed during the meeting to the WTO Secretariat, which consolidates them and forwards them to the candidate country. Further fact-finding meetings may be held as necessary before some members of the working party begin to negotiate with the applicant. The candidate must also submit additional material with respect to the SPS and TBT agreements.[64] Questions that must be answered by the acceding country in the survey concerning sanitary and phytosanitary measures and so-called technical barriers to trade relate to a wide array of standards that have to meet scientific criteria of risk assessment. The idea is to ensure the quality and safety of agricultural and other products that are being traded.

Although the SPS agreement (and similarly the TBT agreement) does not stipulate certain minimum acceptable standards to which all WTO members must adhere, it nevertheless requires that the standards maintained at the border by a WTO member meet such requirements. In the words of one expert, this essentially means that the SPS agreement "places a heavier burden on developing than on industrial countries—this resulting from the standards already in place in the industrial countries more-or-less being established as the standard to which the developing countries must comply."[65] Naturally, for the majority of the acceding countries, which normally are developing and/or underdeveloped economies, this entails a complete overhaul and eventual reform of many existing industry standards, agricultural productions, and manufacturing facilities.

To sum up, despite the inherently legal nature of the WTO, the accession process follows an unpredictable path of difficult negotiations in which the acceding country is faced with often strenuous demands for introducing sweeping changes to its economic and legal institutions. The rules of the game are decided by the existing WTO members that form the working party on accession. WTO members are legally free to conduct the negotiations in any way they deem necessary. As a result, the Singapore issues that failed to be accepted by the majority of WTO membership remain very much part of the WTO accession negotiations.

In December 1999, Jordan finally completed its WTO accession negotiations. Even though its application was first sent in 1994, the process did not get into its substantive stage until 1996. When the ratification process was completed, Jordan became a WTO member in April 2000.[66] Overall it took six years and four months for Jordan to accede to the WTO.[67] At the time when the Jordanian accession was in its final stages, President Clinton was facing an increasingly hostile US Congress. As we remember from the discussion in Chapter 2. he was not able to receive an extension of the fast-track negotiating authority beyond the time necessary to complete the Uruguay Round. In order to secure congressional support for further trade liberalization, Clinton promised to negotiate the US-Jordan free-trade agreement with provisions obliging the Jordanian government to protect the environment and maintain high labor standards.[68]

Labor and environmental issues have been divisive in the context of multilateral talks. Since the collapse of the 1999 WTO Ministerial Conference in Seattle, it was absolutely clear that Clinton's talk advocating the inclusion of labor provisions in the WTO was a nonstarter.[69] The only way to make the labor standards and the environment into inseparable elements of trade agreements—as demanded by the domestic US constituency—was to place such issues on the negotiating table during bilateral trade talks. The US-Jordan free-trade agreement was negotiated throughout 2000, but it was not approved by the US Congress until early fall of 2001. It is truly a historic agreement because of the precedent of formally including the environmental provision and the labor provision within the body of the text, thereby making them subject to the dispute settlement mechanism set out in the agreement.[70]

The immediate impact of this precedent was the inclusion of similar provisions in all bilateral free-trade agreements negotiated by the United States after the congressional approval of the US-Jordan deal. In addition, all of these newly negotiated bilateral agreements follow the pattern established during the WTO accession process. The agreements include provisions concerning the investment to create a secure, predictable legal framework for US investors. They also contain groundbreaking anticorruption measures in government contracting that are modeled on the Agreement on Government Procurement.

During the George W. Bush administration (2001–2008), the United

States has completed free-trade agreements with the following countries: Chile, Singapore, Australia, Costa Rica, the Dominican Republic, El Salvador, Guatemala, Honduras, Nicaragua, Morocco, Bahrain, Peru, Colombia, Panama, and the Republic of Korea.[71] Negotiations were launched with Malaysia, the United Arab Emirates, Oman, Thailand, and the five nations of the Southern African Customs Union: Botswana, Lesotho, Namibia, South Africa, and Swaziland. However, at the end of 2008, these free-trade agreements had not been completed.[72] The United States is certainly not alone in engaging in bilateral negotiations to achieve its required foreign trade policy objectives. Since 2001 the European Commission has negotiated thirty-seven bilateral free-trade agreements. All of them contain strong provisions addressing the Singapore issues, most notably investment. Many agreements contain a trade sustainability assessment with provisions to deal with the environment.[73]

The surge in the number of bilateral agreements negotiated by the United States and the EC is meant to compensate for the faltering Doha Round multilateral talks. In the bilateral setting, the major industrial countries retain their privileged position. The trade deals negotiated under such conditions leave small countries vulnerable to accept far-reaching provisions on issues that are not yet covered by the formal WTO agreements. In a similar way, the WTO accession process allows all existing members to place unprecedented demands on countries trying to accede to the WTO. This again works in favor of the economically powerful countries that have consistently used the accession negotiations to advance their own economic and political agendas. They are doing this by requiring the candidates to undergo major reforms processes and by asking them to make commitments on obligations well exceeding those of the current members of the WTO. Both developments, the growth of bilateral deals and the power-driven WTO accession negotiations, allow the United States and the EC to coerce a growing number of individual countries into signing more comprehensive trade deals. Consequently, when a significant number of countries accepts the Singapore issues and the provisions concerning the environment and labor standards in the bilateral deals or during the WTO accession negotiations, the United States and the EC will be able to successfully introduce them again on the multilateral agenda of the WTO.

Conclusion

During the 1996 Singapore Ministerial Conference the industrialized countries pushed toward creating additional WTO agreements on investment, trade facilitation, competition policy, and government procurement. More recently, with the growing recognition of the role played by trade policy in the economic development of societies, calls for linking trade with the environment and labor standards have been gaining momentum. Developing countries, however, refuse any substantial talks involving these issues.

The growing influence of developing countries in the WTO means that it would be virtually impossible for the industrialized countries to unilaterally push for the introduction of new agreements. Consequently, a new approach has been applied by a number of the industrialized countries in their attempt to enlarge the scope of the WTO. This new approach sees the United States and the EC actively advocating for the inclusion of the new issues when negotiating terms of accession for new WTO members. Additionally, even more sweeping demands are placed on the existing WTO members that are asked to negotiate bilateral trade deals with the United States and the European Communities. While the European Commission is particularly interested in strong provisions on investment and competition policies, the United States uses the bilateral deals to also advance environmental and labor standards.

There are two converging factors that are responsible for seeking a different approach when contemplating inclusion of new trade-related issues into the WTO. The first one is the changing dynamics inside the WTO that allow developing countries to shape the agenda of the WTO decisionmaking processes, which in this case corresponds to an unambiguous rejection of any additional new agreements. The second is the transformation of the power relations in the world economy that sees the European Communities and the United States as having somehow diminished positions as economic partners.

Because of the lack of rules and clear procedures, the WTO accession process has increasingly become dominated by political and self-interested economic considerations of the developed states. The absence of a specific institutional and legal framework guiding the WTO accession facilitates asymmetrical power games played between the existing WTO members and the acceding country. Such power games lead to the placing of excessive demands on the candidate country. The WTO accession process is often used to introduce new obligations on an acceding country as a way of setting a precedent for future multilateral negotiations. In a very similar way, bilaterally made new trade commitments are widening the scope of the legal trade obligations with which a growing number of WTO members now have to comply.

Notes

1. UNCTAD, *International Investment Agreements: Key Issues* (Geneva: United Nations, 2004), pp. 11–14.
2. See Article III and Article XI of GATT 1947.
3. Patrick Low and Arvind Subramanian, "Beyond TRIMs: A Case for

Multilateral Action on Investment and Competition Policy?" in Will Martin and Alan Winters (eds.), *Uruguay Round and the Developing Countries* (Cambridge, UK, and New York: Cambridge University Press, 1996), pp. 380–408.

4. The OECD has thirty members as of May 2008.

5. UNCTAD, *International Investment Agreements: Key Issues,* p. 14.

6. Cynthia Day Wallace, "The Legal Environment for a Multilateral Framework on Investment and the Potential Role of the WTO," *Journal of World Investment* 3, no. 2 (2002): 291–294.

7. WTO, *Report (2001) of the Working Group on the Relationship Between Trade and the Investment to the General Council* (WT/WGTI/5/Add.1) (October 22, 2001).

8. Ibid., p. 3.

9. Ibid., p. 4.

10. Brian Hindlay, "What Subjects Are Suitable for WTO Agreement?" in Daniel L. M. Kennedy and James D. Southwick (eds.), *The Political Economy of International Trade Law* (Cambridge, UK: Cambridge University Press, 2002), p. 165.

11. John Croome, *Reshaping the World Trading System—A History of the Uruguay Round* (Geneva: World Trade Organization, 1995), pp. 77–78, 378.

12. WTO, *Hong Kong Ministerial Declaration—Doha Work Programme* (WT/Min/[05]/W/3/Rev.2) (December18, 2005).

13. Low and Subramanian, "Beyond TRIMs," p. 393.

14. Bernard Hoekman and Peter Holmes, "Competition, Developing Countries and the WTO," in Peter Lloyd and Chris Miller (eds.), *The World Economy—Global Trade Policy 1999* (Oxford, UK: Blackwell Publishers, 1999), pp. 170–171.

15. Patrick Macklem, "Labor Law Beyond Borders," *Journal of International Economic Law* 5, no. 3 (2002): 605–606.

16. Thomas W. Hertel, Fan Zhai, and Zhi Wang, "Implications of WTO Accession for Poverty in China," in Deepak Bhattasali, Shantong Li, and Will Martin (eds.), *China and the WTO: Accession, Policy Reform, and Poverty Reduction Strategies* (Washington, DC: World Bank and Oxford University Press, 2004), p. 283.

17. Jagdish Bhagwati, *The Wind of the Hundred Days—How Washington Mismanaged Globalization* (Cambridge, MA: MIT Press, 2000), pp. 273–275.

18. Chantal Thomas, "Trade-Related Labor and Environmental Agreements," *Journal of International Economic Law* 5, no. 4 (2002): 791.

19. International Labour Organization, "About the ILO, Who We Are: ILO History" (October 2000), www.ilo.org/public/english/about/history.htm (accessed February 1, 2008).

20. Thomas, "Trade-Related Labor," p. 802.

21. Bernard M. Hoekman and Michel M. Kostecki, *The Political Economy of the World Trading System: The WTO and Beyond,* 2nd ed. (New York: Oxford University Press, 2001), p. 451.

22. Michael J. Trebilcock and Robert Howse, *The Regulation of International Trade,* 2nd ed. (London and New York: Routledge, 1999), pp. 445–446.

23. Ibid., pp. 454–455.

24. Ibid., p. 456.

25. Ibid.

26. Macklem, "Labor Law Beyond Borders," p. 626.

27. Ibid., pp. 627–630.

28. Ibid., p. 630.

29. WTO, "Recent Developments in Multilateral Environmental Agreements," Committee on Trade and Environment (July 8, 1998), pp. 7–8.

30. Thomas, "Trade-Related Labor," p. 793.

31. Ibid., p. 794.

32. GATT quoted in Trebilcock and Howse, *The Regulation of International Trade,* p. 398.

33. Panel report quoted in ibid., p. 408.

34. Gary P. Sampson, "Effective Multilateral Agreements and Why the WTO Needs Them," in Peter Lloyd and Chris Milner (eds.), *The World Economy: Global Trade Policy 2001* (Oxford, UK: Blackwell Publishers, 2002), p. 23.

35. Ibid., p. 24.

36. Trebilcock and Howse, *The Regulation of International Trade,* p. 420.

37. Gregory C. Shaffer, "'If Only We Were Elephants': The Political Economy of the WTO's Treatment of Trade and Environmental Matters," in Kennedy and Southwick, *The Political Economy of International Trade Law,* pp. 357–359.

38. Ibid., pp. 366–367.

39. Ibid., p. 386.

40. Jan McDonald, "'It's Not Easy Being Green': Trade and Environmental Linkages Beyond Doha," in Ross P. Buckley (ed.), *The WTO and the Doha Round: The Changing Face of World Trade* (The Hague, Netherlands: Kluwer Law International, 2003), pp. 158–159.

41. WTO, *Technical Note on the Accession Process* (WT/ACC/7/Rev.2) (November 1, 2000), pp. 18–20.

42. WTO, *Report of the Working Party on the Accession of Ecuador* (WT/L/77) (July 14, 1995), Paragraph 81, also pp. 32–33.

43. WTO, *Report of the Working Party on the Accession of Ecuador*. The Protocol of Accession of Ecuador is included within the report (pp. 32–33). This is the case in every subsequent report.

44. WTO, *Report of the Working Party on the Accession of Bulgaria* (WT/ACC/BGR/5) (September 20, 1996).

45. WTO, *Report of the Working Party on the Accession of the Kyrgyz Republic* (WT/ACC/KGZ/26) (July 31, 1998).

46. WTO, *Report of the Working Party on the Accession of Estonia* (WT/ACC/EST/28) (April 9, 1999).

47. WTO, *Report of the Working Party on the Accession of Jordan* (WT/ACC/JOR/33) (December 3, 1999).

48. WTO, *Report of the Working Party on the Accession of Georgia* (WT/ACC/GEO/31) (August 30, 1999).

49. WTO, *Report of the Working Party on the Accession of Croatia* (WT/ACC/HRV/59) (June 29, 2000).

50. WTO, *Report of the Working Party on the Accession of Albania* (WT/ACC/ALB/51) (July 13, 2000).

51. WTO, *Report of the Working Party on the Accession of Lithuania* (WT/ACC/LTU/52) (November 7, 2000).

52. WTO, *Report of the Working Party on the Accession of China* (WT/MIN[01]/3) (November 10, 2001).

53. WTO, *Minutes of the General Council* (WT/GC/M/23) (October 22, 1998).

54. The protocol entered into force on October 18, 1967. *Protocol for the Accession of Poland,* GATT, Basic Instruments and Selected Documents (BISD) 15 Supplement, pp. 46, 52; and *Report of the Working Party on Accession of Poland,* adopted on June 26, 1967 (L/2806), pp. 109–112.

55. WTO, *Technical Note on the Accession Process* (WT/ACC/10/Rev.3) (November 28, 2005), pp. 48–49, 160.

56. See Article XII in Appendix 2.

57. This is in no way an automatic move. For example, when it came to designating a chairman of the working party on the accession of China, it took several months of intensive consultations to reach a consensus. Finally, Pierre-Louis Girard, the then Swiss ambassador to GATT, was nominated in 1987.

58. WTO, *Technical Note on the Accession Process,* (WT/ACC/10) (December 21, 2001), p. 9.

59. WTO, *Technical Note on the Accession Process* (WT/ACC/10/Rev.3), p. 37.

60. WTO, *The WTO Accession Process* (WT/ACC/1) (March 24, 1995).

61. See, for example, the following WTO documents available in the WTO document database: *Memoranda on Accessions* of Ecuador (L/7202), Kyrgyz Republic (WT/ACC/KGZ/3), Georgia (WT/ACC/GEO/3), Albania (WT/ACC/ALB/3), Oman (WT/ACC/OMN/2).

62. WTO, *The WTO Accession Process,* p. 11.

63. WTO, *The WTO Accession Process and Preparation of Services'Schedules* (WT/ACC/5) (October 31, 1996).

64. The WTO Agreement on the Application of Sanitary and Phytosanitary Measures (SPS) and the WTO Agreement on Technical Barriers to Trade (TBT).

65. Michael J. Finger and Philip Schuler, "Implementation of Uruguay Round Commitments: The Development Challenge," in Bernard Hoekman and Will Martin (eds.), *Developing Countries and the WTO: A Pro-active Agenda* (Malden, MA: Blackwell Publishing, 2001), p. 121.

66. WTO, *Report of the Working Party on the Accession of Jordan.*

67. WTO, *Technical Note on the Accession Process* (WT/ACC/10/Rev.3), p. 6.

68. Howard Rosen, "Free Trade Agreements as Foreign Policy Tools: The US-Israel and US-Jordan FTAs," in Jeffrey J. Schott (ed.), *Free Trade Agreements—US Strategies and Priorities* (Washington, DC: Institute for International Economics, 2004).

69. John S. Odell, "The Seattle Impasse and Its Implications for the World Trade Organization," in Kennedy and Southwick, *The Political Economy of International Trade Law,* p. 420.

70. Rosen, "Free Trade Agreements as Foreign Policy Tools," p. 67.

71. The free trade agreements with Colombia, Panama, and the Republic of Korea have been in principle completed, however, as of November 2008, the US Congress has not yet ratified them.

72. For additional details concerning these bilateral trade deals and to read the full text of the agreements, please visit the Office of the US Trade Representative at www.ustr.gov.

73. For additional details concerning these bilateral trade deals and the full text of the agreements, please visit the Office of the US Trade Representative at http://www.ustr.gov.

CHAPTER 8

The Developing Countries in the Global Economy

One significant weakness that characterizes all three key international economic organizations—the IMF, the World Bank, and GATT (WTO)—is their institutional limitation in addressing the asymmetries in the world economy. This problem stems from the fact that when they were first created in the 1940s they were mainly intended to serve the needs of the industrialized nations. It was a weakness not only because the developed countries acquired a sense of entitlement with respect to what these organizations should do. More important, they were never properly institutionally equipped to deal with a fast-growing membership and demands for equal participation voiced by new members, which were poor countries in the developing world. As newly independent and reforming developing countries became signatories to GATT, the dilemma emerged on how to reconcile their ambitions with the realities of the power-driven trade system. Until the WTO was established, GATT remained a club where the top trading nations effectively dominated.

While the WTO offers a promise of a rules-based multilateralism for all its members, one cannot help but wonder how realistic this promise is in terms of delivering concrete economic benefits to all its members. The majority of WTO members are developing countries. Consequently, the challenge of integrating vastly diverse economies under one set of rules in a way that all members can participate in shaping these rules has taken a central stage in the discussions about the future of the WTO. The principle of judicial equality vastly enhanced the role developing countries are playing in the WTO. In fact, as the previous chapters have repeatedly demonstrated, the zone of democratic competition that now exists inside the WTO decisionmaking structures has allowed developing countries to severely curtail the dominant position of the top industrialized countries. Does such changed dynamics in the WTO also reduce the economic inequalities in the world economy?

One of the main themes of this work suggests that indeed changes have been taking place on the global economic stage. These transformations in power relations relate to the emergence of the new power economies in Asia and Latin America. Countries that particularly stand out are India, Brazil, and China. As these countries are becoming new economic giants that increasingly influence the pattern of international trade flows, they also use their newly acquired confidence to shape the agenda inside the WTO. One unintended consequence of the rising international influence of these new economies is their relationship with other developing countries.

This brings me to the two main dilemmas of this chapter. The first dilemma is how to translate the gains achieved under the international trade law of the WTO into gains of economic prosperity and multilateral cooperation that promote sustainable economic development among all WTO members. The second dilemma is to determine what will be the future role of the new top trading nations, especially China, in terms of its involvement in the world economy and the WTO. What model of economic development will China embrace given its prominent role in and outside the WTO?

To investigate the above dilemmas, I will first examine the history behind the debate regarding the link between trade and development in GATT. For decades under GATT, international trade relations evolved around the issues of market access. This meant that the regulatory and macroeconomic policy decisions taking place inside individual countries were left to the discretion of individual contracting parties as long as their trade policies did not violate the GATT principle of nondiscrimination and other established standards. Countries settled for it to the point of treating GATT as a technical agreement attended by trade practitioners who, in turn, were working with an understanding that they should only preoccupy themselves with the interpretation of the agreed rules. Such an approach left countries with a considerable degree of autonomy over their domestic economies, but, on a somewhat negative note, this technical attitude about GATT resulted in separating international trade policy from the domestic developmental concerns of individual states. This separation is no longer possible under the WTO since many of its agreements directly impact WTO members' domestic policies and regulations. This chapter looks closely at China, exploring its position in the WTO and in the world trading system. It also examines China's attitudes toward economic development. The model of economic growth that is advocated by China becomes an interesting case study of the linkage between foreign trade objectives and domestic development strategies of the emerging economic power.

Development, Developing Countries, and the World Trading System

Very early on, as far as the history of GATT is concerned, negotiators were in fact asked to formally reconcile trade and development. The first calls came at the 1947 Havana Conference, during which the final draft of the ITO Charter was being negotiated. Fifty-six countries were represented in Havana, and more than half of them were poor developing economies. A group of Latin American states insisted on keeping many protectionist measures in place to allow them to pursue their own independent development strategies. In proposing additions to the charter, this group wanted to create a special autonomous economic development committee to facilitate the application of special escape clauses that would allow the use of development-oriented protectionist measures. In the end, negotiators agreed to include in the ITO Charter a provision for the promotion of economic development by the establishment of new preferences between countries.[1]

The Havana Charter, however, was not ratified, and the ITO never came into being. The inability of countries to establish the ITO as the third major economic organization corresponded to the abandonment of some of its essential standards. Proponents of the ITO believed that the organization had to necessarily pursue both economic and political objectives. Many of ITO's ambitious goals centered on the idea that international trade impacts domestic economies to such an extent that a multilateral trade deal should contain provisions dealing with a variety of developmental issues. The GATT preamble, on the other hand, only referred to economic objectives. GATT was intended to be only a part of a major organization, but it became an awkward foundation of an infant system. It was saved because it guarded tariff reductions negotiated by countries that hoped to play a leading role in the emerging postwar economic order. Very little consideration was given at the time to the needs of the people in Africa and Asia, especially since vast portions of these continents remained then under colonial control.

Following the debacle of the ITO, a number of countries decided to keep GATT in order to save the tariff cuts they already had negotiated together. The principle actors behind this effort were nine countries, which first ratified GATT on January 1, 1948.[2] GATT was a limited agreement consisting of thirty-eight articles without any adequate provisions to deal with issues of development. As a result, countries that participated in the world trading system under GATT were under no obligation to address development-related issues. For example, Article XVIII of GATT recognizes the need for government intervention when the implementation of economic policies facilitating development requires it. However, the agreement only vaguely recognized the needs of poor countries and there was no commitment for addressing them. The contracting parties to GATT only agreed that "there is need for positive efforts designed to ensure that less-developed CONTRACTING PARTIES secure a share in the growth in international trade commensurate with the needs of their economic development" (GATT 1947, Article XXVI, Para 3).

The geopolitical context of the early years of GATT was then fundamentally different from the circumstances surrounding the first decade of the WTO. GATT was shaped by the economic priorities of its founders and was framed by their legal tradition. We have already identified three major weaknesses of GATT in the previous chapter. It should be noted that these weaknesses—the provisional nature of GATT, its limited scope, and its lack of formal institutional and procedural structures—in fact benefited the leading industrial nations. Various recommendations in support of establishing a more formal procedural framework for GATT were proposed but never went far enough. The dominant countries in the system favored the provisional GATT, which allowed them to maintain, for example, trade preferences while trading with the developing world, as in the case of several European countries, or GATT-inconsistent legislation concerning antidumping laws, as in the case of the United States. To become functional, GATT gradually set up informal procedures and principles. In the absence of clear rules, diplomacy defined the decisionmaking in GATT. It was a form of diplomacy that was rooted in asymmetrical power relations that took advantage of a culture of informality that pervaded GATT. With it, the emerging asymmetry of opportunity started to characterize the position of developing countries in the world trade system. In the words of Rorden Wilkinson:

> The emergence and subsequent consolidation of a culture of informality was just one of the GATT's emerging defects. More troubling was the emerging asymmetry of opportunity arising from the way in which the General Agreement was deployed as an instrument of liberalization. From the outset, the GATT evolved as an industrial nations club. Its original design as a mechanism for facilitating trade-led US growth and Allied reconstruction ensured that the GATT was better suited to enhancing the economic opportunities of its industrial CONTRACTING PARTIES than the primary, agricultural and textile producing economies of their developing counterparts.[3]

Throughout its history, GATT reflected the weaknesses of its origins. Asymmetry of opportunity became embedded in its framework by maintaining the tacit hierarchy that favored the interests of dominant industrialized nations. This hierarchy would not be shaken until the establishment of the WTO.

The promise of the rules-based system under the WTO offered an exciting opportunity, and developing countries responded to the challenge by active participation in the WTO agenda setting. Such participation undermined the dominant position of the industrialized countries. It also initiated a struggle between the North and the South aimed at addressing the historical asymmetry that long characterized the GATT era. The institutional flaws of the WTO became even more pronounced and detrimental to the functioning of the trade system given the growing activism of developing countries. Such activism, as we have seen in earlier chapters, at least was producing some results and culminated with the Doha Declaration that firmly recognized the importance of developmental concerns.

Before the WTO, the issues of development always stayed on the sidelines. Still, a number of initiatives were put forward to deal with the widening asymmetry of the system as more newly independent countries in Africa and Asia joined GATT. The first of them was the 1958 GATT study, otherwise called the Harberler Report, that recognized the precarious situation of the poor countries. The report even justified the use of temporary import restrictions by developing countries given their economic situation. However, in practical terms, the Harberler Report only resulted in a call for a special and differential system for developing countries. In 1971 a distinctive waiver for all developed countries was established to allow for the Generalized System of Preferences (GSP). In 1979 a formal decision was reached known as the "Enabling Clause," with which developed countries could provide "special and differential treatment" to developing countries that normally was prohibited under the GATT principle of nondiscrimination.[4]

This solution did very little to remedy the economic problems experienced by poor countries. In terms of allowing developing countries to participate in the GATT decisionmaking processes, it had arguably the reverse effect. Michael Hart and Bill Dymond observe:

> The failure of developing countries to accept disciplines, such as they were, and their insistence on special status gave industrialized countries the excuse to practice real discrimination, even when this was inconsistent with GATT's rules. By insisting they had rights but no obligations, developing countries surrendered their capacity to pursue those rights with any significant results.[5]

Even the establishment of the United Nations Conference on Trade and Development in 1964 and the short-lived new international economic order proposed in 1974 did not help to bring the developmental concerns onto the GATT agenda. On the contrary, GATT maintained its technical focus on trade in goods and distanced itself from more difficult areas of trade, like trade in textiles and agriculture, which are of vital importance to poorer countries, becoming essentially "anti-developmental in focus."[6]

Tempted with the option of receiving the benefits of special and differential treatment, developing countries most likely felt a disincentive to become active and demanding participants. Thus, the Enabling Clause and the GSP in some respect solidified the hierarchy and the inequality among GATT's contracting parties. This arrangement had consequences. As Debra Steger writes:

> In pursuing the agenda of special and differential treatment, developing countries withdrew from the trading system and allowed the development of special trade regimes by the developed countries in agriculture and textiles that were adverse to the interests of the developing countries. As a result, the trading system that evolved under GATT was two-tiered and unbalanced.[7]

This hierarchy was abolished when the WTO, a formal legal organization, was established. The next step for developing countries would be to ensure that WTO agreements actually positively enhanced the socioeconomic development of their societies.

Development as an issue was not singled out during the Uruguay Round. The quest to make the organization more democratic started soon after the WTO was born, when various coalitions of developing countries formed temporarily or more permanently in order to engage WTO membership on different issues. The quest for making the WTO more development-friendly was accelerated by the implementation problems experienced by developing countries. Struggling to comply with a variety of new WTO obligations, poorer countries started to complain in the context of their status as developing countries with no adequate resources to meet the administrative and regulatory requirements of some WTO agreements. Although the preambles of all WTO agreements appear to imply a special treatment for developing countries, in reality it is hard to tell what that means. The WTO legal framework does not even contain a definition of a developing country, although its texts repeatedly refer to the needs of developing countries.[8] Apart from some extension given when implementing new obligations, developing countries felt routinely overwhelmed in their attempt to be in compliance with the WTO rules.

Tensions were slowly building within the organization in the month leading to the 1999 Ministerial Conference in Seattle. While the industrialized countries were favoring discussion on additional agreements on investment, competition policy, trade facilitation, and even labor and environment, developing countries felt increasingly dissatisfied with the prohibitive costs of the WTO implementation process. For developing countries, any new agreement was not an option until their past demands on agriculture and present implementation problems were tackled.

As a result, the decisionmaking process started to break down. The principle of consensus was ipso facto democratic, but it was also visibly unworkable because of the inability to coordinate talks among over 130 WTO members at the time. Past solutions to such problems were now alienating many developing countries. For example, the WTO officials would engage in the so-called Green Room discussions in which the chair of a particular negotiating group or committee leads a meeting consisting of the representatives from all major developed countries and only a selected number of developing countries. This kind of arrangement was used several times in the past. But given the judicial equality of all WTO members, those developing countries that were not included in the process rejected it.

This started a dynamic of open contestation of practices that no longer needed to be tolerated by now legally empowered developing countries. It was argued that with the Green Room the highly political process of selecting the developing countries' representatives was in actuality unfair, and most of them felt marginalized. Developing countries did not, however, reject the principle of consensus.[9] This is understandable since the inherently democratic principle of consensus allows weaker states to maintain their judicial equality under the WTO. However, the price of doing so turned out to be very high: the collapse of the Seattle meeting, which, according to one observer "has fallen victim to the GATT's success in integrating developing countries more fully into the trading system and requiring them to be full partners in new trade agreements."[10]

The 1999 Seattle Ministerial Conference openly challenged the way the system operated in the past and forced reevaluation of trade priorities of the industrialized nations. It also placed the WTO at the center of the debate about globalization. Internally, the hostilities between the rich trading states and the rest of the membership were becoming more pronounced. Outside on the streets of Seattle, civil society groups staged huge protests against the WTO. These protests would start to create a malevolent image of an organization that was previously known only to a few. The Seattle meeting was shut down without reaching any agreement. However, Jeffrey J. Schott and Jayashree Watal provide us with the most accurate description of what actually happened in 1999:

> Seattle will be remembered as the city where street demonstrations stopped global trade talks cold. But the Seattle protesters don't deserve such notoriety. The meeting actually fell victim to serious substantive disagreements among the member countries of the World Trade Organization over the prospective agenda for new trade talks. These policy differences probably could have been bridged if the WTO's decision-making process had not broken down. Much of the damage to the WTO was self-inflicted.[11]

Following the ministerial meeting, developing countries continued to insist on linking development with trade by recognizing the developmental aspect of the WTO implementation process. A year after the Seattle meeting, the General Council of the WTO started to address the implementation concerns of developing countries with the goal of bridging the North-South differences in the WTO.[12] Under the leadership of India and Brazil, a number of developing countries turned the implementation problems into a developmental agenda for action. The changing dynamics in the WTO eventually resulted in the Doha Declaration.

From Doha to Hong Kong and Back to Geneva

The 2001 Doha Declaration weighs heavily on the world trade system. The disintegration of negotiations during the Fifth WTO Ministerial Conference in Cancun in September 2003 has been attributed to the developed countries' refusal to meaningfully address the concerns of developing countries embodied in the Doha Declaration. The declaration made a commitment to launch a broad-based round of multilateral trade negotiations with the overarching goal of addressing the developmental concerns of WTO members.[13] In Doha, WTO members also adopted the Declaration on the TRIPs Agreement and Public Health to respond to the problem of access to affordable life-saving medicines in the developing world.[14] To address the problems with implementing the WTO agreements by developing countries, the Decision on Implementation-Related Issues and Concerns was also adopted.[15] Together, these three documents are the backbone of the Doha Development Agenda (DDA), which comprises a number of requests from developing countries. These requests concern the implementation of the Uruguay Round Agreement as well as issues of technical assistance and capacity building. The Doha Round of multilateral negotiations, launched within the framework of the Doha Declaration, was supposed to address these requests.

The Cancun Ministerial Conference ended with accusations that the developed countries were not serious about the Doha Round. After a few acrimonious days of talks, the draft of the final declaration tabled by the chairman of the Cancun meeting, Mexican foreign minister Luis Ernesto Derbez, shocked most of the representatives from developing countries. It completely disregarded their proposals on the issues most critical to the developing world: agriculture, investment, government procurement, trade facilitation, competition policy, cotton, industrial tariffs, and development. This is what the final hours of the meeting looked like after the presentation of the failed draft of the Cancun Declaration:

> Far from bringing positions together, the draft widened the differences still further, and developing country ministers, incensed at having been so arro-

> gantly brushed aside, fought back. At the Heads of the Delegations meeting which followed, delegation after delegation spoke up, tearing the draft to shreds for ignoring the strong and repeated messages the developing world had sent throughout the previous three days.[16]

After several futile attempts to rescue the negotiations, the next day Derbez closed the meeting with no declaration. The main issues of the Doha Round that were left unresolved after Cancun were picked up in preparation for the Sixth WTO Ministerial Conference that took place in Hong Kong in December 2005.

Developing countries under the leadership of India and Brazil fully utilized their legal status in the WTO to resist the tactics by the industrialized countries to play down the developmental concerns and effectively shut down the Cancun ministerial meeting. Brazil and India then used their position to restart the talks again. The Doha Round was revived thanks to the 2004 July Framework Agreement, an initiative of the so-called group of Five Interested Parties, which included Brazil, India, the EU, the United States, and Australia.[17] This shows the strength in the position of developing countries, and it is in sharp contrast to the past when only the Quad countries (the United States, the EU, Japan, and Canada) had determined the agenda of the negotiations.

With the Hong Kong meeting approaching, developing countries became very active in shaping the negotiating agenda. In fact, the meeting started with an unprecedented show of solidarity among developing countries. All the different alliances and groups that had formed over the years among developing members of the WTO (the G-20, the G-33, the LDCs, the African Group, and the Small Economies) gathered together to express their desires for the Hong Kong Declaration to be consistent with the developmental mandate of the Doha Round. The Hong Kong Ministerial Conference did make some progress in advancing the round, but the final results were rather disappointing.

To summarize, developing countries as a group demanded that the EC and the United States make substantial commitments on agriculture. This entailed increased access to their markets for agricultural products from the developing world. It also meant a reduction in domestic subsidies and other forms of support that had been practiced in rich countries, which distorted world prices of agricultural products to the detriment of poor countries. From the developing countries' perspective, agriculture always has been at the top of their priorities. Nondiscriminatory trade in agricultural products could significantly benefit many poor societies. The Doha Declaration renewed the commitment to advance agricultural negotiations. The declaration provides for (1) substantial improvements in market access for all agri-food products, (2) the elimination of export subsidies within a reasonably short period of time, and (3) substantial reductions in all forms of production and trade-distorting support. Paragraph 13 of the Doha Ministerial Declaration states that "special and differential treatment for developing countries shall be an integral part of the negotiations" to enable developing countries "to effectively take account of their development needs, including food security and development." However, the modalities for commitments and special and differential treatment were never established before being assigned the deadline of March 2003.

Despite a successful attempt to revitalize the talks in July 2004, the ministerial-level talks in Geneva with the United States, the EU, Brazil, India, and Australia fell apart on October 19, 2005. Negotiators were unable to narrow their differences on agricultural tariff reduction. It appeared that the EU's insufficient offer and its package of unprecedented demands were effectively stalling the talks. To complicate things even more, the EU wanted to see satisfactory progress on nonagricultural market access (NAMA) and services before offering any further concessions in agriculture.

Some progress was nevertheless achieved in Hong Kong. The Hong Kong Declaration commits members to eliminate all forms of agricultural export subsidies by 2013. This date is in line with the EC's position since the 2003 reform of its CAP plans to eliminate many of such subsidies by 2013. Furthermore, countries are expected to make cuts to overall trade-distorting domestic subsidies and other programs. The negotiators started to classify different categories of such support (Amber Box, Blue Box, and de minimis exempted support), but they were unable to agree on criteria assessing the level of these different forms of domestic subsidies.[18] Since the Hong Kong meeting, additional allowable subsidies (Green Box) have been added in the course of negotiations that turned into disagreements over process and modalities rather than discussions about substance.[19] The Amber Box refers to the most trade-distorting domestic subsidies that provide direct price support and other measures that award farmers for an increase in production.[20] The Blue Box includes subsidies that are trade-distorting but farmers make a promise to reduce their production upon receiving them. There are disagreements surrounding this last classification, for many countries believe that the Amber Box is more appropriate in this context. The Green Box subsidies are allowed without limits because they are not considered to be trade distortive. Green Box subsidies must be government funded. They include, for example, marketing services, support in the time of disaster, and agricultural research.

In terms of the actual benefits accrued to developing countries, the outcome of the Hong Kong compromise was clearly uncertain. First of all, the actual elimination of export subsidies was dependent upon the completion of the modalities by the end of April 2006. In addition, WTO members had to submit comprehensive draft schedules of commitments based on them by

July 31, 2006. The text also required WTO members to develop modalities on food aid, export credit programs, and the practices of exporting state trading enterprises by the end of April 2006. None of these deadlines were met.

Another issue area closely connected to agriculture is cotton. Although, cotton was never explicitly mentioned in the original Doha Declaration, cotton subsidies were singled out as an issue and became a vital part of the Doha Round. In May 2003 four African least-developed countries—Benin, Burkina Faso, Chad, and Mali—called for the elimination of all export subsidies, tariffs, and other trade-distorting domestic support programs for cotton. They also demanded compensation for losses until the phase-out was complete. This so-called Cotton Initiative claimed that subsidies maintained by the developed countries had depressed world prices to the point that African countries no longer could export their cotton at a profit.[21]

The Hong Kong Ministerial Declaration commits all developed states to eliminate export subsidies on cotton by the end of 2006. This commitment mainly impacts the United States, as it is the only country that still uses such measures. The United States in fact agreed to give duty-free and quota-free market access to cotton exports from the least-developed countries. However, the African countries in question do not export cotton to the United States, but instead they have to compete against subsidized cotton in Asian markets, and hence they are mainly interested in reduction of domestic cotton subsidies. Unfortunately, the demand of African countries for immediate reductions in domestic cotton subsidies in the United States, and elsewhere, was put on hold until the overall domestic agricultural subsidies reductions, and their implementation schedules, were finally negotiated. Much to the dismay of the poor African states, the United States refused to address the cotton issue in isolation thus leaving it at the mercy of the rest of the agricultural negotiations.

Another prominent issue that emerged during the Hong Kong meeting was "aid for trade." This concept can be traced back to an April 2005 statement by the IMF and World Bank, in which the representatives of both organizations formulated their support for it. In fact, according to the note, these organizations have been preoccupied with this idea for some time now: "The World Bank is engaged across the five fronts of 'aid for trade': (i) technical assistance; (ii) capacity building; (iii) institutional reform; (iv) investments in trade-related infrastructure; and (v) assistance to offset adjustment costs, such as fiscal support to help countries make the transition from tariffs to other sources of revenue."[22]

The Hong Kong initiative toward the poorly defined "aid for trade" creates some worries among the poorer WTO members. They worry that the developmental aspects of the Doha Round eventually will be relegated to the IMF and World Bank—in other words, outside the WTO rules. The Hong Kong Declaration states, "Aid for Trade cannot be a substitute for the development benefits that will result from a successful conclusion to the DDA, particularly on market access. However, it can be a valuable complement to the DDA."[23] Then again, given the uncertainties surrounding the outcome of the Doha Round, the aid for trade program can be used by the developed nations as their way out of negotiating specific developmental issues in the WTO.

One of the best-known achievements at the Hong Kong meeting was the commitment by the developed countries to provide duty-fee and quota-free market access for nonagricultural exports from least-developed countries beginning in 2008.[24] This was the result of the NAMA negotiations. Still, developing members of the WTO were not satisfied. They pointed out that the developed countries would be able to keep up to 3 percent of all the tariff lines outside of this commitment. This option can keep the most important exports from the poor countries in permanent limbo, since there is no deadline for extending the commitment to all product lines.

Responding to the requests from developing countries at the 2005 Ministerial Conference in Hong Kong, WTO members agreed to eliminate agricultural export subsidies and promised to establish full modalities on agriculture. Major progress was also made on Special Products, where developing countries would have flexibility to self-designate for reduced tariff cuts based on food security, livelihood security, and rural development concerns; and on a Special Safeguard Mechanism, which developing countries would be able to use to protect themselves against import surges. Unfortunately, the discussion about what formula should be used in designating the Special Products has not been resolved. In a similar way, the promise to establish full modalities on agriculture has not materialized as of October 2008. The failure to resolve these issues largely contributed to the collapse of the Doha negotiations.

Developing countries have traditionally focused their attention on the WTO Agreement on Trade-Related Aspects of Intellectual Property Rights (TRIPs). The Doha Declaration on the TRIPs Agreement and Public Health has partially addressed the problem of inaccessibility of medicines by the poor nations prior to the Hong Kong meeting. The ensuing negotiations advanced this issue much further, as was explained in Chapter 6. The Doha Declaration has also that mandated WTO members examine traditional knowledge and folklore, and also the relationship between the TRIPs agreement and the CBD. In preparation for the Hong Kong meeting, a group of developing countries under the leadership of India attempted to place these issues on the negotiating agenda. India called for changes to the TRIPs agreement to require that patent applicants disclose the origin of genetic resources and associated traditional knowledge along with evidence of prior informed consent and benefit sharing in their application. This proposal was strongly rejected by the United States, Canada, and Australia. In the end, the Hong Kong Declaration only acknowledges the work undertaken on the TRIPs-CBD relationship.

The progress of services negotiations has been very slow. Under the Doha Declaration, WTO members were to submit their services request lists by June 30, 2002, and their initial offers of service market access by March 31, 2003. Only a limited number of developing countries had done so, claiming the huge implementation costs in other areas and the uncertainty of benefits. Upon the insistence of industrialized nations, the initial draft of the Hong Kong Declaration contained provisions (Annex C) requiring that all WTO members enter into plurilateral negotiations with the goal of achieving some measurable results.

Because of fierce resistance from developing countries, again under the leadership of India, Brazil, and China, the language of Annex C has been considerably weakened. Overall, Paragraph 26 of the Hong Kong Declaration asserts that negotiations, which were to be placed in full gear during 2006, are nevertheless to be conducted "with appropriate flexibility for individual developing countries as provided for in Article XIX of the GATS." Developing countries were able to limit the scope of the ongoing services negotiations, and as of December 2008 no progress was made.

Following the Hong Kong Ministerial Conference, countries continued to talk despite growing problems. As deadline after deadline was not met, the talks eventually ran out of steam on June 21, 2007. Brazil and India placed strong demands on the traditionally unchallenged leaders of the world trade system—the EC and the United States. These demands concerned agriculture, which by spring 2006 became the single most important issue in the Doha Round. India and Brazil ultimately walked out of the negotiations when these demands were not met. The problem is that for many other developing countries these demands were an expression of India's and Brazil's self-interest rather than a multilateral spirit. Since the Hong Kong Ministerial Conference, at the center of the Doha Round were secret talks conducted only among the new great four: Brazil, India, the EC, and the United States. China, as a relatively new WTO member, has been playing a supportive role when formulating the proposals representing the position of developing countries as a group.

The differences of opinion persisted, especially with respect to the classification of various measures of domestic support (Amber, Green, and Blue Boxes). There is also an argument for special and differential treatment for developing countries, which would allow them to maintain higher levels of domestic support in order to ensure sustainability of their agricultural sector. On the other side of the conflict, the European nations and the United States are slow to reduce their own subsidies as they try to maintain some high tariffs on certain agricultural products from the developing world. Just as the developing countries are trying to address their developmental needs, the top trading nations are facing political pressures and demands for protection from their agricultural lobbies.

The year 2007 was to be the final one of the Doha Round because the fast-track authority granted by the US Congress to the George W. Bush administration was expiring at the end of June that year. Without the US president's fast-track authority, countries became reluctant to negotiate with the United States, because the final deal would have to be scrutinized by Congress and in the process subject to possible modifications. Such modifications would most likely not be acceptable to countries that negotiated the deal the first time, and the Doha Round, together with the progress achieved under its mandate, was therefore put into the "freezer" in June 2007. In the jargon of the WTO, it means that the talks are put on hold until, possibly in a few years time, the fast-track authority is granted again to the US administration and, most important, there is a renewed interest among WTO members to restart the talks.

As per WTO rules, the seventh semi-annual ministerial meeting was scheduled to take place at the end of 2007. The deflated mood among WTO members has been partially responsible for scaling down the usual tradition of organizing large Ministerial Conferences in different parts of the world. Uncertain about the options facing the Doha Round negotiations, the WTO Secretariat organized the July 2008 mini-ministerial meeting in Geneva. The meeting centered on talks conducted among the G7 (Australia, Brazil, China, the EU, India, Japan, and the United States). Although some progress was made, the resulting proposal was rejected, and in the fall of 2008 the Doha Round was officially put on hold. As the profound financial crisis of October 2008 was unfolding, there were indications that the need for global economic cooperation once again would provide an impetus for the WTO negotiating parties to come back to the table in the spring of 2009. Sixty years after GATT was negotiated, multilateralism is facing its biggest challenge. Ironically, 2008 was also the year in which China hosted the summer Olympic Games. Since its accession to the WTO in 2001, China has been dominating the news as the largest trading partner of the United States and also a source of the biggest US trade deficit ever. As the world economy is undergoing transformations in power relations, one cannot stop wondering about the future role of China in the WTO. Officially, China was not part of the WTO's top negotiating group between the Cancun ministerial meeting and the spring of 2007. The most visible leaders of this group were India and Brazil, with China slowly becoming more vigorous on the WTO stage. To gain some understanding of China's role in the WTO and by extension in the world economy, the rest of this chapter will concentrate specifically on China.

China in the WTO

November 11, 2001, marks the date when China, after more than fifteen years of long and difficult negotiations, finally acceded to the WTO. The length of the process should not come as a surprise. Full implementation of WTO agreements is a nonnegotiable prerequisite to join the WTO, but this arduous process often requires the introduction of comprehensive domestic reforms by the acceding state. In the case of China, the accession process was particularly challenging given the country's past history as a politically oppressive state with a centrally run economy of over a billion people and a vast territory.

In 1947, the Chinese National Government under the leadership of General Chiang Kai-shek was an ally of the United States and Britain and became one of the twenty-three original signatories of GATT. The postwar period was a turbulent time in China. Most of its population lived in extreme poverty and distrusted the government in power. With antigovernment sentiment growing, Mao Zedong provided an intellectual leadership that galvanized the masses and eventually led to the communist takeover in December 1949. The government of Chiang Kai-shek escaped to the island of Formosa, now known as Taiwan, where the general announced the continuation of the Chinese National Government. He also contested the legitimacy of the new communist government of Mao Zedong on the mainland. In 1950, Chiang Kai-shek sent a message to the GATT headquarters in Geneva to withdraw China from GATT.[25] In 1965, Taiwan requested and was granted observer status to GATT. In 1971, however, this observer status was removed by the contracting parties[26] following a decision by the UN General Assembly that recognized the People's Republic on the mainland as the only legitimate government of China.[27]

During the 1950s, communist China pursued a series of economic reforms designed to hasten industrialization and create a self-sufficient and isolated economy. Such grandiose economic reforms, exemplified in the Great Leap Forward, would not only inflict much harm to the Chinese economy, but also cause the deaths of many millions through famine and forced collectivization. However, it was only after the excesses of the Cultural Revolution, the later death of Mao Zedong in 1976, and the emergence of Deng Xiaoping as the de facto leader of China that the great power would embark on market-oriented reforms.

A turning point in the economic relations between China and the United States was the historic visit by President Richard Nixon to China in February 1972. This event changed the course of foreign policy toward China from estrangement to engagement. In 1978, Deng Xiaoping officially introduced the Open Door Policy that initiated gradual economic liberalization and implemented an export-oriented model of development. In 1982, the People's Republic of China was granted observer status in GATT, and in June 1986, China requested "resumption" of its GATT contracting party status on the basis that the withdrawal notice sent by the Taiwanese government was illegitimate. China did not regain its status but was asked to negotiate new terms of accession. From the first meeting in Punta del Este in

1986, China had been a full participant in the Uruguay Round and signed the Marrakesh Agreement Establishing the World Trade Organization on April 15, 1994, subject to ratification. This move, however, was legally meaningless with respect to becoming a WTO member.

In March 1987, GATT formally established a working party on China's accession.[28] The negotiations showed signs of solid progress until June 1989, when the negotiations stalled for almost three years following the Tiananmen Square uprising. The brutal suppression of the prodemocracy movement by the Chinese government elicited hostile reactions in North America and Europe that spoke against continuing trade relations with China. Despite the sustained criticism, the accession negotiations resumed in the spring of 1992 but proceeded slowly.

On an interesting note, we should draw a connection between the progress of Chinese negotiations and the developments in the Uruguay Round talks. China started its accession under the limited GATT framework. Until the breakthrough of 1992, the fate of the round and the prospects of designing new agreements were uncertain. The early stages of the Chinese accession under GATT mainly centered on the traditional issues of market access for manufacturing products. Yet, by the end of 1992, the round gained momentum and suddenly the possibility of crafting multilateral agreements on intellectual property and services was becoming a reality. As these developments led to the transformation of the GATT system into the much more formal WTO, which was based in the principle of single undertaking, members of the working party on Chinese accession would feel compelled to enlarge the scope of negotiations by including the new issues. As the accession was progressing, by 1993 China was subjected to additional demands concerning a wide range of domestic reforms necessary to ensure implementation of all WTO agreements.

In 1997, Hong Kong returned to China as its Special Administrative Region. China was becoming an irresistible land of investment for major US and European corporations seeking new markets and cost-efficient manufacturing options. For such corporations, Chinese accession to the WTO conveyed a sense of security about the future of their investment. China was determined to join the WTO not only to secure the flow of foreign direct investment, but most important, to be able to shape the policy agenda of the WTO.

Politics again played a detrimental role in May 1999 when China walked out of the advanced negotiations after NATO forces damaged its embassy in Belgrade.[29] At about the same time, Taiwan successfully finalized, in principle, its WTO accession negotiations and reached an agreement with all the members of its working party. However, the Chinese government expressed concerns and disappointment at the prospect of the WTO finalizing the Taiwan accession negotiations ahead of China.[30] This led to an understanding between WTO members and the government in Taiwan that its accession process would be put on hold until mainland China finalized its own negotiations. By responding to this request, WTO membership confirmed an influential role of China in the world economy. China was not even in the WTO but was able to exert pressures on its trading partners to stall the Taiwanese accession indefinitely.

China's bid for WTO accession involved multilateral negotiations with members of the working party and bilateral negotiations with key WTO members, which were extended to all WTO members upon accession. The final period of negotiations (1994–2001) was very frustrating at times. Eventually, on September 17, 2001, China successfully completed the process when all interested members of the WTO accepted its level of reforms and deemed the number of commitments made by China as sufficient.

The accession process further advanced the economic, administrative, and regulatory reforms that the Chinese government had been introducing since 1978. The first set of reforms was carried out to spur robust economic growth in a country long plagued by economic regression and bad central planning. It would be a mistake, however, to view Deng Xiaoping's reforms in the same light as the perestroika reforms that Mikhail Gorbachev would initiate in the next decade to resuscitate the stagnant Soviet Union. Unlike perestroika, with its accompanying policy of glasnost, the loosening of state control over economic life in China did not walk hand-in-hand with reforms that sought greater openness and transparency in the political institutions of the state. In a word, economic rights were not provided along with political rights. Moreover, despite perestroika's appeals to restructuring the centrally planned Soviet economy, it still retained a top-down approach directed by the government that permitted a lot of economic decisionmaking in key sectors in the hands of state-owned enterprises. Even price controls remained. The Chinese reforms, on the other hand, saw greater decentralization that empowered local cooperatives and municipalities to invest in industrialization and export-oriented trade sectors. While there were still bureaucrats who were asked to oversee the development of the economy, they operated more under the conditions of the market rather than in inflexible central planning:

> Chinese leaders over the last two decades have found a unique way to introduce and encourage entrepreneurial activity in an economy that once was centrally planned. Whether by design or by necessity, Beijing has decentralized economic and political decision-making to the provincial and municipal governments, which in turn have used their expanded freedom to engage in productive ventures as well as to grant licenses, incentives, and other favors to certain local privately owned "champions." . . . Importantly, however, at the same time, Chinese government officials have tolerated the formation of countless numbers of other entrepreneurial venues that have sprung up largely in the eastern, richer half of China, and by at least one measure, small and medium-sized enterprises by 2003 accounted for half of the economy's GDP.[31]

It was in 1986, as both industrial and agricultural output began to considerably rise because of the reforms, that the government applied to rejoin GATT. Already, China had signed bilateral trade agreements that contained most-favored-nation principles, and its applications for membership in the World Bank and IMF were accepted without much travail.[32] Nevertheless, although the inclusion of the world's most populous country in the global economy was especially appealing for its market potential, there was so much consternation about the risks of trade diversion and the subsequent losses of industry, the continued high presence of government in economic life, subsidization, and human rights that the talks about membership in the GATT/WTO dragged for a decade and a half in acrimony and tediousness.

One of the major sticking points throughout the negotiations concerned intellectual property rights. Many countries expressed worries that the weakness of intellectual property rights in China would encourage domestic firms to counterfeit foreign goods, thus potentially reducing substantially any gains foreign companies could make in a liberalized Chinese economy. In fact, there was a time that intellectual property pirating was so bad that almost all US software products sold in China were either unlicensed copies or pirated.[33] Large firms that rely on research and development have also repeatedly claimed that their investment in China was discouraged by the weak enforcement of intellectual property rights. Of course, an environment in which copyright infringements are rampant and patents are violated routinely would be just as harmful to domestic firms as well. Not only would they lose incentive for technological innovation, for there is little point in creating something new that will only be stolen, but also counterfeiters would undermine the brand-name recognition companies strive for, and the quality of goods circulating within the Chinese goods economy might suffer as a result.[34]

However, intellectual property rights could impede economic development, for they permit able firms to control parts of the market and thus may incline the market toward monopolization. As explained earlier, this may be a problem particularly for developing economies where foreign firms are more likely to seek protection for their products. Furthermore, the mass copying and distributing of products, especially in software and entertainment products, entails large pools of labor that are devoted to those tasks. The sudden and strict enforcement of intellectual property rights in a country like China where many are employed in such illicit industries could mean severe market dislocations arising from increased unemployment.[35]

Nonetheless, China has passed a number of laws and introduced administrative procedures to enforce intellectual property rights in compliance with TRIPs. China's accession commitments include the revising of trademark and copyright law to clarify collective marks and certificate marks that may respectively be used jointly and distinctively. Compensation for any violations against trademarks and copyrights is also extended. Furthermore, foreign companies can bring their cases to local copyright bureaus.[36]

A major problem with China in regard to the use of intellectual property rights is the lack of effective enforcement procedures that would ensure observance of the laws concerning intellectual property rights. While strides have been made in raising the maximum monetary sanctions and enabling courts to provide "injunctions and orders for seizure of suspected infringing goods," the problem of enforcement is likely to persist for a while.[37] The size of the economy, the volume of economic activity therein, and the lack of diffusion of technology around the country (which, despite its high rates of growth as of late, continues to have a low per-capita income) remain serious obstacles to protecting intellectual property rights. Indeed, copyright and trademark infringements continue to be profitable in the poorer regions of China where illicit enterprises employ significant numbers of workers.[38] As part of the WTO accession process, however, China committed itself to "the vigorous application by Chinese authorities of the enforcement legislation in order to considerably reduce the existing high levels of copyright piracy and trademark counterfeiting. Action should include the closure of manufacturing facilities as well as markets and retail shops that had been the object of administrative convictions for infringing activities."[39] Such an unprecedented and difficult-to-implement commitment was made in response to the demands of WTO members. In total, China made almost twenty commitments in the area of intellectual property rights alone.[40] This means that if the violations of intellectual property continue in the areas where WTO commitments were made, China may be facing a formal complaint in the WTO, which could lead to a trade dispute under the DSU.

While much has been made about the rise of the standard of living in China and the rapid process of the development there, it is sometimes forgotten that the rate of growth is very uneven in between various sectors of the economy and, by extension, different regions of the country. Over half of rural households in China derive their livelihoods from agriculture.[41] Nowhere is this fact more clear than in the interior, where much of the society lives in a rural setting and therefore depends on agriculture for its income. Generally speaking, thanks to new technologies and policies that have helped improve efficiency, farmers have increased their output and earned higher incomes. On closer inspection, however, statistics reveal that those farmers whose livelihoods depend primarily on agriculture in fact experienced a decline in their net incomes for consecutive years in the mid-1990s. Indeed, because of existing tax burdens and their declining incomes, farmers have been forced to find other sources of income and cut back production expenses.[42] Further deterioration of their incomes may breed social unrest and therefore challenge the central government. The situation had thus motivated the government to implement reforms to restructure the agricultural industry in hopes of increasing the income of farmers by improving overall product quality and expanding agriculture processing.[43] Studies have shown, however, that it is possible that six million workers will still shift away from working in agriculture to find employment elsewhere.[44] Despite the reform initiatives pursued by the central government, the combination of less protectionism in agriculture and the rise of retail prices of nonagricultural products would have a negative impact on farmers' households.[45] Overall, there is a danger of creating two fundamentally different Chinas: one urban China dominated by booming industries and represented by spectacularly modern skyscrapers, and another China that is rural and indigent.

Accession negotiations on services liberalization in China were particularly challenging. Most service sectors used to be state-run and were traditionally poorly developed in China. Prior to the beginnings of Deng Xiaoping's implementation of economic reform programs, financial services were completely state-controlled, as the central government's state-owned banking system received all deposits. Upon those transformative reforms, however, there was a loosening of the one-bank system that eventually included the emerging presence of commercial branches of foreign banks. Financial intermediaries also began to operate, and stock exchanges in Shanghai and Shenzhen were established as the domestic financial market became more diversified and less controlled by the state. In the years leading to China's accession to the WTO, there was further restructuring of the People's Bank of China, and more regulations were added to improve financial governance.[46] It was at this time as well that concerns were raised over whether China was ready to open its door to the foreign competition in various services that was sure to come with accession to the WTO. Financial services still remained undeveloped, while the four large (state-run) banks lacked profitability and transparency. There were few formal ties that would link foreign and domestic banks, and the rural banking system was poorly run and neglected.

China, nevertheless, made commitments to liberalize its financial sector in order to, as some would argue, spur "technological innovation that would lower the cost of financial services and permanently bolster growth"[47] and create greater efficiencies in the economy. But, to continue on the theme of China's uneven development, much of the impact that financial liberalization would have would certainly be felt much greater along the rim than in the interior due to the geographical discriminatory policies and commitments of the central government. China managed to maintain severe geographical restrictions stipulating where foreign firms can establish their commercial presence. However, such restrictions had been phased out in the insurance and banking sectors by 2004 and 2006, respectively.[48] The large central banks, too, could face considerable challenges due to the high proportion of their loans being nonperforming and possibilities for having negative capital. Indeed, some of the domestic critics of China's membership in the WTO have included not only factory managers who fear the consequences of foreign competition, but also bank managers, who have warned of the possibilities of bankruptcy and subsequent job losses.[49]

China's accession to the WTO required the state, pursuant to the GATS, to undertake liberalizing reforms in the service sectors to increase market access and reduce discriminatory treatment that favors domestic companies. Interestingly, some of the commitments that China made in terms of coverage of market access are higher than those of most other countries, especially in such sectors as professional services, telecommunications, distribution services, and education services.[50] While China has made significant efforts to eliminate discrimination against foreign firms, regulations concerning licensing and qualifications may offer a small margin of leeway for more subtle forms of discrimination. Quantitative restrictions are still permitted for use in legal, medical, and retailing services.[51] The most explicit barrier to foreign firms, however, is the requirement to enter into joint ventures in order to restrict foreign ownership. Many such restrictions are to be eliminated, although in telecommunications and life insurance, they will remain as negotiated in China's accession to the WTO—arguably to cut adjustment costs, prevent rent appropriation, and help local owners "learn by collaborating."[52] The geographical limitations that have made China's awesome economic growth so disparate will be phased out in a number of sectors, although the relaxation of such constraints will likely have arrived a bit late and the relative poverty of the interior will likely persist into the future.[53] Like much of the economic liberalization pursued by China, such reforms do not occur overnight and are instead implemented gradually so as to mitigate any adverse effects. They are further complemented by another set of reforms and new regulations designed to reduce market failures in information asymmetry, improve and guarantee quality standards, and provide universal access to certain services.[54]

The telecommunications industry in China has for a long time also been under the sole control of the state through the Ministry of Ports and Telecommunications with only Telecom providing basic telecommunications services. To reform the industry, the government sought to transform the structure of the monopolistic one into one that would be characterized by limited competition. It was for this reason that Unicom was created as a competitor to Telecom in 1994. Indeed, to induce a more oligopolistic structure in the industry, Telecom was broken up into Telecom, China Mobile, and ChinaSat. These companies would specialize in fixed-line telephone networking, mobile phone business, and satellite, respectively. The results of these changes were to include not only lower prices for consumers, but also a substantial loss in profitability.[55] For example, China Mobile saw its revenues decline by a third. Moreover, the dominance of these state-owned firms continues to persist, as evidenced by Telecom's dominance of 99 percent of the fixed-line market.[56]

Accession to the WTO became significant for the telecommunications industry in China, for the industry was regarded as a national priority. Nevertheless, upon significant international pressure, China has made commitments "to open the telecom market to foreign participation, and bring the domestic regulatory and business environment in line with international standards."[57] Certainly, China has opened up value-added services, domestic and international services, and mobile telephony, albeit with restrictions delimiting foreign ownership and investment up to 50 percent after six years of accession and initial limits on the geographical scope of the market access, to be gradually phased out.[58] The caps on foreign investment thus mean that foreign firms would be more careful and selective in their allocations of investment dollars, and some aspects of industry, such as the fixed-line subsector, are too dominated by a single domestic firm for foreign firms to enter at all. Competition, therefore, looks to remain largely between domestic state-owned enterprises in the foreseeable future.

As far as other service sectors are concerned, China made only limited liberalizing commitments in legal services and in the controversial audiovisual sector by significantly restricting the ability of foreign firms to establish a commercial presence in China. No commitments were made in the health and social services sector.[59]

China's compliance with its commitments to the WTO agreements may be institutionally hampered by the lack of legal transparency in the administrative processes. This is important, for "if the relevant rule is only known to domestic producers, foreign producers cannot have knowledge of whether or not the rule is discriminatory in its effect, and whether the rule can represent its interests or not."[60] The dubious and selective forms of law enforcement perpetuated by various state departments and ministries compound this problem with the legal system of China.[61] There is also little recourse to the Chinese judiciary, as it lacks the independence to be able to discharge its duties of enforcing laws impartially. Even when laws and regulations are proclaimed by the central government, there is no guarantee that they will be observed at the local level, given the disregard that subcentral governments are known to have on occasion for the central government's rules.[62]

Another interesting issue concerning China and the WTO is the dominant role of state-owned enterprises (SOEs). Their importance in the Chinese economy is striking when one considers that recent estimates suggest they account for over a third of the Chinese GDP. As Qingjiang Kong put it by analyzing Article XVII of GATT, which is now part of the WTO:

> The risk is that action by an SOE has the potential to undermine the fundamental rules of the GATT. For the most part, the GATT assumes that economic decision-making is made by producers and consumers based on price, but SOEs do not always make decisions based on price. It is not difficult to see SOEs that consume computer chips purchasing all of their computer chips from State-owned chips manufacturers. This would not only contravene the primary requirement of Article XVII, i.e., that State enterprises shall make purchases or sales "solely in accordance with commercial considerations," but also effectively undermine the GATT's Article III national treatment provision. Similar arguments can be made about how SOEs may engage in behavior that would undermine the GATT Article I commitment of MFN treatment, the Article II commitment to a schedule of concessions, and the Article XI commitment against maintaining quantitative restrictions. Given that the reason for purchases or sales by State enterprises is not transparent, none of these disciplines could be effective.[63]

Although the telecommunications industry, discussed above, may be cited as an extreme example, a large number of state-owned enterprises in various manufacturing sectors are a barrier to entry by many foreign firms. In the textile industry, which produces more than 20 percent of China's exports and employs over 7.5 million people, almost 18 percent of the enterprises are state-owned.[64] Most important, if many Chinese-based corporations are in fact at least partially state-owned, how can one ensure fair competition between private international companies, which operate without any governmental support, and the state-backed Chinese companies? Responding to requests by WTO members, China made the following commitment as part of its accession negotiations:

> The representative of China further confirmed that China would ensure that all state-owned and state-invested enterprises would make purchases and sales based solely on commercial considerations, e.g., price, quality, marketability and availability, and that the enterprises of other WTO Members would have an adequate opportunity to compete for sales to and purchases from these enterprises on non-discriminatory terms and conditions. In addition, the Government of China would not influence, directly or indirectly, commercial decisions on the part of state-owned or state-invested enterprises, including on the quantity, value or country of origin of any goods purchased or sold, except in a manner consistent with the WTO Agreement.[65]

Despite this commitment, one cannot help but be skeptical about its implementation. It may simply be logistically impossible to prove any intervention of the Chinese government in the operation of the Chinese company, which is closely linked by virtue of ownership to its government.

Whatever one might write about the continuing disparities that may exist in Chinese society, or the pervasive presence of state-owned corporations, the accession to the WTO should bear positive consequences as the total welfare gain is projected to be US$40 billion and has increased its share of the world import markets from 5.8 percent in 2001 to 6.4 percent in 2007.[66] The expansion of Chinese merchandise trade (due to increased demand), coupled with the reduction of quotas on textiles and clothing by China's trading partners in Western Europe and North America, should have favorable results for the Chinese economy. Indeed, since China joined the WTO, the country has maintained a stellar rate of economic growth. Of course, the inclusion of the world's biggest market is not without some costs to others. The removal of quotas and other trade barriers once designed to restrain Chinese textiles and clothing manufacturers could mean trade diversion for many Latin American countries and some other Asian countries, namely Vietnam.[67] Responding to the concerns expressed by WTO members, given the fact that China has the largest share of the global trade in textiles and clothing, special restrictions (safeguards) were placed on Chinese trade in textiles. This may allow other developing countries to compete on world markets. These safeguards partially expired in 2008, with the rest to expire in 2013.[68]

Many critics of China's presence in the WTO still wonder to what extent the Chinese economic miracle is the result of low labor standards and poor environmental regulations. As the dominant producer of textiles and clothing, China has been accused of having unfair trade advantage by exploiting workers, who are already paid comparatively low wages when contrasted with salaries elsewhere in the world. And yet no commitment was requested by WTO members on this issue. Keeping labor-related concerns out of the WTO negotiations has been consistent with past practices under GATT. The government of China would never allow it to be the first country to make such a commitment.

China is one of the most vocal critics of bringing environment and labor issues under the purview of the WTO. This resistance has great implications for the world economy, for without China's participation, a multilateral agreement on trade and environment would not work. China is an emergent economic giant, but it is also a major environmental polluter. Furthermore, China is being accused of purposely keeping low labor standards to maintain comparative advantage over its trading partners.

As the front-runners of the Industrial Revolution and the most technologically advanced states, the developed countries were first to acknowledge the need for regulations aimed at ensuring responsible conduct of their private and corporate citizens when using natural resources. According to the position by developing countries, the high levels of economic development achieved by the top Western economies make environmental and labor laws affordable for them. In contrast, countries struggling with a multiplicity of developmental problems cannot place environmental and labor concerns ahead of concerns over extreme poverty, famine, and health epidemics. The position held by China and other developing countries is difficult to contest. And yet, if at this historic moment of human progress the world community is not able to arrive at an understanding concerning the unchecked pursuit of economic development, the quality of life everywhere may deteriorate to the point that economic progress could become meaningless.

Economic realists conclude that the new powerful role played by China on the world's economic stage would make it eventually impossible to push aside environmental and labor concerns. On November 13, 2005, an explosion at a chemical plant in northeast China resulted in total poisoning of the Songhua River, which is the main source of water for the city of Harbin. The government kept silent about the incident until the situation got out of control ten days later and the city of Harbin was forced to shut down running water to its 3.8 million people. Since the spill of 100 tons of benzene and other chemicals flowing down the Songhua River was expected to reach the Russian border city of Khabarovsk, the Chinese officials were forced to build a dam on a waterway at the juncture of two rivers on the Chinese-Russian border.[69] The cost of this operation was tremendous. Afterward, the Chinese officials requested environmental assessments of many of its chemical plants. One can only hope that the high price of cleaning the damage of the chemical spill and the public outcry that accompanied this disaster will provide a powerful incentive for stronger environmental laws in China.

In December 2005, a coal-mine blast in northern China left at least seventy-four workers dead. It was the third major coal-mine disaster in China since early November that year. The explosion occurred in Tangshan, a city in Hebei Province. It was unclear how many miners were underground when the explosion happened, and the confusion over how many miners were killed is disheartening. Apparently, rescuers searching for miners that perished in another disaster a week before struggled unsuccessfully for days to get an accurate count of how many miners were working at the time of the blast. This underscores the negligence of safety protocols and poor state of the industry. It appears that in 2004 more than 6,000 miners were killed in fires, floods, cave-ins, and explosions in China. Poor labor standards, lack of enforcement, and obsolete equipment are among the factors that are often blamed for the industrial accidents in China.

The most devastating coal-mine accident in recent years occurred in February 2005 in northeastern Liaoning Province, when an explosion killed 214 miners. The accident prompted Premier Wen Jiabao to criticize the industry and its poor safety record, which is the worst in the world.[70] It was later reported that the government found the situation intolerable and admitted that there was an urgent need to introduce strict labor codes and harsh penalties for violating them in order to prevent future industrial accidents in China.

Still, the Chinese government resists international pressure to become a signatory to major international environmental conventions. It also flatly rejects any discussions about labor standards in the WTO context.

Conclusion

The objective of keeping the developmental issues out of GATT became a norm possibly because of the initially small number of countries that were signatory to the agreement. For the better part of its history, GATT was an exclusive club under the dominant leadership of the industrialized nations. The main developmental issues during its early years concerned the reconstruction of postwar Europe. Only when former colonies in Africa and Asia were becoming independent did the issues of socioeconomic development gain a new meaning. GATT, however, was slow to adapt to these new realities of international relations. After all, the system was structurally biased in favor of the industrialized nations, and hence its negotiating agenda habitually reflected their economic priorities. Small developing economies that joined GATT were clearly at a disadvantage in terms of their ability to be influential players within the system. It was not until the creation of the WTO that opportunities opened up for developing countries through the judicial equality embedded in the new organization. Under the new institutional arrangement of the WTO, they felt encouraged not only to formulate their own demands, but also to contest proposals submitted by the industrialized nations. Consistent pressure applied by developing countries eventually led to the launching of the Doha Round of multilateral negotiations, which for the first time in the history of the world trade system firmly recognized the link between development and trade.

Within the WTO, the relationship between development and WTO-guided trade policies is now under the scrutiny of its members. The 2001 Doha Ministerial Declaration constituted one of the pivotal moments for the WTO and the globalizing economy. Its importance rested upon two factors: (1) the declaration formally recognized the link between trade and development, and (2) it demonstrated the new influence of developing countries within the WTO.

But even if the institutional dynamics within the WTO have been permanently altered in favor of developing countries that are now able to take advantage of their legal equality under the WTO system, the asymmetries in the world trading system have not yet been remedied. Perhaps because of its spectacular economic growth, enormous size, and huge population, China receives a lot of attention in this context. During the long accession process, China repeatedly refused to negotiate any new WTO-plus obligations that would touch upon the environmental and labor aspects of its trade regime.

Mainly because of the size of its economy, China was able to resist many of the invasive demands for liberalization and additional commitments that were desired by the WTO members.

The growing presence of developing countries—most notably China—in the WTO means that it will be virtually impossible to introduce new agreements, in particular on labor and environment. We may speculate that economic liberalization will mean less government control over society and a greater awareness about policies in place in China, and a growing social activism could provide incentives for higher standards and accountability. But critics of China and its role in the WTO are naturally skeptical. They do not believe in the positive scenario of self-restraint; instead, they claim that the Chinese economic growth is both socially and environmentally unsustainable. It is also worrisome to think what that means in terms of China being an economic success story and a potential model of economic development for the rest of the developing countries in the global economy.

Notes

1. Clair Wilcox, *A Charter for World Trade* (New York: Macmillan, 1949), pp. 47–49.

2. Australia, Belgium, Canada, Cuba, France, Luxembourg, the Netherlands, the UK, and the United States. In 1947 Cuba was in a very close economic relationship with the United States.

3. Rorden Wilkinson, *The WTO: Crisis and the Governance of Global Trade* (London and New York: Routledge, 2006), p. 47.

4. Peter-Tobias Stoll and Frank Schorkopf, *WTO—World Economic Order, World Trade Law* (Leiden, Netherlands: Martinus Nijhoff Publishers, 2003), pp. 39–40.

5. Michael Hart and Bill Dymond, "Special and Differential Treatment and the Doha 'Development' Round," *Journal of World Trade* 37, no. 2 (2003): 415.

6. Rorden Wilkinson, "The WTO in Crisis—Exploring the Dimensions of Institutional Inertia," *Journal of World Trade* 35, no. 3 (2001): 406.

7. Debra P. Steger, *Peace Through Trade—Building the WTO* (London: Cameron May, 2004), p. 21.

8. "*Recognizing* further that there is need for positive efforts designed to ensure that developing countries, and especially the least developed among them, secure a share in the growth in international trade commensurate with the needs of their economic development." Preamble to the Agreement Establishing the World Trade Organization, in WTO, *The Results of the Uruguay Round of Multilateral Trade Negotiations* (1995).

9. John S. Odell, "The Seattle Impasse and Its Implications for the World Trade Organization," in Daniel L. M. Kennedy and James D. Southwick (eds.), *The Political Economy of International Trade Law* (Cambridge, UK, and New York: Cambridge University Press, 2002), p. 422.

10. Jeffrey J. Schott and Jayashree Watal, "Decision Making in the WTO," in Jeffrey J. Schott (ed.), *The WTO After Seattle* (Washington, DC: Institute for International Economics, 2000), p. 284.

11. Ibid., p. 283.

12. WTO, *General Council: Implementation-Related Issues and Concerns* (WT/L/384) (December 19, 2000).

13. WTO, *Ministerial Declaration* (WT/MIN/[01]/DEC/W/1) (November 14, 2001).

14. WTO, *Declaration on the TRIPS Agreement and Public Health* (WT/MIN/[01]/DEC/W/2) (November 14, 2001).

15. WTO, *Implementation-Related Issues and Concerns* (WT/MIN/[01]/DEC/W/10) (November 14, 2001).

16. Fatoumata Jawara and Aileen Kwa, *Behind the Scenes at the WTO—The Real World of International Negotiations: The Lessons of Cancun* (London and New York: Zed Books, 2004), p. xvi.

17. WTO, *Doha Work Programme* (WT/L/579) (August 2, 2004).

18. WTO, *Hong Kong Ministerial Declaration—Doha Work Programme* (WT/MIN[05] W/3/Rev.2) (December 18, 2005).

19. "Modalities" is the term used by WTO officials when referring to targets (including numerical targets) for achieving the objectives of the negotiations, as well as methodological issues related to rules.

20. Developed countries are allowed to have only 5 percent of their domestic subsidies classified as Amber Box, while developing countries are allowed 10 percent.

21. WTO, *Negotiations on Agriculture—Poverty Reduction: Sectoral Initiative in Favour of Cotton* (TN/AG/GEN/4) (May 16, 2003).

22. *Aid for Trade: Competitiveness and Adjustment Joint Note by the Staffs of the IMF and the World Bank,* April 12, 2005, www.worldbank.org.

23. WTO, *Hong Kong Ministerial Declaration—Doha Work Programme* (WT/MIN[05] W/3/Rev.2), Paragraph 57.

24. Ibid., Annex F.

25. A. Neil Tait and Kui-Wai Li, "Trade Regimes and China's Accession to the World Trade Organization," *Journal of World Trade* 31, no. 3 (1997): 98.

26. Harold K. Jacobson and Michael Oskenberg, *China's Participation in the IMF, the World Bank, and GATT: Toward a Global Economic Order* (Ann Arbor: University of Michigan Press, 1990), pp. 63–64.

27. UN, *UN General Assembly—Resolution 2758—Restoration of the Lawful Rights of the People's Republic of China in the UN* (October 26, 1971).

28. WTO, *Technical Note on the Accession Process* (WT/ACC/10) (December 21, 2001), p. 11.

29. "China, U.S. Continue WTO Talks," *Xinhua News,* April 22, 1999. Also, Gill Bates, "Limited Engagement," *Foreign Affairs* 78, no. 4 (1999): 65–76.

30. "Beijing, Taipei Wage Psychological Warfare," *Globe and Mail,* August 16, 1999.

31. William J. Baumol, Robert E. Litan, and Carl J. Schramm, *Good Capitalism, Bad Capitalism and the Economics of Growth and Prosperity* (New Haven, CT, and London: Yale University Press, 2007), p. 146.

32. Qingjiang Kong, "Enforcement of WTO Agreements in China: Illusion or Reality?" *Journal of World Trade* 35, no. 6 (2001): 1182.

33. Ibid., p. 1186.

34. Keith E. Maskus, "Intellectual Property Rights in the WTO Accession Package: Assessing China's Reforms," in Deepak Bhattasali, Shantong Li, and Will Martin (eds.), *China and the WTO: Accession, Policy Reform, and Poverty Reduction Strategies* (Washington, DC: World Bank and Oxford University Press, 2004), p. 55.

35. Ibid., pp. 56–57.

36. Ibid., pp. 52–53.
37. Ibid., p. 59.
38. Ibid., p. 60.
39. WTO, *Technical Note on the Accession Process* (WT/ACC/10), pp. 142–143.
40. In contrast, most of other countries that have acceded to the WTO since 1995 made on average one single commitment with respect to intellectual property rights protection. For comparison, see ibid., pp. 139–144.
41. Chen Xiwen, "China's Agricultural Development and Policy Readjustment After Its WTO Accession," in Bhattasali, Li, and Martin, *China and the WTO*, p. 71.
42. Ibid., p. 72.
43. Ibid., pp. 74–75.
44. Elena Ianchovichina and Will Martin, "Economic Impacts of China's Accession to the WTO," in Bhattasali, Li, and Martin, *China and the WTO*, p. 218.
45. Ibid., p. 220.
46. Deepak Bhattasali, "Accelerating Financial Market Restructuring in China," in Bhattasali, Li, and Martin, *China and the WTO*, pp. 182–183.
47. Ibid., p. 187.
48. Aaditya Mattoo, "The Services Dimension of China's Accession to the WTO," in Bhattasali, Li, and Martin, *China and the WTO*, p. 125.
49. Kong, "Enforcement of WTO Agreements," p. 1189.
50. Mattoo, "The Services Dimension of China's Accession to the WTO," p. 119.
51. Ibid., p. 129.
52. Ibid., p. 131.
53. Ibid., pp. 131–132.
54. Ibid., pp. 132–134.
55. Debbie Mrongowius and Mari Pangestu, "Telecommunications Services in China: Facing the Challenges of WTO Accession," in Bhattasali, Li, and Martin, *China and the WTO*, pp. 161–162.
56. Ibid., p 162.
57. Ibid., p. 166.
58. Ibid.
59. WTO, *Technical Note on the Accession Process* (WT/ACC/10), pp. 160–183.
60. Kong, "Enforcement of WTO Agreements," p. 1190.
61. Ibid., p. 1191.
62. Ibid., p. 1192.
63. Ibid., p. 1196.
64. Mark Willams, Kong Yuk-Choi, and Shen Yan, "Bonanza or Mirage? Textiles and China's Accession to the WTO," *Journal of World Trade* 36, no. 3 (2002): 577–578.
65. WTO, *Technical Note on the Accession Process* (WT/ACC/10), p. 49.
66. Ianchovichina and Martin, "Economic Impacts of China's Accession," p. 221.
67. Ibid.
68. Willams, Yuk-Choi, and Yan, "Bonanza or Mirage?" pp. 577–591.
69. "China Mulls Dam for Toxic Spill," *Xinhua News Agency*, December 5, 2005.
70. "Dozens Dead in China Mine Blast—Casualties Grow in Latest Disaster to Strike Mining Industry," *Xinhua News Agency*, December 10, 2005.

PART 4

Conclusion

CHAPTER 9

The Future of the Expanding World Trade Organization

One of the most astonishing decades of the twentieth century was the period between 1985 and 1995. In the mid-1980s, the news media were still lamenting the Iron Curtain dividing the world into the two spheres of influence: the capitalist West and the communist East. It was the time when only a few would dare to hope for a world that could turn away from ideological differences and military competitions toward cooperation aimed at eradicating economic inequalities and ensuring democratic representation for all. But only several years later, that unexpected moment in fact came. The demise of the Soviet bloc at the beginning of the 1990s propelled former enemies and friends alike to work together and provided an impetus for a renewed multilateral approach to global economic affairs. As states began to collaborate with each other on a level unseen since the years immediately following World War II, their emphasis was on enhancing the role of international law and on strengthening global institutions in managing international relations.

It was arguably a coincidence that at the time when turbulent political changes were transforming the world, representatives of the over hundred signatories to GATT were in the middle of the Uruguay Round of multilateral trade negotiations. The round was supposed to expand the world trading system into new areas of economic activities, but its first few years were showing slow progress, because perhaps there was no clear vision regarding the future of GATT. Just when the talks appeared to be faltering, negotiators were confronted with the new geopolitical realities that came with the end of the Cold War. In this unique moment of history, the idea of globalization—understood in terms of closer economic integration of all states—provided a distinctive rationality for the creation of the WTO. From geopolitical shifts to novel inventions in communication and transport technologies, economic globalization was becoming a symbol of new patterns in international trade. Negotiators of the Uruguay Round submitted new proposals, which created the much-needed momentum for the round's completion. They also decided to transform a provisional GATT into a fully legally binding WTO.

In the minds of the negotiators, the WTO was a logical response to the sweeping transformations in the global economy. Not only was the WTO declared to be a universal organization open to all countries, it also brought under its framework new trade issues that seemed to characterize the unprecedented growth in transnational economic activities, most notably services and intellectual property. The increased importance of global trade in services led to the designing of a unique multilateral agreement that would serve as a basis for negotiating the opening of a whole range of domestic service sectors to foreign competition. The growing prominence of research-based new technologies and the fear of piracy in the fields of computer software and entertainment products led multinational companies to lobby hard for the inclusion in the WTO of an agreement that would mandate the enforcement of a minimum level of intellectual property rights protection worldwide. The WTO became a formal legal organization with its own dispute settlement mechanism that is based on the principle of compulsory adjudication. The unified dispute settlement body responsible for adjudicating WTO trade disputes connects all new WTO agreements with other agreements relating to the trade in goods, including the old GATT.

Since it was established, the dynamics inside the WTO and the challenges created by the implementation of new WTO agreements have mirrored some of the most compelling tensions that have been taking place in international economic relations. The incredible developments that have taken place in the WTO since 1995 provide us with great insights into the changing dynamics in the world economic order. They also allow us to contemplate many questions about globalization, the future of multilateralism, the political and economic relations between the industrialized economies and developing countries, and the domestic implications of the progressive codification of international economic law. A code of WTO legal rules can now constrain the behavior of its member states by way of monitoring and supervising the implementation of the existing rules and commitments countries made in joining the organization. As David M. Blumental observes, "The premises of a global economy—interdependence and transparency—have permanently altered the notions of absolute sovereignty, escalating the natural tension between states' sovereignty and domestic policy and adherence to international norms."[1] Indeed, it is one of the consequences of the new world economy that international trade law now intrudes far more directly into matters that were previously considered to be under the sole jurisdiction of the state.

This book has analyzed the most politically controversial WTO agreements. It has also investigated the dynamics behind the decisionmaking processes inside the WTO. It was interesting to see how the WTO, as a microcosm of the changes taking place in the world economy, reflects the reconfiguration of the power relations on the global economic stage. This shift, however, brings with it the ongoing struggle of adaptation and resistance with those developing members of the WTO that are trying to assert themselves as active and influential participants within the WTO.

The book has been organized around three main themes. The first theme considers the WTO as a response to the geopolitical and socioeconomic transformations that began to manifest themselves toward the end of the 1980s. The second theme considers the WTO to be an unfinished project, especially when it comes to its decisionmaking processes. The third theme sees a number of developing countries as primary movers behind shifting power relations in the international trade system. I would like to draw some conclusions based on the investigation that followed these three themes throughout the pages of this book.

My first observation reflects on the historical timing of the WTO: the globalizing moment of the 1990s. Traditionally, the practice of GATT relied on principles of reciprocity and diplomacy, which often translated into behind-closed-doors power-driven politics, and could not ensure the rule of law in the absence of the principle of judicial equality and compulsory adjudication of trade disputes. WTO legal rules for the first time in the history of GATT introduced the principle of judicial equality for all WTO members and the practice of compulsory adjudication once a complaint by an injured party is accepted as valid to initiate a formal trade dispute. Furthermore, the WTO code includes provisions allowing for the authorization of sanctions should they become necessary to remedy the violation of agreed rules. Thus the WTO marks an important event in the tradition of international relations by attempting to move them away from diplomatic power-based management toward the rules-based mechanisms of global governance.

The establishment of the WTO was rationalized as a victory of the legal approach that would guarantee a rules-based multilateralism for all and provide tangible benefits for every WTO member. However, soon after the initial enthusiasm evaporated, the implementation problems experienced by developing WTO members questioned the practical implications of creating an organization that puts so many obligations on countries that have neither the resources nor the expertise to cope with them. The global policymakers have been misguided in separating the economic arguments and legal considerations from the countries' needs and traditions.

The WTO implementation process was intended to help countries reform their domestic economies so they could fully benefit from membership in the multilateral trading system. Sadly, the depth and the multiplicity of obligations relating to new WTO agreements have put tremendous pressure on developing countries. We have examined this problem in the context of a number of WTO agreements. As a result, questions must be asked about whether poorer countries would ever be able to overcome many formidable barriers of implementation—like absence of institutional infrastructure, insufficient legal expertise, limited financial resources, challenges of life-threatening epidemics, administrative paralysis, high unemployment, lack of regulatory transparency, limited regulatory capacity—in order to benefit from WTO membership.

The most controversial WTO agreements contain provisions that stress the importance of domestic regulations with respect to the implementation and enforcement of WTO obligations by its members. The regulatory reforms, however, are difficult and must be done in a thoughtful way to address the multiplicity of economic, social, and political issues. It would be a mistake, for example, to fully liberalize telecommunication, transportation, and financial services sectors and open a country to unregulated inflow of foreign services suppliers without first having designed laws that set standards and monitor investors' activities so their behavior does not become predatory. In order to be effective, the new laws and regulations must be created in the context of the individual developmental strategies of WTO members and not based on abstract legal blueprints.

Many positive changes occur and policies are drafted when the urgency of the moment forces action, but there is also a risk in rushing a new project too quickly. Called from the start by many diplomats in Geneva "an escape into the future," the WTO's ambitious agreements were not matched by the relevant institutional reforms. The decision to create the WTO was made in a hurry as the trajectory of the Uruguay Round became altered by the sudden changes in international relations. The world trading system appeared obsolete and awkward under the provisional GATT when the world was embracing the idea that the forces of globalization demanded global solutions. The rush to complete the Uruguay Round before the final deadline in December 1993 left many agreements unfinished, subject to future negotiations, or pressed into existence without a proper examination of their potential impact on socioeconomic development in many developing countries.

This brings me to the second theme of the book. The WTO remains an unfinished project for a number of reasons. The first and most obvious one has to do with negotiations and agreements that were left to be completed in the next round. The WTO agreement on agriculture must be mentioned first in this context. However, the GATS was also an interesting experiment that did not produce the expected results. The new negotiations on liberalization of service sectors have not been advancing well since they were launched in

2000. Furthermore, as our inquiry has shown, there is so much work to be done when it comes to the agreement on textiles and clothing, the antidumping agreement, and TRIMs. Serious implementation problems eventually led to a modification of TRIPs; however, not all of the intellectual property rights issues have been resolved by the WTO membership. Subjects such as indigenous knowledge, farmers' rights, and compulsory licensing have remained unsettled since the time of the Uruguay Round.

Second, there is also a dilemma of adding new issues to the WTO legal framework. The four Singapore issues—government procurement, investment, competition policy, and trade facilitation—were strongly advocated by the developed countries as far back as the Uruguay Round. Moreover, the growing attention paid to the environment and labor standards creates enormous pressure to address them within the WTO. Both civil society activists and business groups continue to press their governments to expand the WTO. Many consider the WTO to be unfinished precisely because of the uncertain position of these new issues on the WTO agenda. Yet, strong opposition of developing countries prevents the addition of any new agreements.

Therefore, the third reason why the WTO is in need of reforms has to do with its weak institutional structure. The unfinished business in this respect relates to a gap between the enormous scope of WTO agreements and the GATT-era principle of consensus it still operates under. This principle, as was demonstrated in this book, is in itself deeply democratic. Nevertheless, in combination with the principle of single undertaking, which is new to the WTO, decisionmaking by consensus can lead to institutionally paralyzing struggles between competing countries. Currently, there is no institutional mechanism in place that would allow for an exit strategy once such struggles turn into a mutually hostile contest over who controls the WTO agenda setting. The WTO needs to be completed in the sense of preserving the most promising achievement of the WTO—the principle of judicial equality—without compromising the effectiveness of the organization.

The third theme of the book follows developing countries in their quest to reshape the world trading system. The negotiators of the Uruguay Round have forged an organization that offers judicial equality to all its members, which is not a small commitment given the large membership of the WTO. The initial resistance of the major trading nations against such an organization provided early clues about its potential to reduce domination of the industrialized states in controlling the agenda of the WTO. Indeed, the rules-based WTO opened up a zone of democratic competition within its decisionmaking processes.

Since the WTO came into existence, democratic contestation by developing countries resulted not only in resisting the agenda setting by the previously unchallenged developed countries, but also in the release of the Doha Declaration. This declaration formed a basis for the Doha Development Round of multilateral negotiations. The declaration incorporates some of the crucial demands of the developing members of the WTO. The changing dynamics inside the world trading system also revealed how powerful some of the rapidly developing countries have become. India, Brazil, and China now hold as much bargaining power inside the WTO, and more broadly in the global economy, as the United States and the EC. However, this also means that none of the main players in the WTO can unilaterally push through their demands. On June 21, 2007, the Doha Round was partially suspended due to the failure of WTO members to reach a compromise on a number of issues, most notably on trade in agriculture. The gradual deterioration of the negotiations has proven that the WTO is quite poorly equipped, institutionally speaking, to deal with the large number of conflicting demands.

Since the WTO was born, developing countries previously marginalized under GATT took advantage of their legal equality to resist pressures from the developed world concerning further trade liberalization. Various, and often fluid, alliances were created among developing members of the WTO in an effort to turn the tables and demand that the rich countries start paying attention to the needs of economically weak countries. This is exactly how the Doha Round of multilateral trade negotiations came into existence. It was launched at the fateful 2001 WTO Ministerial Conference in Doha, Qatar, only weeks after the September 11 attacks. It was a meeting that heralded a renewed spirit of multilateralism in the name of refocusing trade policies to take into consideration the developmental concerns of WTO members. At the same meeting, the completion was announced of a more-than-a-decade-long accession process of China to the WTO.

More than seven years later, the historically influential Western nations now stand strangely weak as actors in the global economy. At the same time, the most prominent developing countries are gradually recognizing the impact of their new role in the WTO. The Doha Round, which was supposed to be about development in the context of a wide range of issues relating to several WTO agreements, turned into a scuffle that mainly concerned agriculture and modalities on market access. It appears that by becoming more democratic internally the WTO decisionmaking has become characterized by struggles between the developed and developing countries. The traditionally powerful nations continue to pressure developing countries via bilateral deals and backroom politics.[2] Meanwhile, some developing countries resent these actions and respond by submitting new proposals in the WTO. It is quite possible that the move to reform the organization will begin with initiatives by India, China, and Brazil.

Indeed, this is not 1947, and all WTO members must understand how much the world has changed since GATT was signed. The recent transformations in the world economy demand the reexamination of the institutional weaknesses of the WTO in the context of the altered power relations in the global economy. The long-unchallenged economic dominance of the West over the world trading system is over. It is time to pragmatically reform international institutions to allow for better coordination of the complex global economic transactions that occur on a quotidian basis among all trading nations. Alternatively, we may witness a sustained retreat from multilateralism in favor of regional and bilateral trade treaties that have already been proliferating. However, as Clair Wilcox told us before, bilateralism "begets discrimination in international commerce. It enables states with larger bargaining power to gain at the expense of weaker ones. It tends to shift the emphasis in commercial relations from economics to politics."[3] Sooner or later such power-based management of international trade tends to be detrimental for all actors involved.

What to do next? Perhaps this is the time for trading countries to take a long, hard look at whether they want to conduct their trade policies in the spirit of multilateralism, regionalism, or self-interested logic. And although the world economy has always contained elements of all three, the general attitude tended toward the coordination of economic activities among its most advanced economies. It would be a shame if multilateralism were to be replaced by multipolarity, with a number of influential economic states engaging with each other in nasty power economics. Nonetheless, the reforms of the WTO should begin with defining what are the present expectations of WTO members with respect to multilateralism. Multilateralism does not have to mean the rigid application of one set of trade obligations that must legally bind all WTO members to the same degree. The legalization of the WTO allowed the developing countries to become active participants in the WTO decisionmaking; however, it also increased the level of obligations and costs of signing new agreements. As one set of scholars put it, "The downside of increased legalization in this instance lies in the inevitable uncertainties of economic interactions between states and in the need for flexibility to deal with such uncertainty without undermining the trade regime as a whole."[4]

I realize, however, that in advocating greater flexibility in the WTO, one may be accused of turning away from the principles of international law toward a system based on power. The following excerpt well illustrates this point:

> Some bemoan the increasing judicialization of GATT and its successor, the WTO. Apart from the usual fears of turning everything over to the lawyers, many trade diplomats are concerned that legalities will drive flexibility out of the system. Perhaps this is true, but it remains to be seen whether this is undesirable: one person's flexibility is another's unbridled

> discretion. The power to be flexible included the power to twist, if not to ignore, the rules. A flexible trade regime grounded in diplomacy is a regime dominated by the powerful, who usually are convinced of the benignity of their own policies and intentions, sometimes justifiably so. Still, as Professor Francis Allen has said, "In this sinful world, when the lion and the lamb lie together the lamb is usually in the interior of the lion." . . . The results seem inevitable; in any political regime *the strong are likely to have their way.* For this reason, the well-being of the lambs, paradoxically, is likely to be furthered by a modest approach to developing WTO law, as is the well-being of the WTO legal system itself.[5]

While I realize the dangers, I still argue that the principle of consensus and the principle of single undertaking—the two principles on which the WTO is based—are inherently incompatible given the reality of the expanding WTO. They are incompatible because of the number of WTO members, the scope of WTO obligations, and the underdeveloped institutional framework of the organization. What I am suggesting is not the return to the old system, but rather creating a new one that would ensure the space for democratic competition in the WTO decisionmaking bodies, but would also permit individual countries to opt out from additional and unwanted obligations. My first suggestion is to relax the principle of single undertaking. There is nothing wrong with allowing a group of countries to negotiate plurilateral agreements that only bind the interested parties. Eventually, other countries may join if they find such agreements beneficial for their own developmental and trade needs. Alternatively, the principle of consensus could be replaced by the formal acceptance of a voting scheme where the absolute majority would prevail. The reforms suggested would introduce a necessary degree of flexibility that would resolve the games played in the WTO by the states stuck between the bureaucratic layers of WTO principles and practices and would allow their individual priorities to be voiced by way of democratic representation in the WTO.

The story of the WTO reveals that international institutions must be brought front and center to the analysis of the international political economy. Such institutions are important because it is through them that countries have made and will continue to make their own economic history. The WTO is the medium through which international trade flows are organized. But the WTO inevitably is also a global social entity created in response to a particular historical moment. We have examined how the organization is trying to account for the changes taking place in the world economy. It is precisely through an organizational form like the WTO that we can observe global market behavior of small and big countries. This is why we continue to study international organizations such as the WTO to better understand the changing dynamics in the global political economy.

Notes

1. David M. Blumental, "Applying GATT to Marketizing Economies: The Dilemma of WTO Accession and Reform of China's State-Owned Enterprises (SOEs)," *Journal of International Economic Law* 2, no. 1 (1999): 114.

2. Fatoumata Jawara and Aileen Kwa, *Behind the Scenes at the WTO—The Real World of International Negotiations: The Lessons of Cancun* (London and New York: Zed Books, 2004), pp. xxxviii–xli.

3. Clair Wilcox, *A Charter for World Trade* (New York: Macmillan, 1949), pp. 18–19.

4. Judith Goldstein and Lisa L. Martin, "Legalization, Trade Liberalization, and Domestic Politics: A Cautionary Note," *International Organization* 54, no. 3 (2000): 620–621.

5. David Palmeter, *The WTO as a Legal System: Essays on International Trade Law and Policy* (London: Cameron May, 2003), pp. 367–368.

APPENDIX 1

Selected Provisions of the 1947 General Agreement on Tariffs and Trade

Article XVII: State Trading Enterprises

1. (a) Each contracting party undertakes that if it establishes or maintains a State enterprise, wherever located, or grants to any enterprise, formally or in effect, exclusive or special privileges, such enterprise shall, in its purchases or sales involving either imports or exports, act in a manner consistent with the general principles of non-discriminatory treatment prescribed in this Agreement for governmental measures affecting imports or exports by private traders.

(b) The provisions of sub-paragraph (a) of this paragraph shall be understood to require that such enterprises shall, having due regard to the other provisions of this Agreement, make any such purchases or sales solely in accordance with commercial considerations, including price, quality, availability, marketability, transportation and other conditions of purchase or sale, and shall afford the enterprises of the other CONTRACTING PARTIES adequate opportunity, in accordance with customary business practice, to compete for participation in such purchases or sales.

(c) No contracting party shall prevent any enterprise (whether or not an enterprise described in sub-paragraph (a) of this paragraph) under its jurisdiction from acting in accordance with the principles of sub-paragraphs (a) and (b) of this paragraph.

2. The provisions of paragraph 1 of this Article shall not apply to imports of products for immediate or ultimate consumption in governmental use and not otherwise for resale or use in the production of goods for sale. With respect to such imports, each contracting party shall accord to the trade of the other CONTRACTING PARTIES fair and equitable treatment.

3. The CONTRACTING PARTIES recognize that enterprises of the kind described in paragraph 1 (a) of this Article might be operated so as to create serious obstacles to trade; thus negotiations on a reciprocal and mutually advantageous basis designed to limit or reduce such obstacles are of importance to the expansion of international trade.

Article XXVIII bis: Tariff Negotiations

1. The CONTRACTING PARTIES recognize that customs duties often constitute serious obstacles to trade; thus negotiations on a reciprocal and mutually advantageous basis, directed to the substantial reduction of the general level of tariffs and other charges on imports and exports and in particular to the reduction of such high tariffs as discourage the importation even of minimum quantities, and conducted with due regard to the objectives of this Agreement and the varying needs of individual CONTRACTING PARTIES, are of great importance to the expansion of international trade. The CONTRACTING PARTIES may therefore sponsor such negotiations from time to time.

APPENDIX 2

Selected Provisions of the Marrakesh Agreement Establishing the World Trade Organization

Article I: Establishment of the Organization

The World Trade Organization (hereinafter referred to as "the WTO") is hereby established.

Article II: Scope of the WTO

1. The WTO shall provide the common institutional framework for the conduct of trade relations among its Members in matters related to the agreements and associated legal instruments included in the Annexes to this Agreement.

2. The agreements and associated legal instruments included in Annexes 1, 2 and 3 (hereinafter referred to as "Multilateral Trade Agreements") are integral parts of this Agreement, binding on all Members.[1]

3. The agreements and associated legal instruments included in Annex 4 (hereinafter referred to as "Plurilateral Trade Agreements") are also part of this Agreement for those Members that have accepted them, and are binding on those Members. The Plurilateral Trade Agreements do not create either obligations or rights for Members that have not accepted them.

4. The General Agreement on Tariffs and Trade 1994 as specified in Annex 1A (hereinafter referred to as "GATT 1994") is legally distinct from the General Agreement on Tariffs and Trade, dated 30 October 1947, annexed to the Final Act Adopted at the Conclusion of the Second Session of the Preparatory Committee of the United Nations Conference on Trade

and Employment, as subsequently rectified, amended or modified (hereinafter referred to as "GATT 1947").

Article III: Functions of the WTO

1. The WTO shall facilitate the implementation, administration and operation, and further the objectives, of this Agreement and of the Multilateral Trade Agreements, and shall also provide the framework for the implementation, administration and operation of the Plurilateral Trade Agreements.

2. The WTO shall provide the forum for negotiations among its Members concerning their multilateral trade relations in matters dealt with under the agreements in the Annexes to this Agreement. The WTO may also provide a forum for further negotiations among its Members concerning their multilateral trade relations, and a framework for the implementation of the results of such negotiations, as may be decided by the Ministerial Conference.

3. The WTO shall administer the Understanding on Rules and Procedures Governing the Settlement of Disputes (hereinafter referred to as the "Dispute Settlement Understanding" or "DSU") in Annex 2 to this Agreement.

4. The WTO shall administer the Trade Policy Review Mechanism (hereinafter referred to as the "TPRM") provided for in Annex 3 to this Agreement.

5. With a view to achieving greater coherence in global economic policy-making, the WTO shall cooperate, as appropriate, with the International Monetary Fund and with the International Bank for Reconstruction and Development and its affiliated agencies.

Article IV: Structure of the WTO

1. There shall be a Ministerial Conference composed of representatives of all the Members, which shall meet at least once every two years. The Ministerial Conference shall carry out the functions of the WTO and take actions necessary to this effect. The Ministerial Conference shall have the authority to take decisions on all matters under any of the Multilateral Trade Agreements, if so requested by a Member, in accordance with the specific requirements for decision-making in this Agreement and in the relevant Multilateral Trade Agreements.

2. There shall be a General Council composed of representatives of all the Members, which shall meet as appropriate. In the intervals between

meetings of the Ministerial Conference, its functions shall be conducted by the General Council. The General Council shall also carry out the functions assigned to it by this Agreement. The General Council shall establish its rules of procedure and approve the rules of procedure for the Committees provided for in paragraph 7.

Article VIII: Status of the WTO

1. The WTO shall have legal personality, and shall be accorded by each of its Members such legal capacity as may be necessary for the exercise of its functions.

2. The WTO shall be accorded by each of its Members such privileges and immunities as are necessary for the exercise of its functions.

Article IX: Decision-Making

1. The WTO shall continue the practice of decision-making by consensus followed under GATT 1947.[2] Except as otherwise provided, where a decision cannot be arrived at by consensus, the matter at issue shall be decided by voting. At meetings of the Ministerial Conference and the General Council, each Member of the WTO shall have one vote. Where the European Communities exercise their right to vote, they shall have a number of votes equal to the number of their member States[3] which are Members of the WTO. Decisions of the Ministerial Conference and the General Council shall be taken by a majority of the votes cast, unless otherwise provided in this Agreement or in the relevant Multilateral Trade Agreement.[4]

Article XII: Accessions

1. Any State or separate customs territory possessing full autonomy in the conduct of its external commercial relations and of the other matters provided for in this Agreement and the Multilateral Trade Agreements may accede to this Agreement, on terms to be agreed between it and the WTO. Such accession shall apply to this Agreement and the Multilateral Trade Agreements annexed thereto.

2. Decisions on accession shall be taken by the Ministerial Conference. The Ministerial Conference shall approve the agreement on the terms of accession by a two-thirds majority of the Members of the WTO.

3. Accession to a Plurilateral Trade Agreement shall be governed by the provisions of that Agreement.

Notes

1. Annexes are not included here. In the original documents, Annex 1 contains the Multilateral Agreements on Trade in Goods, the General Agreement on Trade in Services (GATS), and the Agreement on Trade-Related Aspects of Intellectual Property Rights (TRIPs); Annex 2 contains the Dispute Settlement Understanding (DSU); and Annex 3 contains the Trade Policy Review Mechanism.

2. The body concerned shall be deemed to have decided by consensus on a matter submitted for its consideration, if no Member, present at the meeting when the decision is taken, formally objects to the proposed decision.

3. The number of votes of the European Communities and their member States shall in no case exceed the number of the member States of the European Communities.

4. Decisions by the General Council when convened as the Dispute Settlement Body shall be taken only in accordance with the provisions of paragraph 4 of Article 2 of the Dispute Settlement Understanding.

APPENDIX 3
Abbreviations

ASEAN	Association of Southeast Asian Nations
ATC	Agreement on Textiles and Clothing (WTO)
AU	African Union
BIT	bilateral investment treaty
CAP	Common Agricultural Policy (EU)
CBD	Convention on Biological Diversity
CTE	Committee on Trade and the Environment (WTO)
DDA	Doha Development Agenda
DSU	Dispute Settlement Understanding (WTO)
EC	European Communities
EU	European Union
FAO	Food and Agricultural Organization (UN)
FDI	foreign direct investment
G8	Group of 8
GATS	General Agreement on Trade in Services
GATT	General Agreement on Tariffs and Trade
GMO	genetically modified organism
GSP	Generalized System of Preferences
IBRD	International Bank for Reconstruction and Development
ILO	International Labour Organization
IMF	International Monetary Fund
IPRs	intellectual property rights
ISI	import substitution industrialization
ITO	International Trade Organization
LDC	least-developed country
MAI	Multilateral Agreement on Investment

MEA	Multilateral Environmental Agreement
MFA	Multi-Fibre Arrangement
MFN	most-favored-nation
NAFTA	North American Free Trade Agreement
NAMA	nonagricultural market access
NGO	nongovernmental organization
NIEO	new international economic order
OECD	Organization for Economic Cooperation and Development
PhRMA	Pharmaceutical Research and Manufacturers of America
SDR	special drawing right
SPS	sanitary and phytosanitary
TBT	technical barriers to trade
TPRM	Trade Policies Review Mechanism
TRIMs	Agreement on Trade-Related Investment Measures
TRIPs	Agreement on Trade-Related Aspects of Intellectual Property Rights
UN	United Nations
UNCTAD	United Nations Conference on Trade and Development
UPOV	International Union for the Protection of New Varieties of Plants
USTR	United States trade representative
WHO	World Health Organization
WIPO	World Intellectual Property Organization
WTO	World Trade Organization

Bibliography

Abbott, Frederick M. (1998). "The Enduring Enigma of TRIPS: A Challenge for the World Economic System," *Journal of International Economic Law* 1, no. 4.

——— (2002). "The TRIPS Agreement, Access to Medicines, and the WTO Doha Ministerial Conference," *Journal of World Intellectual Property* 5, no. 1.

Abreu, Marcelo de Paiva (1996). "Trade in Manufactures: The Outcome of the Uruguay Round and Developing Country Interests." In *The Uruguay Round and the Developing Countries,* edited by Will Martin and L. Alan Winters. Cambridge, UK: Cambridge University Press.

Acheson, Keith, and Christopher Maule (2001). *Much Ado About Culture—North American Trade Disputes*. Ann Arbor: University of Michigan Press.

Adlung, Rolf (2005). *Public Services and the GATS*. WTO Working Paper, ERSD-2005-03.

Albin, Cecilia (2001). *Justice and Fairness in International Negotiation.* Cambridge, UK: Cambridge University Press.

Alford, William P. (1995). *To Steal a Book Is an Elegant Offence—Intellectual Property Law in Chinese Civilization.* Stanford, CA: Stanford University Press.

Anderson, Kym, and Lee A. Jackson (2005). "What's Behind GM's Trade Disputes?" *World Trade Review* 4, no. 2.

Ashcraft, Richard (1996). "Lockean Ideas, Poverty, and the Development of Liberal Political Theory." In *Early Modern Conceptions of Property,* edited by John Brewer and Susan Staves. London and New York: Routledge.

Barnett, Michael, and Martha Finnemore (2004). *Rules for the World: International Organizations in Global Politics*. Ithaca, NY: Cornell University Press.

Barton, John H., Judith L. Goldstein, et al. (2006). *The Evolution of the Trade Regime: Politics, Law, and Economics of the GATT and the WTO.* Princeton, NJ: Princeton University Press.

Bates, Gill (1999). "Limited Engagement," *Foreign Affairs* 78, no. 4.

Baumol, William J., Robert E. Litan, and Carl J. Schramm (2007). *Good Capitalism, Bad Capitalism and the Economics of Growth and Prosperity.* New Haven, CT, and London: Yale University Press.

Bhagwati, Jagdish (1998). "Poverty and Reforms: Friends and Foes?" *Journal of International Affairs* 52, no. 1.

——— (2000). *The Wind of the Hundred Days—How Washington Mismanaged Globalization*. Cambridge, MA: MIT Press.

Bhattasali, Deepak (2004). "Accelerating Financial Market Restructuring in China." In *China and the WTO: Accession, Policy Reform, and Poverty Reduction Strategies*, edited by Deepak Bhattasali, Shantong Li, and Will Martin. Washington, DC: World Bank and Oxford University Press.

Blumental, David M. (1999). "Applying GATT to Marketizing Economies: The Dilemma of WTO Accession and Reform of China's State-Owned Enterprises (SOEs)," *Journal of International Economic Law* 2, no. 1.

Boughton, James M. (1998). "Harry Dexter White and the International Monetary Fund," *Finance and Development* 35, no. 3.

Bray, Donald W., and Marjorie Woodford Bray (2002). "Beyond Neoliberal Globalization: Another World," *Latin American Perspectives* 29, no. 6: 117–126.

Breskovski, Vassil (1993). "Bulgaria and the GATT—A Case Study for Accession," *World Competition* 17, no. 2.

Brown, Chad P., Bernard Hoekman, and Caglar Ozden (2003). "The Pattern of US Antidumping," *World Trade Review* 2, no. 3.

Cameron, Maxwell A., and Brian W. Tomlin (2000). *The Making of NAFTA—How the Deal Was Done*. Ithaca, NY: Cornell University Press.

Cass, Deborah Z. (2005). *The Constitutionalization of the World Trade Organization—Legitimacy, Democracy, and Community in the International Trading System*. Oxford, UK: Oxford University Press.

Chan, Anita, and Robert J. S. Ross (2003). "Racing to the Bottom: International Trade Without a Social Clause," *Third World Quarterly* 24, no. 6: 1011–1028.

Chang, Ha-joon (1998). "Globalization, Transnational Corporations, and Economic Development: Can the Developing Countries Pursue Strategic Industrial Policy in a Globalization World Economy?" In *Globalization and Progressive Economic Policy*, edited by Dean Baker, Gerald Epstein, and Robert Pollin. Cambridge, UK, and New York: Cambridge University Press.

Cohen, Benjamin J. (1998). *The Geography of Money*. Ithaca, NY: Cornell University Press.

Correa, Carlos M. (2000). *Intellectual Property Rights, the WTO and Developing Countries—The TRIPS Agreement and Policy Options*. Penang, Malaysia: Third World Network.

Cottier, Thomas (1998). "The Protection of Genetic Resources and Traditional Knowledge: Towards More Specific Rights and Obligations in World Trade Law," *Journal of International Economic Law* 1, no. 4.

Croome, John (1995). *Reshaping the World Trading System—A History of the Uruguay Round*. Geneva: World Trade Organization.

Das, Dilip K. (2000). "Debacle at Seattle—The Way the Cookie Crumbled," *Journal of World Trade* 34, no. 5.

Deardoff, Alan V., and Robert M. Stern (1983). "Economic Effects of the Tokyo Round," *Southern Economic Journal* 49, no. 3.

Desta, Melaku Geboye (2005). "The Integration of Agriculture into WTO Disciplines." In *Agriculture in WTO Law*, edited by Bernard O'Connor. London: Cameron May.

Feketekuty, Geza (2000). "Improving the Architecture of GATS." In *GATS 2000—New Directions in Services Trade Liberalization*, edited by Pierre Sauve and Robert M. Stern. Washington, DC: Brookings Institution Press.

Finger, J. M. (1974). "GATT Tariff Concessions and the Exports of Developing Countries—United States Concessions at the Dillon Round," *Economic Journal* 84, no. 335.

Finger, Michael J., and Philip Schuler (2001). "Implementation of Uruguay Round Commitments: The Development Challenge." In *Developing Countries and the WTO: A Pro-active Agenda*, edited by Bernard Hoekman and Will Martin. Malden, MA: Blackwell Publishing.

Footer, Mary E., and Christopher Beat Graber (2000). "Trade Liberalization and Cultural Policy," *Journal of International Economic Law* 3, no. 1.

Francois, Joseph F., Bradley McDonald, and Hakan Nordstrom (1996). "The Uruguay Round: A Numerically Based Qualitative Assessment." In *The Uruguay Round and the Developing Countries*, edited by Will Martin and L. Alan Winters. Cambridge, UK: Cambridge University Press.

Friedman, Milton (1982). *Capitalism and Freedom*. Chicago: University of Chicago Press.

Fukuyama, Francis (1996). *Trust—The Social Virtues and the Creation of Prosperity*. New York: Penguin Books.

GATT (General Agreement on Tariffs and Trade) (1979). *Agreement on Measures to Discourage the Importation of Counterfeit Goods* (L/4817). July 31.

"General Agreement on Tariffs and Trade," *International Organization* 16, no. 4 (1962).

Goff, Patricia M. (2007). *Limits to Liberalization—Local Culture in a Global Marketplace*. Ithaca, NY: Cornell University Press.

Goldstein, Judith, and Lisa L. Martin (2000). "Legalization, Trade Liberalization, and Domestic Politics: A Cautionary Note," *International Organization* 54, no. 3.

Goldstein, Judith, Miles Kahler, Robert O. Keohane, and Anne-Marie Slaughter (2000). "Introduction: Legalization and World Politics," in "Legalization and World Politics," a special issue of *International Organization* 54, no. 3.

Goldstein, Paul (1994). *Copyright's Highway—From Gutenberg to the Celestial Jukebox*. New York: Hill and Wang Publishers.

Grynberg, Roman, and Roy Mickey Joy (2000). "The Accession of Vanuatu to the WTO—Lessons for the Multilateral Trading System," *Journal of World Trade* 34, no. 6.

Habermas, Jürgen (1996). *Between Facts and Norms: Contributions to a Discourse Theory of Law and Democracy*. Cambridge, MA: MIT Press.

Hart, Michael, and Bill Dymond (2003). "Special and Differential Treatment and the Doha 'Development' Round," *Journal of World Trade* 37, no. 2.

Hartwick, Elaine, and Richard Peet (1999). *Theories of Development*. New York: Guilford Press.

Hathaway, Dale E., and Merlinda D. Ingco (1996). "Agricultural Liberalization and the Uruguay Round." In *The Uruguay Round and the Developing Countries*, edited by Will Martin and Alan Winters. Cambridge, UK, and New York: Cambridge University Press.

Haus, Leah A. (1992). *Globalizing the GATT—The Soviet Union's Successor States, Eastern Europe, and the International Trading System*. Washington, DC: Brookings Institution.

Helliwell, John F. (2002). *Globalization and Well-Being*. Vancouver, BC: UBC Press.

Hindlay, Brian (2002). "What Subjects Are Suitable for WTO Agreement?" In *The Political Economy of International Trade Law*, edited by Daniel L. M. Kennedy and James D. Southwick. Cambridge, UK, and New York: Cambridge University Press.

Hirst, Paul, and Grahame Thompson (1999). *Globalization in Question: The International Economy and the Possibilities of Governance.* Cambridge, UK: Polity Press.

——— (2002). "The Future of Globalization," *Cooperation and Conflict* 37, no. 3: 249.

Hoekman, Bernard (1996). "Assessing the General Agreement on Trade in Services." In *The Uruguay Round and the Developing Countries,* edited by Will Martin and Alan Winters. Cambridge, UK, and New York: Cambridge University Press.

Hoekman, Bernard, and Peter Holmes (1999). " Competition, Developing Countries and the WTO." In *The World Economy—Global Trade Policy 1999,* edited by Peter Lloyd and Chris Miller. Oxford, UK: Blackwell Publishers.

Hoekman, Bernard, and Michel M. Kostecki (2001). *The Political Economy of the World Trading System: The WTO and Beyond,* 2nd ed. Oxford, UK, and New York: Oxford University Press.

Howse, Robert, and Kalypso Nicolaidis (2001). "Legitimacy and Global Governance: Why Constitutionalizing the WTO Is a Step Too Far." In *Efficiency, Equity, Legitimacy: The Multilateral Trading System at the Millennium,* edited by Roger B. Porter, Pierre Sauve, Arvind Subramanian, and Americo Beviglia Zampetti. Washington, DC: Center for Business and Government at Harvard University and Brookings Institution Press, 2001.

Hudec, Robert (1993). *Enforcing International Trade Law: The Evolution of the Modern GATT Legal System.* Salem, NH: Butterworth Legal Publishers.

Ianchovichina, Elena, and Will Martin (2004). "Economic Impacts of China's Accession to the WTO." In *China and the WTO: Accession, Policy Reform, and Poverty Reduction Strategies,* edited by Deepak Bhattasali, Shantong Li, and Will Martin. Washington, DC: World Bank and Oxford University Press.

International Labour Organization. (2000). "About the ILO, Who We Are: ILO History" (October). www.ilo.org/public/english/about/history.htm (accessed June 1, 2007).

Irwin, Douglas A. (1995). "The GATT in Historical Perspective," *American Economic Review* 85, no. 2.

Ito, Takatoshi, and Anne O. Krueger (eds.) (2003). *Trade in Services in the Asia Pacific Region.* Chicago: University of Chicago Press.

Jackson, John H. (1997). *The World Trading System: Law and Policy of International Economic Relations.* Cambridge, MA: MIT Press.

Jackson, John H., and Sylvia A. Rhodes (1999). "United States Law and China's Accession Process," *Journal of International Economic Law* 2, no. 3.

Jackson, Lee A., and Kym Anderson (2005). "What's Behind GM's Trade Disputes?" *World Trade Review* 4, no. 2 (2005).

Jacobson, Harold K., and Michael Oskenberg (1990). *China's Participation in the IMF, the World Bank, and GATT: Toward a Global Economic Order.* Ann Arbor: University of Michigan Press.

James, Harold (2003). *The End of Globalization: Lessons from the Great Depression.* Cambridge, MA: Harvard University Press.

Jawara, Fatoumata, and Aileen Kwa (2004). *Behind the Scenes at the WTO—The Real World of International Negotiations: The Lessons of Cancun* (London and New York: Zed Books, 2004).

Kahler, Miles (2005). "Defining Accountability Up: The Global Economic

Multilaterals." In *Global Governance and Public Accountability*, edited by David Held and Mathias Koenig-Archibugi. Oxford, UK, and Malden, MA: Blackwell Publishing.

Kawamoto, Akira (1997). "Regulatory Reform on the International Trade Policy Agenda," *Journal of World Trade* 31, no. 4.

Kenen, Peter B. (1994). *Managing the World Economy: Fifty Years After Bretton Woods*. Washington, DC: Institute for International Economics.

Kennedy, Daniel L. M., and James D. Southwick (eds.) (2002). *The Political Economy of International Trade Law.* Cambridge, UK: Cambridge University Press.

Keohane, Robert O., and Joseph Nye (1977). *Power and Interdependence: World Politics in Transition.* Boston: Little Brown.

——— (1984). *After Hegemony: Cooperation and Discord in the World Political Economy*. Princeton, NJ: Princeton University Press.

Kondo, Edson K. (1995). "The Effect of Patent Protection on Foreign Direct Investment," *Journal of World Trade* 29, no. 6.

Kong, Qingjiang (2001). "Enforcement of WTO Agreements in China: Illusion or Reality?" *Journal of World Trade* 35, no. 6.

Kongolo, Tshimanga (2001)."Public Interest Versus the Pharmaceutical Industry's Monopoly in South Africa," *Journal of World Intellectual Property* 4, no. 5.

Kostecki, Michel M. (1978). *East-West Trade and the GATT System.* New York: St. Martin's Press.

Krasner, Stephen D. (ed.) (1983). *International Regimes.* Ithaca, NY: Cornell University Press.

——— (1991). "Sovereignty," *Foreign Policy* 122.

Krugman, Paul R., and Maurice Obstfeld (1997). *International Economics: Theory and Policy*, 4th ed. Boston: Addison Wesley.

Lanoszka, Anna (2001). "The WTO Accession Process—Negotiating Participation in a Globalizing Economy," *Journal of World Trade* 35, no. 4.

Low, Patrick, and Arvind Subramanian (1996). "Beyond TRIMs: A Case for Multilateral Action on Investment and Competition Policy?" In *The Uruguay Round and the Developing Countries*, edited by Will Martin and Alan Winters. Cambridge, UK, and New York: Cambridge University Press.

Luff, David (2004). "Current International Trade Rules Relevant to Telecommunication Services." In *WTO and Global Convergence in Telecommunications and Audio-Visual Services*, edited by Damien Geradin and David Luff. Cambridge, UK, and New York: Cambridge University Press.

Macklem, Patrick (2002). "Labor Law Beyond Borders." *Journal of International Economic Law* 5, no. 3.

Marchetti, Juan A. (2004). "Developing Countries in the WTO Services Negotiations," Table 1, Chart 1. In *WTO Working Paper*, ERSD-2004-06.

Marko, Mary (1998). "An Evaluation of the Basic Telecommunications Services Agreement," CIES Policy Discussion Paper 98/09.

Martin, Will, and Alan Winters (1996). "The Uruguay Round: A Milestone for Developing Countries." In *The Uruguay Round and the Developing Countries*, edited by Will Martin and Alan Winters. Cambridge, UK, and New York: Cambridge University Press.

Maskus, Keith E. (2000). *Intellectual Property Rights in the Global Economy*. Washington, DC: Institute for International Economics.

——— (2004). "Intellectual Property Rights in the WTO Accession Package: Assessing China's Reforms." In *China and the WTO: Accession, Policy*

Reform, and Poverty Reduction Strategies, edited by Deepak Bhattasali, Shantong Li, and Will Martin. Washington, DC: World Bank and Oxford University Press.

Maskus, Keith E., and Jerome H. Reichman (2004). "The Globalization of Private Knowledge Goods and the Privatization of Global Public Goods," *Journal of International Economic Law* 7, no. 2.

Matsushita, Mitsuo, Petros C. Mavroidis, and Thomas J. Schoenbaum (2003). *The World Trade Organization: Law, Practice and Policy*. Oxford, UK, and New York: Oxford University Press.

Mattoo, Aaditya (1997). "National Treatment in the GATS: Corner Stone or Pandora's Box?" *Journal of World Trade* 31, no. 1.

——— (2000). "Financial Services and the WTO: Liberalization Commitments of the Developing and Transition Economies," *World Economy* 23, no. 3.

Mattoo, Aaditya (2004). "The Services Dimension of China's Accession to the WTO." In *China and the WTO: Accession, Policy Reform, and Poverty Reduction Strategies*, edited by Deepak Bhattasali, Shantong Li, and Will Martin. Washington, DC: World Bank and Oxford University Press.

Mavroidis, Petros C. (2005). *The General Agreement on Tariffs and Trade—A Commentary*. Oxford, UK, and New York: Oxford University Press.

May, Christopher, and Susan K. Sell (2006). *Intellectual Property Rights—A Critical History*. Boulder, CO, and London: Lynne Rienner Publishers.

McDonald, Jan (2003). "'It's Not Easy Being Green': Trade and Environmental Linkages Beyond Doha." In *The WTO and the Doha Round: The Changing Face of World Trade*, edited by Ross P. Buckley. The Hague: Kluwer Law International, pp. 158–159.

McGrady, Benn (2004). "TRIPS and Trademarks: The Case of Tobacco," *World Trade Review* 3, no. 1.

McRae, Donald (2000). "The WTO in International Law: Tradition Continued or New Frontier?" *Journal of International Economic Law* 3, no. 1.

Mearsheimer, John J. (2001). *The Tragedy of Great Power Politics*. New York: W. W. Norton.

Moravcsik, Andrew (1999). "New Statecraft? Supranational Entrepreneurs and International Cooperation," *International Organization* 53, no. 2.

Mrongowius, Debbie, and Mari Pangestu (2004). "Telecommunications Services in China: Facing the Challenges of WTO Accession." In *China and the WTO: Accession, Policy Reform, and Poverty Reduction Strategies*, edited by Deepak Bhattasali, Shantong Li, and Will Martin. Washington, DC: World Bank and Oxford University Press.

Mukerji, Asoke (2000). "Developing Countries and the WTO—Issues of Implementation," *Journal of World Trade* 34, no. 6.

Murphy, Craig N. (2002). "The Historical Process of Establishing Institutions of Global Governance and the Nature of Global Polity." In *Towards a Global Polity*, edited by Morten Ougaard and Richard Higgott. London and New York: Routledge.

Narlikar, Amrita (2003). *International Trade and Developing Countries: Bargaining Together in GATT and WTO*. London and New York: Routledge.

——— (2006). "Fairness in International Trade Negotiations," *World Economy* 29, no. 8.

Noland, Marcus (1999). "Learning to Love the WTO," *Foreign Affairs* 78, no. 5.

Odell, John S. (2000). *Negotiating the World Economy*. Ithaca, NY: Cornell University Press.

——— (2002). "The Seattle Impasse and Its Implications for the World Trade Organization." In *The Political Economy of International Trade Law*, edited by Daniel L. M. Kennedy and James D. Southwick. Cambridge, UK, and New York: Cambridge University Press.

Odell, John S., and Susan K. Sell (2006). "Reframing the Issue: The WTO Coalition on Intellectual Property and Public Health, 2001." In *Negotiating Trade—Developing Countries in the WTO and NAFTA*, edited by John S. Odell. Cambridge, UK, and New York: Cambridge University Press.

Organization for Economic Cooperation and Development (2003). "The Doha Development Agenda: Tariffs and Trade." OECD Policy Brief (August 23). www.oecd.org/dataoecd/35/49/8920463.pdf (accessed July 6, 2007).

Ostry, Sylvia (1997). *The Post–Cold War Trading System: Who's on First?* Chicago: University of Chicago Press.

——— (2001). "World Trade Organization: Institutional Design for Better Governance." In *Efficiency, Equity, Legitimacy: The Multilateral Trading System at the Millennium*, edited by Roger Porter, Pierre Sauve, Arvind Subramanian, and Americo Beviglia Zampetti. Washington, DC: Brookings Institution Press.

——— (2002). "The Uruguay Round North-South Bargain: Implications for Future Negotiations." In *The Political Economy of International Trade Law*, edited by Daniel L. M. Kennedy and James D. Southwick. Cambridge, UK, and New York: Cambridge University Press.

Otten, Adrian (1998). "Implementation of TRIPS Agreement," *Journal of International Economic Law* 1, no. 4.

Paiva Abreu, Marcelo de (1996). "Trade Manufactures: The Outcome of the Uruguay Round and Developing Country Interests." In *The Uruguay Round and Developing Countries*, edited by Will Martin and Alan Winters. Cambridge, UK, and New York: Cambridge University Press.

Palast, Gregory (2001). "The WTO Agreement on Services," *The Observer*, April 15.

Palmeter, David (2003). *The WTO as a Legal System: Essays on International Trade Law and Policy*. London: Cameron May.

Patel, Chandrakant (2003). "Single Undertaking: A Straitjacket or Variable Geometry?" T.R.A.D.E. Working Paper, no. 15. Geneva: South Center.

Patterson, Eliza R. (1986). "Improving GATT Rules for Nonmarket Economies," *Journal of World Trade Law* 20, no. 2.

Pauly, Louis W. (1997). *Who Elected the Bankers? Surveillance and Control in the World Economy*. Ithaca, NY: Cornell University Press.

Perlow, Gary H. (1981). "The Multilateral Supervision of International Trade: Has the Textiles Experiment Worked?" *American Journal of International Law* 75, no. 1.

Petersmann, Ernst-Ulrich (1998). "From the Hobbesian International Law of Coexistence to Modern International Law: The WTO Dispute Settlement System," *Journal of International Economic Law* 1, no. 2.

——— (1998) "GATT Law on State Trading Enterprises: Critical Evaluation of Article XVII and Proposals for Reforms." In *State Trading in the Twenty-First Century*, edited by Thomas Cottier and Petros C. Mavroidis. Ann Arbor: University of Michigan Press.

——— (2000). "The WTO Constitution and Human Rights," *Journal of International Economic Law* 3, no. 1.

Primo Braga, Carlos A. (1996). "Trade-Related Intellectual Property Issues: The

Uruguay Round Agreement and Its Economic Implications." In *The Uruguay Round and the Developing Countries*, edited by Will Martin and Alan Winters. Cambridge, UK, and New York: Cambridge University Press.

Raffaelli, Marcelo (1998). "Bringing Textiles and Clothing into the Multilateral Trading System." In *The Uruguay Round and Beyond: Essays in Honour of Arthur Dunkel*, edited by Jagdish Bhagwati and Mathia Hirsh. Berlin and Heidelberg: Springer-Verlag.

Rawls, John (1996). *Political Liberalism*. New York: Columbia University Press.

——— (1999). *The Law of Peoples*. Cambridge, MA: Harvard University Press.

Reichman, Jerome H. (1998). "Securing Compliance with the TRIPS Agreement After US v India," *Journal of International Economic Law* 1, no. 4.

——— (1998). "Universal Minimum Standards of Intellectual Rights Protection Under the TRIPS Component of the WTO Agreement." In *Intellectual Property and International Trade: The TRIPS Agreement*, edited by Carlos M. Correa and Abdulqawi A. Yusuf. Boston and London: Kluwer Law International.

Richardson, Bennett (2005). "Sticky Situation for Japan's Rice Policy," *Asia Times*, July 28.

Rodrik, Dani (1998). "Why Do More Open Economies Have Bigger Governments?" *Journal of Political Economy* 106, no. 5.

Rosen, Howard (2004). "Free Trade Agreements as Foreign Policy Tools: The US-Israel and US-Jordan FTAs." In *Free Trade Agreements—US Strategies and Priorities*, edited by Jeffrey J. Schott. Washington, DC: Institute for International Economics.

Ruggie, John G. (1982). "International Regimes, Transactions and Change: Embedded Liberalism in the Postwar Economic Order," *International Organization* 36 (Spring).

Ryan, Michael P. (1998). *Knowledge Diplomacy: Global Competition and the Politics of Intellectual Property*. Washington, DC: Brookings Institution Press.

Salazar Brandao, Antonio P. Eugenio Diaz-Bonilla, Bruce L. Gardner, Devinder Sharma, and Alan Swinbank (2003). "A Dialogue: Trade Liberalization in Agriculture," *SAIS Review* 23, no. 1.

Sampson, Gary P. (2002). "Effective Multilateral Agreements and Why the WTO Needs Them." In *The World Economy: Global Trade Policy 2001*, edited by Peter Lloyd and Chris Milner. Oxford: Blackwell Publishers.

Scharpf, Fritz (1999). *Governing in Europe—Effective and Democratic?* New York and Oxford: Oxford University Press.

Scholte, Jan Aart (2005). *Globalization—A Critical Introduction*, 2nd ed. Basingstoke, UK: Palgrave.

Schott, Jeffrey J., and Jayashree Watal (2000). "Decision Making in the WTO." In *The WTO After Seattle*, edited by Jeffrey J. Schott. Washington, DC: Institute for International Economics.

Schraeder, Peter J. (2004). *African Politics and Society—A Mosaic in Transformation*, 2nd ed. Belmont, CA: Thomson & Wadsworth, pp. 70–71.

Schuh, Edward G. (2002). "Developing Country Interests in WTO Agricultural Policy." In *The Political Economy of International Trade Law*, edited by Daniel L. M. Kennedy and James D. Southwick. Cambridge, UK, and New York: Cambridge University Press.

Schumpeter, Joseph A. (1976). *Capitalism, Socialism and Democracy*. New York: Harper Perennial.

Sell, Susan K. (2003). *Private Power, Public Law—The Globalization of Intellectual Property Rights*. Cambridge, UK, and New York: Cambridge University Press.

Shaffer, Gregory C. (2002). "'If Only We Were Elephants': The Political Economy of the WTO's Treatment of Trade and Environmental Matters." In *The Political Economy of International Trade Law*, edited by Daniel L. M. Kennedy and James D. Southwick. Cambridge, UK, and New York: Cambridge University Press.

Shapiro, Ian (2003). *The State of Democratic Theory*. Princeton, NJ: Princeton University Press.

Steger, Debra P. (2004). *Peace Through Trade: Building the WTO*. London: Cameron May.

Steward, Terence P. (ed.) (1993). *The GATT Uruguay Round—A Negotiating History (1986–1992)*, vol. 1. Deventer, Netherlands: Kluwer Law and Taxation Publishers.

Stiglitz, Joseph E. (2001). "Two Principles for the Next Round or, How to Bring Developing Countries in from the Cold." In *Developing Countries and the WTO: A Pro-active Agenda*, edited by Bernard Hoekman and Will Martin. Malden, MA: Blackwell Publishing.

Stiles, Kendall (1996). "Negotiating Institutional Reform: The Uruguay Round, the GATT, and the WTO," *Global Governance* 2, no. 1.

Stoll, Peter-Tobias, and Frank Schorkopf (2006). *WTO—World Economic Order, World Trade Law*. Leiden, Netherlands, and Boston: Martinus Nijhoff Publishers.

Sutherland, Peter D. (1998). "Globalisation and the Uruguay Round." In *The Uruguay Round and Beyond—Essays in Honour of Arthur Dunkel,* edited by Jagdish Bhagwati and Mathias Hirsch. Berlin: Springer Publishing.

Tait, A. Neil, and Kui-Wai Li (1997). "Trade Regimes and China's Accession to the World Trade Organization," *Journal of World Trade* 31, no. 3.

Tangermann, Stefan (2002). "Agriculture on the Way to Firm International Trading Rules." In *The Political Economy of International Trade Law*, edited by Daniel L. M. Kennedy and James D. Southwick. Cambridge, UK, and New York: Cambridge University Press.

Templeman, Lord Sydney (1998). "Intellectual Property," *Journal of International Economic Law* 1, no. 4.

Thomas, Chantal (2002). "Trade-Related Labor and Environmental Agreements," *Journal of International Economic Law* 5, no. 4.

Trebilcock, Michael J., and Robert Howse (1999). *The Regulation of International Trade,* 2nd ed. London and New York: Routledge.

Trebilcock, Michael, and Julie Soloway, (2002). "International Trade Policy and Domestic Food Safety." In *The Political Economy of International Trade Law*, edited by Daniel L. M. Kennedy and James D. Southwick. Cambridge, UK, and New York: Cambridge University Press.

UNCTAD (2004). *International Investment Agreements: Key Issues*. Geneva: United Nations.

Van Brabant, Josef M. (1998). "Eastern Europe and the World Trade Organization: The Present Position and Prospects for Accession." In *Eastern Europe and the World Economy—Challenges of Transition and Globalization*, edited by Iliana Zloch-Christy. London: Edward Elgar Publishing.

——— (1998). *The Political Economy of Transition: Coming to Grips with History and Methodology*. London and New York: Routledge.

Van den Broek, Naboth (2003). "Power Paradoxes in Enforcement and Implementation of World Trade Organization Dispute Settlement Reports," *Journal of World Trade* 37, no. 1.

Vermulst, Edwin, and Paul Waer (1999). "EC Anti-Subsidy Law and Practice After the Uruguay Round—A Wolf in Sheep's Clothing?" *Journal of World Trade* 33, no. 3.

Wallace, Cynthia Day (2002). "The Legal Environment for a Multilateral Framework on Investment and the Potential Role of the WTO," *Journal of World Investment* 3, no. 2.

Walters, Robert S., and David H. Blake (1992). *The Politics of Global Economic Relations*. Englewood Cliffs, NJ: Prentice Hall, 1992.

Weiss, Freidl (2002). "WTO Decision-Making: Is It Reformable?" In *The Political Economy of International Trade Law*, edited by Daniel L. M. Kennedy and James D. Southwick. Cambridge, UK, and New York: Cambridge University Press.

Wilcox, Clair (1949). *A Charter for World Trade*. New York: Macmillan.

Wilkinson, Rorden (2001). "The WTO in Crisis—Exploring the Dimensions of Institutional Inertia," *Journal of World Trade* 35, no. 3.

——— (2006). *The WTO: Crisis and the Governance of Global Trade*. London and New York: Routledge.

Williams, Mark, Kong Yuk-Choi, and Shen Yan (2002). "Bonanza or Mirage?: Textiles and China's Accession to the WTO," *Journal of World Trade* 36, no. 3.

Winham, Gilbert R. (1986). *International Trade and the Tokyo Round Negotiation*. Princeton, NJ: Princeton University Press.

——— (1998). "Explanations of Developing Country Behavior in the GATT Round Negotiation," *The World Economy* 21, no. 3.

Woznowski, Jan (1974). *Polska w GATT (Poland and the GATT)*. Warsaw: PWE.

WTO (1994). *Schedule of Specific Commitments—Canada* (GATS/SC/16), April 15.

——— (1994). *Schedule of Specific Commitments—United States* (GATS/SC/90), April 15.

——— (1995). "Annex 1B: General Agreement on Trade in Services." In *The Results of the Uruguay Round of Multilateral Trade Negotiations*. Geneva: WTO.

——— (1995). "Annex 1C: Agreement on Trade-Related Aspects of Intellectual Property Rights." In *The Results of the Uruguay Round of Multilateral Trade Negotiations*. Geneva: WTO.

——— (1995). "Annex 2: Understanding on Rules and Procedures Governing the Settlement of Disputes." In *The Results of the Uruguay Round of Multilateral Trade Negotiations*. Geneva: WTO.

——— (1995). "The Preamble." In *The Results of the Uruguay Round of Multilateral Trade Negotiations*. Geneva: WTO.

——— (1995). *Report of the Working Party on the Accession of Ecuador* (WT/L/77).

——— (1995). *The Results of the Uruguay Round of Multilateral Trade Negotiations*. Geneva: GATT/WTO.

——— (1995). *The WTO Accession Process* (WT/ACC/1), March 24.

——— (1996). *India—Patent Protection for Pharmaceutical and Agriculture Chemical Products—Complaint by the United States* (WT/DS50), July 2.

——— (1996). *Report of the Council for TRIPS* (IP/C/8), November 6.

——— (1996). *Report of the Working Party on the Accession of Bulgaria* (WT/ACC/BGR/5), September 20.

——— (1996). *Second Protocol to the Agreement on Trade in Services (Financial Services)—Done at Geneva on October 6, 1995* (WT/Let/93), June 21.

——— (1996). *The WTO Accession Process and Preparation of Services Schedules* (WT/ACC/5), October 31.

——— (1998). *Fifth Protocol to the Agreement on Trade in Services (Financial Services)—Done at Geneva on 27 February 1998* (WT/Let/221), May 21, and (WT/Let/223), May 27.

——— (1998). *Health and Social Services—Background Note by the Secretariat* (S/C/W/50), September 18.

——— (1998). *Minutes of the General Council* (WT/GC/M/23), October 22.

——— (1998). "Recent Developments in Multilateral Environmental Agreements," Committee on Trade and Environment, July 8.

——— (1998). *Report of the Working Party on the Accession of the Kyrgyz Republic* (WT/ACC/KGZ/26), July 31.

——— (1998). *Schedule of Specific Commitments on Services—The Kyrgyz Republic* (WT/ACC/KGZ/26), July 31.

——— (1999). *Application of the Necessity Test: Issues for Consideration.* Informal Note by the Secretariat, Job 5929, October 8.

——— (1999). *Minutes of October 06, 1999 General Council Meeting* (WT/GC/M/48), October 27.

——— (1999). *Non-Violation Nullification or Impairment Under the TRIPS Agreement—Communication from Canada* (IP/C/W/127), Febuary 10.

——— (1999). *Non-Violation Nullification or Impairment Under the TRIPS Agreement—Communication from Canada, the Czech Republic, the EC, Hungary and Turkey* (IP/C/W/191), June 22.

——— (1999). *Non-Violation Nullification or Impairment Under the TRIPS Agreement—Communication from Cuba, the Dominican Republic, Egypt, Indonesia, Malaysia and Pakistan* (IP/C/W/141), April 29.

——— (1999). *Preparation for the 1999 Ministerial Conference* (JOB [99] 5868 and 6223), October.

——— (1999). *Report of the Working Party on the Accession of Estonia* (WT/ACC/EST/28), April 9.

——— (1999). *Report of the Working Party on the Accession of Georgia* (WT/ACC/GEO/31), August 30.

——— (1999). *Report of the Working Party on the Accession of Jordan* (WT/ACC/JOR/33), December 3.

——— (2000). *Annual Report of the Council for TRIPS* (IP/C/22), December 6.

——— (2000). *Argentina—Certain Measures on the Protection of Patents and Test Data, Complaint by the United States* (WT/DS196/1), May 30.

——— (2000). *Brazil—Measures Affecting Patent Protection—Complaint by the US.* (WT/DS199/1), June 8.

——— (2000). *Communication from China—The Chinese Laws* (WT/ACC/CHN/40), November 9.

——— (2000). *General Council: Implementation-Related Issues and Concerns* (WT/L/384), December 19.

——— (2000). *Report of the Working Party on the Accession of Albania* (WT/ACC/ALB/51), July 13.

——— (2000). *Report of the Working Party on the Accession of Croatia* (WT/ACC/HRV/59), June 29.

——— (2000). *Report of the Working Party on the Accession of Lithuania* (WT/ACC/LTU/52), November 7.

——— (2000). *Request to Join Consultation by the EC* (WT/DS199/2), June 20.

——— (2000). *Request to Join Consultations by the EU* (WT/DS196/2), June 20.

——— (2000). *Request to Join Consultations by Switzerland* (WT/DS196/2), June 21.

——— (2000). Scope and Modalities of Non-Violation Complaints Under the TRIPS *Agreement—Communication from the US* (IP/C/W/194), July 17.

——— (2000). *Technical Note on the Accession Process* (WT/ACC/7/Rev.2), November 1.

——— (2001). *Annual Report of the Council for TRIPS* (IP/C/23), October 5.

——— (2001). *Declaration of the Group of 77 and China on the Fourth WTO Ministerial Conference at Doha, Qatar* (WT/L/424), October 24.

——— (2001). *Declaration on the TRIPS Agreement and Public Health* (WT/Min/[01]/Dec/W/2), November 14.

——— (2001). *Implementation-Related Issues and Concerns* (WT/Min/[01]/Dec/W/10), November 14.

——— (2001). *Ministerial Declaration* (WT/Min/(01)/Dec/W/1), November 14.

——— (2001). *Ministerial Declaration on the TRIPS Agreement and Public Health, a Proposal by the African Group, Bangladesh, Barbados, Bolivia, Brazil, Cuba, Dominican Republic, Ecuador, Haiti, Honduras, India, Indonesia, Jamaica, Pakistan, Paraguay, Philippines, Peru, Sri Lanka, Thailand and Venezuela* (WT/GC/W/450), October 4.

——— (2001). *Mutually Agreed Solution* (WT/DS199/4), July 19.

——— (2001). *Report (2001) of the Working Group on the Relationship Between Trade and the Investment to the General Council* (WT/WGTI/5/Add.1), October 22.

——— (2001). *Report of the Working Party on the Accession of China* (WT/MIN[01]/3), November 10.

——— (2001). *Request for Establishment of the Panel* (WT/DS199/3), January 8.

——— (2001). *Technical Note on the Accession Process* (WT/ACC/10), December 21.

——— (2003). *Negotiations on Agriculture—Poverty Reduction: Sectoral Initiative in Favour of Cotton* (TN/AG/GEN/4), May 16.

——— (2004). *Doha Work Programme* (WT/L/579), August 2.

——— (2004). *United States—Measures Affecting the Cross-Border Supply of Gambling and Betting Services* (WT/DS285/R), November 10.

——— (2005). *Hong Kong Ministerial Declaration—Doha Work Programme* (WT/Min/[05]/W/3/Rev.2), December 18.

——— (2005). *Technical Note on the Accession Process* (WT/ACC/10/Rev.3), November 28.

——— (2005). *United States—Measures Affecting the Cross-Border Supply of Gambling and Betting Services* (WT/DS285/AB/R), April 7.

——— (2007). *United States—Measures Affecting the Cross-Border Supply of Gambling and Betting Services* (WT/DS285/RW), March 30.

——— (2008). *China—Measures Affecting Financial Information Services and Foreign Financial Information Suppliers (Complaint by the US)* (DS373), March 3.

WTO/GATT (1974). Document MTN.3B1. Cited in Mary E. Footer and Christopher Beat Graber (2000), "Trade Liberalization and Cultural Policy," *Journal of International Economic Law* 3, no. 1.

——— (1986). "Basic Instruments and Selected Documents (BISD), Thirty-Third Supplement." In *Ministerial Declaration on the Uruguay Round—Punta del Este*. Geneva: WTO.

——— (1991). *Draft Final Act Embodying the Results of the Uruguay Round of Multilateral Trade Negotiations* (MTN.TNC/W/FA), December 20.

——— (1991). *The Services Sector Classification List*. Document MTN.GNS/W/120, July 10.

Xiwen, Chen (2004). "China's Agricultural Development and Policy Readjustment After Its WTO Accession." In *China and the WTO: Accession, Policy Reform, and Poverty Reduction Strategies*, edited by Deepak Bhattasali, Shantong Li, and Will Martin. Washington, DC: World Bank and Oxford University Press.

Yeutter, Clayton (1998). "Bringing Agriculture into the Multilateral Trading System." In *The Uruguay Round and Beyond: Essays in Honour of Arthur Dunkel*, edited by Jagdish Bhagwati and Mathia Hirsh. Berlin and Heidelberg, Germany: Springer-Verlag.

Zampetti, Americo B. (2003). "Democratic Legitimacy in the World Trade Organization: The Justice Dimension," *Journal of World Trade* 37, no. 1.

Index

About the Book

A comprehensive examination of the World Trade Organization, this new book covers all the basics: the WTO's history, its structure, and its practices and concerns.

Beginning with an overview of the world trading system since the end of World War II, Lanoszka explains the profound changes brought about by the establishment of the WTO. Then, a discussion of the organization's structure, rules, membership criteria, and decisionmaking processes provides the foundation for an exploration of key issues—e.g., agreements dealing with agricultural products, textiles, and dumping—that continue to be sources of international tension.

The rapidly growing global services economy is the topic of an entire chapter, as is the passionately debated subject of intellectual property rights. Emerging issues such as the environment, e-commerce, and the new roles of the developing countries also receive thorough attention.

The book concludes with a look at the most recent developments taking place in the WTO and, more broadly, in the world trading system.

Anna Lanoszka is associate professor of international economic relations at the University of Windsor, Canada. Prior to her academic career, she worked in the Accessions Division of the World Trade Organization.